The Therapeutic Relationship in Psychotherapy Practice

The Therapeutic Relationship in Psychotherapy Practice: An Integrative Perspective explores the key components of the patient–therapist relationship in psychotherapy' as well as how these elements affect the treatment process and outcomes, and what therapists may do to enhance the relationship. Dr. Gelso posits a tripartite model in which the therapeutic relationship is seen as being composed of three interlocking elements: a real or personal relationship, a working alliance, and a transference–countertransference configuration that exist in each and every therapeutic relationship. Focusing on what psychotherapists can do to foster strong and facilitative relationships with their patients, the book includes substantial material drawn from clinical practice, with an ever-present eye on research findings.

Charles J. Gelso, is professor emeritus and senior lecturer in psychology at University of Maryland. He has written widely about the therapeutic relationship over the years, theorizing about and studying key elements of the relationship. Dr. Gelso has been editor of major journals in psychotherapy and has received many top awards in the field.

The Therapeutic Relationship in Psychotherapy Practice
An Integrative Perspective

Charles J. Gelso

LONDON AND NEW YORK

First published 2019
by Routledge
2 Park Square, Milton Park, Abingdon, Oxon OX14 4RN

and by Routledge
711 Third Avenue, New York, NY 10017

Routledge is an imprint of the Taylor & Francis Group, an informa business

© 2019 Taylor & Francis

The right of Charles J. Gelso to be identified as author of this work has been asserted by him in accordance with sections 77 and 78 of the Copyright, Designs and Patents Act 1988.

All rights reserved. No part of this book may be reprinted or reproduced or utilised in any form or by any electronic, mechanical, or other means, now known or hereafter invented, including photocopying and recording, or in any information storage or retrieval system, without permission in writing from the publishers.

Trademark notice: Product or corporate names may be trademarks or registered trademarks, and are used only for identification and explanation without intent to infringe.

British Library Cataloguing-in-Publication Data
A catalogue record for this book is available from the British Library

Library of Congress Cataloging-in-Publication Data
Names: Gelso, Charles J., 1941- author.
Title: The therapeutic relationship in psychotherapy practice : an integrative perspective / Charles J. Gelso.
Description: New York, NY : Routledge, 2019. | Includes bibliographical references and index.
Identifiers: LCCN 2018020855| ISBN 9781138999794 (hardback) | ISBN 9781138999800 (pbk.) | ISBN 9781315658063 (ebook)
Subjects: | MESH: Professional-Patient Relations | Psychotherapeutic Processes | Transference (Psychology)
Classification: LCC RC480.5 | NLM WM 62 | DDC 616.89/14–dc23LC record available at https://lccn.loc.gov/2018020855

ISBN: 978-1-138-99979-4 (hbk)
ISBN: 978-1-138-99980-0 (pbk)
ISBN: 978-1-315-65806-3 (ebk)

Typeset in Bembo
by Taylor & Francis Books

 Printed in the United Kingdom by Henry Ling Limited

Contents

Preface   vi

1   An Integrative Conception of the Therapeutic Relationship: Overview of the Tripartite Model   1

2   The Empathic Way and Benevolent Neutrality   29

3   Building a Real Relationship and Forging a Working Alliance: What Is a Therapist to Do?   52

4   Detecting and Working with Transference   73

5   Know Thyself, Manage Thyself   102

6   Love, Hate, and Other "Inadmissible" Feelings in the Psychotherapist   125

7   Good Therapist, Good Relationship: A Summing Up   140

Index   157

Preface

This book represents a bringing together of ideas I have developed about the patient–therapist relationship over more than five decades of psychotherapy practice and research. In the book, I have aimed to both present and extend what I have been writing and theorizing about over these many years. I have sought to address what seem to me to be some of the most fundamental questions about the therapeutic relationship, such as: What is the relationship? What are its key elements and how do they operate in concert? How is the relationship both the same and different across the major systems of psychotherapy? Most important, what is it about the therapeutic relationship that fosters growth in patients? And finally, what can therapists do to create and enhance a sound therapeutic relationship?

From the point at which I first started conceptualizing this book, my intent has been to write to practitioners. So, while the book is certainly informed by empirical research, I have sought most fundamentally to write a book of clinical theory addressing each of the key topics in a way that is directly clinically relevant. So, although I do not think this is a how-to cookbook, it does focus on what the therapist can and should do to foster the relationship and patient change. As part of this process, I use ample case material from my own practice of psychotherapy and therapy supervision, as well as already published case material. The intent is to make the theoretical material come to life through the discussion of cases.

Throughout my career, I have been able to work with both brief and long-term cases, some of which have lasted for a decade or longer. For example, while I was helping develop the 12-session time-limited therapy program at the University of Maryland's counseling center early in my career, I was also working with patients at a low-fee psychoanalytically oriented clinic in Washington D.C. specializing in long-term therapy with patients who could not afford expensive private treatment. Although some may say that very long-term therapy, work lasting for many years, simply reflects or even fosters patient dependency, I believe such work is necessary and life-changing, perhaps even lifesaving, for some patients, particularly those whose early and enduring life experiences have not allowed for the development of a sound sense of self and self-regard, but instead have created a deeply damaged sense of self and self-regard. Here I am reminded of one of my very long-term patients whose goal in therapy was to "be with someone when I am alone." This kind of change in the development of the self simply does not happen in brief work. So, whereas the case material I use represents a mixture of brief and long-term work, much of what I focus on in this book reflects longer-term therapy.

Although my theoretical leanings are toward a psychoanalytic/psychodynamic approach to conceptualization and treatment, I also have a great respect and appreciation of other approaches, most notably humanistic/experiential and cognitive/behavioral approaches; and I seek to integrate these into my work. Throughout the book, I aim to make observations and inferences that are relevant across the major theoretical systems, and point to how practitioners of the different systems might address certain topics, e.g., transference, differently. In this sense, I believe the theoretical foundation of the book is integrative.

The book begins with a definition of the therapeutic relationship, including both what it is and what it is not. I then explore a model of the therapy relationship that my collaborators and I have worked on since the mid-1980s, what I have called the tripartite model of the therapeutic relationship. In this model, all therapy relationships are seen as consisting of three interlocking elements: a working alliance, what I term a real relationship, and a transference–countertransference configuration. In Chapter 1, I present the latest thinking on this model. In the following five chapters, the elements of the model are examined in greater depth, including how the therapist can work with each element to increase chances of successful treatment.

Within the context of the tripartite model, one may ask whether there are fundamental elements of a therapeutic relationship that make therapy work. In Chapter 2, I examine this question and explore what may be termed The Empathic Way, which is seen as consisting of the therapist's empathy, caring and affirmation, a relational context that is seen as necessary if the therapeutic relationship is to be strong and curative. I also examine what I term benevolent neutrality, which fosters growth when it is provided in the context of the empathic way. When talking about therapist neutrality, the reader will soon see that this is very different from the kind of disinterested, bland neutrality that has become a caricature of an outmoded psychoanalytic treatment.

In the final chapter of the book, I offer A Summing Up (in the words of the great British storyteller, Somerset Maugham). Eleven statements are provided and discussed that seek to bring together key points in the book, and also underscore some important features that have not been sufficiently addressed. I suppose that if you had to read a single chapter, this is it. But if you do, I hope it also whets your appetite to delve into the other chapters.

Writing this book has helped me stretch my clinical thinking, especially in framing clinical theory in a way that is clinically relevant to practitioners. Of course, as always, it is the reader who will decide the extent to which I have succeeded or failed in this effort. Throughout my career, I have had the privilege, indeed the luxury, of working with extraordinary collaborators, including graduate students, at the University of Maryland. I began to name them, but had to stop because the list is too long and the fear too great that I would omit someone. As for the book manuscript, I want to offer my heartfelt thanks to my research assistants, Ms. Erin Hill and Ms. Jillian Lechner, for their diligent and effective editorial work. I depended on them and they always came through. I want to also express my gratitude to George Zimmar, a former publisher at Routledge, for his encouragement of my writing the book and belief in this work. Finally, thanks are due to Olivia Powers and Lillian Rand for shepherding the book through the editorial and production stages in Routledge. I also want to thank Kristina Wischenkamper for her wise and meticulous editing of the manuscript.

1 An Integrative Conception of the Therapeutic Relationship
Overview of the Tripartite Model

This book is about the relationship that exists between psychotherapists and their patients. As has been abundantly clear to practicing psychotherapists for many decades, and confirmed decisively by empirical research in recent decades, the therapeutic relationship is one of the key elements, or more likely the key element, in the therapeutic change process. More than perhaps any other factor, it is responsible for the success or failure of psychotherapeutic treatments. As will be evident throughout this book, the therapeutic relationship is a function of the feelings, attitudes, and behavior that both the patient and the therapist carry with them into the work and then experience with and enact toward each other during the therapy sessions, and even outside of sessions.

In this first chapter, I define the therapeutic relationship and present a model of its key interlocking elements, which are viewed as a fundamental part of all therapeutic relationships, regardless of the therapist's theoretical orientation. Although I draw from empirical research, my intent throughout is to speak primarily to practitioners, both students in training and practicing therapists across the spectrum of experience levels. While there are fundamental features of all therapeutic relationships, it also seems true that how the therapeutic relationship operates depends on a number of factors. For one, the relationship seems to manifest somewhat differently in brief therapy as compared to longer-term work. In my own experience as a practicing psychotherapist over several decades, I have had the advantage of being involved in a number of very long-term therapies, e.g., therapies lasting five years or more, and in some cases longer than a decade. Writing about these long-term therapies, outside of psychoanalysis, is sorely lacking in the field of psychotherapy, especially in the U.S., where pragmatic issues such as insurance reimbursements and excessive reliance on medication, often at the expense of psychotherapy, have contributed to briefer and briefer treatments. Throughout the book, I shall make distinctions between the operations of the therapeutic relationship in briefer and longer psychotherapies.

Another intent of this first chapter, and indeed the entire book, is to examine how the therapeutic relationship and its elements operate and may be addressed by the therapist in the three major theoretical systems that have been the most prominent over the years: psychoanalytic/psychodynamic therapy, humanistic/experiential therapy, and cognitive/behavioral therapy. To be sure, there are many different theories within and outside these three broad orientations, and these will at times be discussed; but for the purposes of this book, the broad orientations, and their views of the therapeutic relationship and how it is best considered and used in therapy, will be generally sufficient.

As mentioned in the Preface, in this chapter and the entire book, I have drawn a great deal from clinical experience, my own and that of others, including the clinical writing of other psychotherapists and the work of student-trainees I have taught and supervised over the years. Although empirical research, both quantitative and qualitative, is inarguably of great importance, it is our clinical experience that allows us to understand research findings in terms of their implications for actual practice. Our clinical experiences thus serve as a guide to making sense of and using research findings. However, it has been my impression over many decades that psychotherapy scientists have not sufficiently appreciated the great importance of clinical experience and observation, whereas I contend that such experience and observation are of fundamental importance in how we practice our science and art, how we interpret research findings, and indeed just what actually gets studied empirically.

The Relationship Defined

Given the enormous amount of writing and research that has been published on the therapeutic relationship over the past half century, it is rather amazing that so little has been done to define explicitly just what the relationship is and what are its elements.

It's Not the Facilitative Conditions and It's More than the Alliance

Most often, the relationship has been conflated and confused with two factors that, however important, could not possibly serve as a definition of the relationship. For example, some have appeared to define the relationship as synonymous with what Carl Rogers many years ago termed as the necessary and sufficient conditions for therapeutic personality change (Rogers, 1957), in particular, what have been viewed as the three therapist-offered conditions of empathic understanding, unconditional positive regard, and congruence. These Rogerian conditions for successful therapy have been repeatedly supported by research and clinical experience as important, more likely crucial, elements of successful treatment of all kinds (Elliott, Bohart, Watson, & Greenberg, 2011; Farber & Doolin, 2011; Kolden, Klein, Wang, & Austin, 2011). However, simple logic tells us that therapist-offered conditions, no matter how important, cannot serve as a proxy for or definition of the therapeutic relationship, which is an inherently bipersonal concept. That is, the relationship in individual psychotherapy is a two-person phenomenon, and cannot be sufficiently defined by only the therapist's positive contributions. It must be defined in terms of the participants' inner experience and behavior with each other.

A second frequent definition of the therapeutic relationship is essentially the working alliance or the alliance between therapist and patient. Following Bordin's classic paper (Bordin, 1979), the alliance is most often defined as the bond between the participants, the extent of their agreement on the goals of therapy, and the extent of their agreement on the tasks that will likely allow for attainment of those goals. This conception does not contain the logical problems inherent in defining the relationship as only therapist-offered conditions. However, defining the therapeutic relationship as simply the working alliance is much too narrow, and misses other key elements. Although the patient–therapist bond is part of this conception, the focus tends to be on that part of the relationship that reflects the conscious and rational work of therapy. The conception misses other elements that are an important part of all therapeutic relationships. It has been my contention over the years that the therapeutic relationship is more than the working alliance and must be defined and conceptualized in a more comprehensive manner to be most useful clinically and theoretically.

When theorizing about the elements of all therapeutic relationships, Jean Carter and I sought to provide a definition that was general, that incorporated the bipersonal nature of relationships, and that would be relevant to all theoretical orientations (Gelso & Carter, 1985, 1994). We defined the relationship as *the feelings and attitudes that therapist and client have toward one another, and the manner in which these are expressed.* Although including "the manner in which they are expressed" in this definition has been criticized for being too general, and including just about everything (Hill, 1994), we have maintained that the expression of the relationship must be included in any definition because without expression, there can be no relationship. However, we have emphasized that the expression of the relationship may be highly subtle, including a wide range of non-verbal behaviors (e.g., postures, gestures, eye movements, and voice tone), as well as clear and direct verbal behavior. This general definition has appeared to receive considerable acceptance, for example, being adopted in the two editions of Norcross' major handbook on therapeutic relationships.

The Therapeutic Relationship and Therapist Techniques

For any construct to be meaningful in practice or science, it must be defined in a way that makes clear what the construct is not, as well as what it is. As Carter and I early noted, "if the relationship consists of *all* things, then there is nothing else – and a definition would be beside the point" (Gelso & Carter, 1985, p. 159). Perhaps the key construct that the relationship must be differentiated from if it is to be meaningful is that of *therapist technique*, the technical part of therapy. We may conceptualize therapist technique as the operations used by therapists to move treatment forward and bring about change. Techniques generally emanate from the therapist's theory of psychotherapy and of how to bring about constructive change in the patient. The person-centered therapist, for example, tends to make much use of the verbal technique, reflection of feeling; the psychodynamic therapist sees interpretation as a key to change; the cognitive-behavioral therapist focuses on behavioral techniques involving direct guidance; and the process-experiential therapist favors empty-chair techniques and two-chair dialogues. Indeed, in order to be considered a unique theory of therapy, the theory must have an accompanying set of techniques that are, to a degree, different from other theories of therapy. This is so even for theories that appear to eschew techniques, e.g., person-centered theory.

Although it seems true that the relationship part of psychotherapy must be differentiated from the technical or technique part, it is also true that the two are intertwined in important ways. Each of the two influences the other. To use the technique of interpretation as an example, the content, emotional tone, depth, specificity, length, timing, and accuracy of interpretations used by the psychodynamic therapist will have much to do with that therapist's feelings and attitudes toward the patient. So the quality and subtleties of the relationship deeply affect all aspects of technique, and all aspects of the techniques that are used just as deeply affect the quality of the therapeutic relationship.

The Tripartite Model: Theory of the Therapeutic Relationship

Anytime two individuals get together with a task or piece of work at hand, one might see their relationship as consisting of three elements: a work part, a personal non-work part, and a part containing all of the projections each makes onto the other based on the projector's distant and recent past. From this basic view has emerged what I have termed over the past three decades a tripartite model of the therapeutic relationship (Gelso & Carter, 1985, 1994; Gelso & Hayes, 1998; Gelso & Samstag, 2008; Gelso, 2014).

The tripartite model of the therapeutic relationship asserts that *all psychotherapy relationships consist of three interlocking elements: what is termed a real or personal relationship, a working alliance, and a transference–countertransference configuration.* This last element, the transference–countertransference configuration, possesses two sub-parts, patient transference and therapist countertransference. In the remainder of Chapter 1, I shall delve into the tripartite model and present an updated conception of it. To begin with, the theory entails four general propositions:

1   *The three elements or components each exist from the first moments of psychotherapy, and even prior to the first session (e.g., in the patient's thoughts and fantasies of his or her would-be therapist) and they unfold in complex ways over the course of all therapies.*
2   *The three elements relate to or interact with one another over the course of all treatments.*
3   *Precisely how the three elements manifest themselves during therapy and how they unfold over the course of therapy is, to an important extent, dependent on the therapist's theory of therapy.*

4   *The three elements must be attended to if psychotherapy of all orientations is to be maximally successful, although how and how much they are addressed will vary according to the therapist's theory and the patient's qualities.*

We now define the elements and clarify how they operate in general and in the three dominant theoretical orientations. In the subsequent chapters, the concepts from Chapter 1 will be elaborated, with a particular focus on what the therapist can do to strengthen and make maximal use of the therapeutic relationship. Case material will be incorporated into these subsequent chapters in an effort to illuminate the constructs clinically.

The Real Relationship: The Foundation

The real or personal relationship is the non-work, person-to-person aspect of the therapeutic relationship. While it does not have to do directly with the work of therapy, it has everything to do with how the two participants "take to" and feel about each other – how they connect as human beings. An awful lot of this connection pertains to the extent to which the persons are "in the same tribe," so to speak, in terms of personal qualities that matter to them, e.g., ways of seeing and experiencing the world, sense of humor, ease of "getting" each other (see Gelso & Silberberg, 2016). The real relationship and its sister concept, the working alliance, are fundamental elements of the therapy relationship, and, clinically speaking, it is hard to imagine therapeutic work being effective in the absence of a sound real relationship and working alliance. In fact, I have viewed the real relationship as the foundation of the therapeutic relationship, in that everything that happens in the work rests on this personal connection between therapist and patient.

We have defined the real relationship as *the personal relationship marked by the extent to which the participants are genuine with one another and perceive each other in ways that are accurate and fitting* (Gelso, 2009, 2014; Gelso & Hayes, 1998; Gelso & Samstag, 2008). Following this definition, the real relationship is seen as having two basic qualities: genuineness and realism. Genuineness refers to the quality of being real and non-phony in the relationship, whereas realism pertains to experiencing and perceiving the other in ways that fit the other, rather than being projections based on the perceiver/experiencer's issues. My collaborators and I have theorized that what matters most in therapy is the strength of the real relationship, and this strength is determined by two ingredients: *magnitude* of the real relationship (or just how much real relationship exists in the overall relationship) and what we term *valence*, the extent to which the participants' feelings and attitudes toward one another are positive. Generally speaking, the greater the magnitude and valence of the real relationship, the stronger it will be, and the more beneficial will be its impact on the work. This assertion has been substantially supported by research over the past decade and a half (see Gelso, 2011, 2014 for reviews of the empirical research).

Some further clarification of the concept of valence needs to be offered here. We have said that the more positive the participants' feelings toward one another, the better. Does this imply that negative feelings will be harmful to the work and thus do not have a place in effective psychotherapy? Experience suggests that negative transference can be an important ingredient of effective therapy of all orientations, particularly if the therapist helps the patient understand and work through where those feelings come from and what they are about. Indeed, one of our studies suggested that the more secure the patient's attachment to the therapist, the more likely were negative feelings that were considered transferential to come into the open (Woodhouse, Schlosser, Crook, Ligiéro, & Gelso, 2003). A clinically sensible interpretation of this finding is that a sound, secure personal attachment to the therapist allows for the emergence and eventual working through of negative transferences.

Thus, negative transference feelings may exist within the broader context of a positive real or personal relationship. However, for the therapy to work maximally, it is suggested that the participants' feelings for one another as persons, their real relationship, must be largely positive.

The real or personal relationship, as I have said, exists from the first moment of contact between therapist and patient. Both participants will have an immediate impression of the person of the other, an immediate feeling for what the other is like as a person. Some of these impressions will be inaccurate, some driven by transference distortions (discussed subsequently). Still, this sense of the other will drive, for example, what, how, and how much the patient reveals to the therapist, and how the therapist thinks about and responds to the patient. In most cases, the real relationship is on the positive side of the valence continuum right from the beginning of treatment, as suggested by several studies (see summary by Gelso, 2014), and it continues to strengthen as the work progresses. However, the real or personal relationship strengthens more in successful psychotherapies than unsuccessful therapies.

The Real Relationship in the Dominant Theoretical Orientations

Does this personal relationship develop differently in therapies of differing theoretical orientations? Although I have theorized that the real relationship is important in all psychotherapy, and probably equally important across the different theoretical approaches, it is also true that the real relationship shows itself differently and is dealt with differently in the three dominant theoretical forms of therapy.

In humanistic/experiential therapies. A major paradox exists regarding the humanistic/experiential view of the real relationship. On the one hand, given its phenomenological and constructivist philosophical underpinning, the idea of something objectively real does not makes sense to the adherents of this approach. So the realism element of the real relationship has never appealed to humanist therapists. However, the idea of a genuine, person-to-person relationship (the genuineness element of the real relationship) appears to be the centerpiece of the work in all such approaches. From the founding fathers of person-centered therapy and gestalt therapy, Carl Rogers and Fritz Perls respectively, down to the present, for example, Les Greenberg's emotion-focused therapy, the I–thou relationship, or the person-to-person relationship has been seen as vitally significant. Techniques certainly are important, especially for gestalt and emotion-focused therapies, but the personal relationship is salient, in the sense that the therapist must be authentic and genuine in the here-and-now, and must not hide behind a professional shield. And the personal relationship is change-inducing in itself.

Does this centrality and salience of the real relationship in humanistic therapies mean that the therapist should tell all? Should the humanistic/experiential therapist communicate whatever s/he feels with all clients at all times? Although it approaches the ludicrous to think that these questions could be answered in the affirmative, a key question for humanistic/experiential therapists is just what should be communicated, to whom, and when. Greenberg's (2002) suggestions go a long way toward answering this question from the humanistic perspective. He recommends that therapists be sure to embed self-disclosures and immediacy comments within a context of empathy and positive regard for the patient; be sure of what they deeply feel and on their intent of helping the patient (rather than themselves) by making the disclosure; be sensitive to the timing of their disclosures; share their intent in making the immediacy communication; and make clear their openness to the exploration of the patient's reactions to the feelings that are shared by the therapist. In sum, within the humanistic/experiential tradition, the therapist's communications of his or her feelings and attitudes toward the patient are to be embedded in a general set of guidelines or parameters. The therapist is much more disciplined about what and how s/he shares feelings and attitudes with the patient than might appear to be the case at first blush.

In the psychoanalytic/psychodynamic therapies. In psychoanalytic/psychodynamic therapies the real relationship is typically more in the background than in the humanistic/experiential therapies. To be sure, the real relationship is important, especially in the currently popular relational approaches (see Eagle, 2011 for a thorough exploration of classical versus contemporary psychoanalysis). For example, when clinicians such as Renik (1999) suggest that analysts "play with their cards face up" or when interpersonal/psychodynamic therapists such as Teyber (2006) and Hill and Knox (2009) discuss therapist immediacy, they are essentially focusing on the therapist sharing what he or she feels in the moment, toward the patient, within the therapeutic relationship. Yalom (2002), whose orientation encompasses both psychodynamic and humanistic traditions, captures this process of sharing within a real relationship when he advocates "talking in the here and now about the here and now." These viewpoints about the therapist sharing what s/he feels in the relationship and about the patient represent some fundamental changes within psychoanalytic thought, actually a sea change of sorts, and are a far contrast from classical psychoanalytic orthodoxy, with its emphasis on the analyst as a black screen. Still, for most psychoanalytic/psychodynamic therapists, the real relationship and therapist immediacy within it are substantially less salient, less up front, than in the humanistic approaches. And there is relatively greater emphasis than in the humanistic approaches on helping the patient understand and work through their feelings and attitudes toward the therapist that represent a carryover from earlier relationships and unresolved conflicts. We are here talking about transference, which will be discussed shortly.

The cognitive/behavioral therapies. The CBT therapist typically does not conceptualize the work and the therapeutic relationship in terms of a real or personal relationship. CBT therapists do, however, increasingly address "the relationship" as a global entity, and an important one at that. As one studies the newer CBT approaches, an attention to the working alliance, which we discuss next, is apparent. Still, in the current literature in the CBT area, it seems evident that at least a part of what these "third wave" CBT therapists are doing is developing strong real or personal relationships with their patients. For example, a major CBT treatment of persons suffering from borderline personality development, often referred to as dialectical behavior therapy or DBT, very clearly attends to the therapist and patient's feelings toward one another as persons (see, for example, Linehan, 1993; McMain & Wiebe, 2013). The same can be said about other CBT approaches, such as Persons' (2008) case formulation approach to CBT.

Although the real or personal relationship between patient and therapist in CBT naturally exists, as it does in all forms of therapy, it is generally not salient, at least in the professional writing by CBT therapists. Instead, it resides in the background, still undergirding the work. The warmth, caring, and compassion that are a part of modern CBT work are both an element of the real relationship and are seen as helpful in CBT. This real relationship represents a way of fostering patients' adherence to therapist instructions and is a curative ingredient in and of itself (see Persons, 2008).

The Working Alliance: The Catalyst

Although I have viewed the real relationship as the foundation of the therapeutic relationship, successful treatment cannot be accomplished if there is only a strong personal relationship. The participants need also to be joined together in a work relationship – to be a team that can trust each other's willingness and ability to do the work of therapy. In keeping with these features, the working alliance may be seen as that part of the total therapeutic relationship that pertains directly to the work connection between the participants. In our earlier work, Jean Carter and I (Gelso & Carter, 1994) defined the working alliance as *the alignment or joining together of the patient's reasonable self or ego with the therapist's analyzing or therapizing self or ego for the purpose of the work, of accomplishing the work of psychotherapy.*

As indicated, both the therapist and the patient contribute to the building of the working alliance. To clarify further, the therapist contributes by showing that he or she cares for and understands the patient and his or her problems. The therapist also contributes to the alliance by showing that he or she can be trusted to be there for the patient, and that he or she has the therapeutic skills to help the patient and the work move forward. Regarding skills, therapists of differing orientations will likely contribute somewhat differently to the alliance. For example, the psychodynamic therapist may solidify the alliance by making "on the money" interpretations; the humanistic therapist by making empathically attuned reflections of feelings or effectively used two-chair techniques; and the CBT therapist by wisely arranging homework assignments. Similarly, differing techniques will foster the alliance for different patients. As suggested in the seminal qualitative study by Bachelor (1995), what constitutes a good alliance was seen differently by different clients. Some viewed the good alliance as consisting primarily of therapist nurturance (e.g., empathy, positive regard, warmth); others saw good alliances as involving client insight that was fostered by the therapist; and a third cluster perceived the alliance as collaboration, where the therapist and client worked together and shared joint responsibility. As for the patient, s/he must trust, at least to a workable degree, the therapist's skills to get the work accomplished and the therapist's caring attitudes and feelings toward the patient. The patient must also be willing to enter an intimate work relationship.

Going back to our definition of the working alliance, the working alliance involves the reasonable side of the client's self or ego joining with the therapist's working side to do what is needed in treatment. Connecting this conception to the seminal work of Bordin (1979), when these sides are joined together, as both a cause and effect of this joining together, there is a sound working bond between the participants, and they are on the same page regarding the goals of the treatment, whether or not these goals have been explicitly stated. They agree that the goals are worth pursuing and that they are viable as goals. In addition, every therapeutic treatment possesses a range of tasks used by the therapist in an effort to attain the goals that have been established. When tasks make good sense to the patient, and it seems to him or her that these tasks will facilitate the attainment of the goals, the alliance is strengthened. Similarly, when the alliance is strong, the patient is more likely to accept the tasks offered by the therapist.

Just like the real relationship, the working alliance typically is strong right from the first session, and in successful treatments, it tends to strengthen as the work progresses, just like the real relationship. Many have suggested that the working alliance solidifies by the third session, but this assertion has been largely spawned by research on brief therapy. In very long-term work, e.g., psychoanalysis, the great clinician Ralph Greenson suggested that the alliance takes about six months to form. It makes sound clinical sense that just how long it takes to form a sound working alliance depends greatly on the demands and duration of the treatment. For long-term, insight-oriented therapy, for example, which demands a great deal from the patient, my experience has been that a few months are required to solidify the working alliance; but for therapy of a few sessions to a few months in duration, the more commonly suggested 3–5 session timetable is realistic.

Although the working alliance seems to have a similar path as the real relationship, the path for the alliance appears actually to be generally rockier and more variable. As the practicing psychotherapist sees regularly, and the research scholar has discovered, the alliance seems to have more peaks and valleys than the real relationship (see research summary by Horvath, Del Re, Flukiger, & Symonds, 2011). Apart from therapists' actual mistakes (e.g., empathic failures, errors in technique), simply doing one's job will at times weaken the alliance. For example, after the initial connection between therapist and patient, as the therapist begins to understand the core issues of the patient and seeks to move forward in clarifying these core issues, the alliance will often weaken. This is because the therapist, in doing the work of therapy, begins to touch on the defenses in the patient that seek to keep certain issues away from consciousness. In CBT terms, the therapist begins to hit the patient's resistances to behavioral changes.

Because of these natural ups and downs in the alliance, Carter and I early theorized that in successful therapy there would be a high–low–high pattern in the alliance, wherein an initially strong alliance would go through a period of weakening, followed by regaining strength (Gelso & Carter, 1985, 1994). However, the best available empirical evidence suggests an interesting twist in alliance development. It appears that in the most successful treatments, there may well be one or more high-low-high patterns, which is often referred to as "tear-and-repair" or "rupture-and-repair" (see reviews by Horvath et al., 2011, and Safran, Muran, & Eubanks-Carter, 2011). Clinically, this makes much sense. Especially in longer-term therapy, there is no reason to believe that only one high–low–high pattern exists. After the alliance solidifies, there will be occasional ruptures in the alliance due to therapist errors or to the inevitable work of therapy, and in the most effective treatments, the therapist is sensitive to these ruptures and seeks to repair them. In Chapter 3 we shall have more to say about this rupture–repair process.

I suggest that it is the therapist's first, and arguably most important, job to foster a sound working alliance. The therapist's second job is to then preserve that alliance. These two jobs apply to therapies of all theoretical orientations. In Chapter 3, I shall delve more into this process of fostering and preserving the working alliance. For now, suffice it to say that developing and preserving the alliance does not mean, indeed goes far beyond, just being caring and agreeable, and taking the patient's side in his or her struggles with the outside world. Doing simply this compromises the integrity of the working alliance and will only temporarily make the patient feel better; it artificially inflates the alliance.

Although I discussed in some detail how the real relationship is differently construed in the three dominant theoretical approaches to therapy, the working alliance is viewed in similar terms across theories. And all approaches acknowledge the importance of this alliance. In fact, the role of the working alliance in more and less successful psychotherapies has been more vigorously investigated empirically than virtually any other construct in psychotherapy. The findings are so consistent that we no longer really investigate if the working alliance matters. Decades of research have answered this question decisively and affirmatively. How much and in what ways does it matter? Those are more interesting questions, ones that we shall take up in Chapter 3.

Transference and Countertransference: Conflict and Projection

Although transference and countertransference tend to feed and play off each other, they each also make separate contributions to the therapeutic relationship and the success or failure of psychotherapy. Thus, we examine them separately in this section, as well as in Chapters 4 and 5.

Transference in Psychotherapy and Life

The concept of transference emanates from psychoanalysis, and many see this concept as Freud's most important discovery. At the same time, transference is a highly controversial concept, both within and outside of psychoanalysis. Psychodynamic/psychoanalytic therapists struggle with its definition, in particular, the extent to which transference emerges solely from the patient or is a product or co-construction of the therapist–patient relationship. Adherents of other theoretical orientations often dismiss transference as an important factor in treatment, at times suggesting that it is nonexistent or an artifact of the power imbalance some see as inherent in psychoanalytic treatment (see Chapter 4).

As for defining transference, my collaborators and I have sought to develop a conception that integrates classical psychoanalytic conceptions with more contemporary relational/self-psychological viewpoints (Gelso & Hayes, 1998; Gelso & Bhatia, 2012). We have defined transference as *the patient's experience and perceptions of the therapist that are shaped by the patient's own psychological structures and past, involving carryover from and displacement onto the therapist of feelings, attitudes, and behaviors belonging rightfully to and originating in earlier significant relationships*. Although the specifics of transference are always in part tied to the person of the therapist, and are influenced by what the therapist perceives and does, the core theme of transference resides in the patient and his or her unresolved conflicts. It is this core theme, or the core conflictual relationship theme in Luborsky's terms, that is carried from the patient's past into the therapeutic relationship that is the heart of transference. The carryover may reflect the patient's fears and aggressive feelings (as in negative transference) or wishes (as in positive or idealizing transferences). In these ways, the transference may be negatively or positively valenced. Bowlby's (1988) conception that is drawn from the developmental theories of Piaget makes a great deal of sense. Here, Bowlby draws on the Piagetian concepts of assimilation and accommodation to explain transference. In assimilation, the patient wraps new information into an existing mental scheme, whereas in accommodation, the pre-existing scheme is modified to take into account the new information. Transference represents a predominance of assimilation.

It has been my contention that transference is a universal – it occurs in all psychotherapies and indeed in all relationships. This viewpoint has been buffered by our review of research findings on the existence of transference in diverse theoretical approaches to treatment (Gelso & Bhatia, 2012). In that review, Bhatia and I found that transference happens in nonanalytic treatments as well as analytic therapies, and in those treatments transference happens about as much as it does in analytic treatments. We also discovered that the content of transference was about the same in psychoanalytic and nonanalytic treatments, and that transference appears to manifest itself, perhaps increasingly so, as sessions increase, whether or not therapists attend to it. So it appears to be there and to play a role in treatment, whether or not therapists "believe in" transference or pay attention to it.

As for the existence of transference in life and relationships outside of psychotherapy, the social psychological research program by Susan Andersen and her colleagues strongly supports that idea that transference shows itself "throughout interpersonal life in perception and behavior. Prior relationships can and do play out in present ones" (Andersen & Pryzbylinski, 2012, p. 381). These findings are consistent with Freud (1912/1953) original conception of transference as occurring in both therapeutic and everyday relationships, but Andersen's work also greatly extends Freud's ideas.

Transference and its Unfolding in Different Therapies

Although transference occurs in all therapies, as well as in relationships outside of psychotherapy, just how it occurs, how much it shapes and colors the treatment, and how it affects treatment outcomes are surely tied with key aspects of the treatment, such as the therapist's theoretical orientation and treatment duration.

Transference in psychodynamic therapies. From its inception in the early part of the 20th century, transference and its resolution have been a fundamental part of psychoanalytic treatment. In fact, for many years, psychoanalysis was viewed as the systematic analysis of the transferences. However, things have changed in psychoanalysis. Stemming from what is often referred to as the relational tilt in present-day psychoanalysis, transference is now more often seen as a co-constructed phenomenon in which both the therapist and the patient contribute to its particular form and meaning. As this has happened, the definition of transference has shifted. For many now, transference is seen as all of the patient's reactions to and about the therapist. What often goes unrecognized in this change is that if transference is all of the patient's reactions to the therapist, the concept of transference itself becomes essentially meaningless. If transference is everything, then from a scientific perspective, it is nothing; for to be meaningful, a construct has to have boundaries that demarcate what it is from what it is not. If psychoanalysis goes down this totalist road, it can do away with this ambiguous term, transference, and simply refer to the patient's reactions to the analyst. However, if we do this, then we shall likely have to break down the concept into different types, and one of the types would need to be those reactions that are a carryover from unresolved conflicts in the patient's childhood, i.e., the definition we provided earlier, or some facsimile of it.

For most psychoanalytic/psychodynamic psychotherapists, transference, as we have defined it, continues to be a highly central concept. Still, most analytic theoreticians would probably agree that transference is not merely the patient's carryover from the past and projection onto the therapist. There is some important degree of co-construction. The dynamic therapist allows for the transference to emerge by not mixing in too much of his or her own personhood, and by maintaining a healthy or empathic neutrality (see Chapter 2). The therapist then seeks to help the patient understand the transference projections onto the therapist, while also understanding how the particular therapist–patient relationship has helped shape the specifics of the transference. This emerging understanding by the patient into the core transference theme helps the patient come to consciously see not only what s/he is carrying from the past into the therapeutic relationship, but also how this is occurring in other significant relationships in his/her life. The connection of the transference source, the therapeutic relationship, and the patient's outside world of relationships is given deliberate attention by the psychodynamic therapist. That is, the dynamic therapist seeks to foster the patient's insight into this triangle of past–therapy relationship–relationships outside of therapy. The patient's understanding of the transference in the context of an empathic, caring therapeutic relationship is also expected to have a healing effect on the patient's core issues. For example, the patient who feels deeply unworthy of being loved comes to understand how this underlying feeling plays out in the therapeutic relationship in terms of the patient's expectations of the therapist and anger toward the therapist for not caring, and how it plays out in his/her significant relationships in life outside of therapy. As this happens, the patient is gaining insight into how s/he came to feel so unworthy and how this feeling and partly conscious belief is not accurate, i.e., that the patient is of course worthy, as we all are!

Transference in the humanistic/experiential therapies. From the early days of Carl Rogers non-directive and then client-centered (Rogers, 1942, 1951), person-centered therapists have expressed much ambivalence as to the usefulness of transference, and indeed of the mere existence of transference. Carl Rogers and Fritz Perls, the founders of person-centered and gestalt therapy respectively, maintained that transference, while a part of some if not all therapies, was not particularly useful. Rogers believed that the therapist's steadfast expression of empathic understanding, unconditional positive regard, and genuineness or congruence overrode any potentially deleterious effects of transference. Indeed, if the therapist consistently experienced and displayed these three attitudes, whatever transference might appear would eventually dissipate. There was not the sense that transference could be used to benefit the treatment.

For the gestalt therapists, there has been an increasing tendency to pay attention to transference (e.g., Yontef & Jacobs, 2011). In reviewing modern gestalt therapy, Murdock (2013) tells us that the gestalt therapist both attends to transference and sees it as co-constructed by therapist and patient. This seems little different from the current relational tilt in psychoanalysis. The key difference is in how the transference is treated in gestalt therapy. It is not interpreted to the patient, but rather treated as a happening in the here and now therapeutic relationship and also as a sign of *unfinished business* in the patient and responded to with a range of gestalt techniques. I shall have more to say about this in Chapter 4.

Transference in cognitive-behavioral therapies. Although therapists practicing one or another of the variants of CBT have been largely indifferent to the idea of transference, there actually has been a strand of this orientation that has viewed transference as an important phenomenon for decades. For example, over four decades ago Goldfried and Davison (1976) discussed transference in behavior therapy as an important factor. They viewed transference in a way that was highly similar to interpersonal psychoanalytic therapists such as Harry Stack Sullivan and Frieda Fromm-Reichmann, but they did not believe that transference was best treated by providing the patient with interpretations and insight. Instead, the behavior therapist was to view transference as a sample of behavior that was likely to also occur outside the consulting room that could be modified through behavioral techniques.

The current third wave of behavior therapy is much more sensitive than earlier approaches to the therapeutic relationship and its importance, and to transference as a phenomenon within the relationship that should be addressed, especially if it may interfere with the behavioral work of treatment. The general approach of CBT therapists to transference is to point it out when it either interferes with the work of CBT or reflects behaviors that interfere with the patient's life outside of therapy. In this sense, it is remarkable just how prescient Goldfried and Davison were.

How transference unfolds. As the therapist who has been in therapy him/herself likely knows, transference ideas begin in most patients when they start thinking of therapists they might contact for treatment. We create images of who this therapist will be, and these images are given color and shape by our basic interpersonal conflicts and themes. When the actual contact is made by phone or email, these preformed transferences continue to develop, and then they become modified during the patient's first meetings. They are modified both by the reality of the therapist, as well as the patient's core issues and conflicts being carried into the treatment and projected onto the therapist.

These beginning transferences seem to differ for psychoanalytically oriented therapy in contrast to nonanalytic therapy. For example, it would appear to make good clinical sense that negative transference would decrease over sessions in successful therapy. And, indeed, that is what was discovered in one of our studies of theoretically diverse, short-term therapies (12-session duration limit; Gelso, Kivlighan, Wine, Jones, & Friedman, 1997). In more successful cases, negative transference increased to about the midpoint of treatment, and then substantially declined in the latter part. However, for less successful cases, negative transference increased throughout treatment. This pattern fits with what most brief therapists know – negative transference that is unresolved during brief work can essentially wipe out the potentially positive effects of treatment.

The clinically reasonable research findings just noted, however, did not hold up in studies of either psychoanalysis lasting several years or brief psychoanalytic treatment (Graff & Luborsky, 1977; Patton, Kivlighan, & Multon, 1997). Transference increased throughout the course of treatment and was associated with positive outcomes. Thus, in therapies in which transference is a key element of the work, as in psychoanalytic treatments, rising transferences may well signify that the work of therapy is being done, whereas in other treatments, rising transference, especially negatively valenced transference, probably suggests that the therapeutic relationship is being harmed, and that the treatment will not be counted as successful.

There is one more bit of information about transference that may be particularly useful in this overview. That is, it seems that when transference is accompanied by patient insight and understanding, it may be helpful in treatments of all orientations and durations. Several field studies in our therapy relationship laboratory at Maryland have supported this notion (see Gelso, 2014). Even negative transference, or perhaps especially negative transference, can be of great benefit to the treatment, provided that the patient comes to understand his or her projections onto the therapist for what they are – carryovers from past significant relationships. This phenomenon underscores the usefulness of therapists of all theoretical orientations helping their patients explore and examine transferences when they emerge and threaten the success of therapy.

Countertransference and Its Management

Unlike transference, it is generally understood and agreed upon that countertransference occurs in all treatments, regardless of theoretical orientation. Although the definitions of countertransference are many and varied, there is also general agreement that it may be for better or worse – that if understood and managed by the therapist, countertransference can benefit the work; but if countertransference is ignored or poorly understood by the therapist, it can hinder or even irreparably damage the therapeutic relationship, and thus the treatment itself.

Just what is meant by this term, countertransference? Like the term transference, there are a number of definitions, and there is considerable confusion about its meaning and how it is to be used by individual therapists. In Chapter 5 the varying definitions shall be explored in some detail. For the current chapter, we examine a fundamental distinction and source of confusion in conceptualizations of countertransference: what Jeffrey Hayes and I (Gelso &

Hayes, 2007) view as an integrative conception versus what may be seen as a totalistic definition.

As for an integrative conception, drawing on Gelso and Hayes (2007), countertransference may be defined as *the therapist's internal or external reactions to the patient shaped by the therapist's unresolved past or present emotional conflicts or vulnerabilities*. These reactions may be triggered by the patient's behavior or by the therapeutic frame. Regarding the latter, simply doing therapy may stir a set of unresolved issues in the therapist. A common countertransference to the therapeutic frame that we see in trainees is the need to be excessively supportive, to the extent that the difficult comments and questions that we often need to offer to our patients are avoided.

As for the therapist's issues being stimulated by the patient's behavior, to be sure, the patient is certainly implicated in the therapist's countertransference, but the therapist's own conflicts and vulnerabilities are the key "hooks" that create the experience and/or enactment of countertransference. This hook may be highly subtle, but in my view, it must be there if we are to consider the reaction countertransferential. This view is in sharp contrast to the totalistic conception of countertransference that has become popular in recent years. From a totalistic perspective, all therapist emotionally based reactions to the patient constitute countertransference. Thus, the therapist's reactions that are a natural response, not based on unresolved conflicts and vulnerabilities, are included in the definition. If the therapist feels angry in response to naturally anger-provoking patient behavior, or sexually turned on in response to highly seductive patient behavior, or drowsy in response to affectively flat patient behavior, this is considered to be a countertransference reaction. This totalistic conception is seriously problematic for three reasons. First, if countertransference is defined as *all* therapist reactions, then the concept and the term become meaningless. Why not then just use the term "therapist reactions"? Thinking about this from a scientific and theoretical perspective, if a construct is defined as all-encompassing, and has no boundaries, implying that it cannot be differentiated from other constructs, if we cannot specify what that construct *is not*, it is scientifically meaningless. Second, by using the term countertransference, we seem to imply that there is something more, that there is something going on in the therapist other than natural and predictable reactions, and that there is something about the therapist that is being brought to bear. Yet a totalistic definition negates this implication. Third, a totalistic conception that makes countertransference a natural and predictable reaction based on the patient's behavior takes the spotlight off the therapist and his or her issues, which is dangerous. We therapists need to keep the spotlight on ourselves and our unresolved conflicts and vulnerabilities if we are to manage our reactions effectively.

Hayes' and my views about countertransference (e.g., Gelso & Hayes, 2007) have often been misunderstood as implying that therapists' reactions that are natural and predictable, and not based on their own conflicts and vulnerabilities, are unimportant. This is a serious misconception of our frame. All therapist reactions are important, whether or not they are based on their own unresolved conflicts or vulnerabilities! It is just that we believe it scientifically and clinically preferable to reserve the term countertransference for instances in which the therapist's conflicts and vulnerabilities are central in their reactions to the patient. All other instances should be studied as well, and need to be considered by all therapists, regardless of theoretical leanings.

Most often the patient's behavior is a trigger that connects to the therapist's unresolved conflicts and vulnerabilities to create internal reactions in the therapist. These internal reactions may or may not then be acted out in the treatment, and whether or not they are acted out depends on the therapist's countertransference management abilities, to which we now turn.

Managing Countertransference

As I have said, countertransference can be for better or worse, which is why Hayes and I subtitled our countertransference book as "Perils and Possibilities." Whether countertransference is an aid or a hindrance depends, to a large extent, on how effectively it is managed. This concept of management has become somewhat controversial. Some have taken it to mean that countertransference should be controlled to the extent that it no longer exists. To the contrary, since we therapists are all flawed human beings, we shall always have unresolved conflicts and vulnerabilities. What we can and must do is our best to understand the conflicts that are being stirred by our patients and use this understanding to aid in our empathically grasping our patients' inner world and behavior. If we listen and observe carefully, we find that our inner reactions, and also our external behavior, tell us a great deal about our patients, how they affect others, how significant others have treated them, and how they react to others. These understandings can be a key part of treatment. Indeed, accumulated empirical evidence provides strong support for the importance of countertransference management in minimizing the potentially damaging effects of countertransference enactments and in facilitating successful treatment (Hayes, Gelso, & Hummel, 2011).

What are the ingredients of countertransference management? Beginning with my work with VanWagoner, Hayes, and Diemer (1991), my collaborators and I have posited five highly interrelated factors as being key to effectively managing countertransference. These factors are seen as constituents of countertransference management. That is, they actually constitute management itself. The factors have trait-like qualities in the sense that they tend to be a part of the therapist and cut across the therapist's patients. Still, they certainly are malleable and can be strengthened by training and the therapist's own personal therapy. The first and perhaps foremost factor in managing countertransference is the therapist's own *self-understanding or self-insight*. Self-insight includes both intellectual or cognitive insight and integrative insight, which combines intellectual self-understanding and emotional awareness. From the time of Plato's maxim, "know thyself," to Freud's assertion that the therapist must go beyond normality and grasp how his or her complexes and unresolved conflicts affect his or her understanding of the patient, the concept of self-insight in healers has been viewed as deeply significant. In Chapter 5, actions that therapists can undertake to facilitate self-insight are discussed. For here, suffice it to say that grasping one's inner experiences and what those experiences are about in the moment when doing psychotherapy needs to be an ongoing effort on the therapist's part. By grasping one's inner experiences, I include the therapist's understanding of what s/he is experiencing during the therapy hour and understanding his/her feelings and thoughts toward and about the patient in the consulting room. Grasping and understanding these experiences is perhaps ultimately the best antidote to acting the feelings out in the hour, which nearly always undermines effective psychotherapy.

A second and related factor in countertransference management is *therapist empathy*. By empathy, I mean the therapist's ability to intellectually understand and to an extent emotionally experience the inner feelings of the patient. The empathic therapist climbs into the patient's world, cognitively grasps it, and metaphorically takes a taste of the patient's experiencing. Empathy also involves a partial and temporary identification with the patient. In this sense, the therapist *becomes* the patient, although only partially and temporarily. Too much identification with the patient entails the therapist losing him or herself in the relationship, which causes great problems in the relationship. Empathy shall be discussed in detail in Chapter 2. It is one of the most thoroughly studied constructs in psychotherapy, and a wide range of research methods have converged to underscore the importance of therapist empathy to successful treatment.

But just how does therapist empathy aid in countertransference management? The therapist who possesses a high degree of empathy, and thus excels at being attuned to the patient's inner experience, is able in a certain sense to override unresolved conflicts that are being triggered by the patient or the therapeutic frame, and stay focused on the patient and his or her inner world and experience. In addition, it seems likely that the highly empathic therapist actually has fewer unresolved conflicts and vulnerabilities because of his or her empathy. Although the resolution of conflicts and vulnerabilities likely fosters empathy, it also seems true that the capacity for empathy helps resolve conflicts and vulnerabilities. In this sense, the empathic therapist has greater understanding and resolution of his or her issues.

A third factor or constituent of effective countertransference management has been termed *self-integration*. Here we refer to the therapist's possession of a unified, basically intact character structure, which includes psychological health. The integrated therapist is able to know "where s/he stops and the patient starts," that is, able to have boundaries between self and other that are firm without being rigid. This therapist can merge with and separate from the patient without getting stuck in either of the two extremes. S/he does not get lost in the patient's identity and yet is personally integrated enough to enter the patient's world without experiencing the terror of losing the self.

The fourth constituent of countertransference management is *anxiety management*. Anxiety management is seen as the ability to recognize, tolerate, and learn from one's anxiety. Note that we are not referring to eliminating or even minimizing anxiety. Effective countertransference management allows anxiety to be experienced in the session, while at the same time being the subject of the therapist's curiosity. The therapist is able to notice his or her anxiety, and rather than trying to get rid of it, is able to also ask, "What is this about?" "What is making me anxious right now?" The answer shouldn't be just, "the patient and her behavior," but most often is "the patient and his behavior touching on this or that issue in me." Then we can ask, "Is this what the patient does to others when they get close?" "Does this reflect what was done to the patient when growing up?" "Is this what the patient feels with significant others?"

The final constituent of countertransference management is termed *conceptualizing ability*. Being able to have a conceptualization of the patient and the treatment process, as well as the self, helps considerably in managing countertransference. For example, understanding that the patient suffers from this or that disorder helps reduce the therapist's potential negative reactions to the patient connected to the patient's behavior stirring up the therapist's vulnerabilities. When teaching students about this factor, I often refer to the narcissistically injured patient who treats the therapist as if he or she were not a person, or who just doesn't care about the therapist as a separate person. Instead, this therapist is only there to mirror the patient's greatness. I believe these are patients with whom therapists often unconsciously seek to break off treatment. This is so because being non-existent is almost intolerable for us therapists. However, learning about narcissistic personality disorders and, for example, the kinds of transferences, or more broadly relationships, they form, helps considerably in modulating countertransference and the impulse to break off work with the patient. In essence, having a cognitive-conceptual handle of the patient and the therapeutic interaction helps us work with rather than act out potentially damaging countertransference.

Five Factors or Two?

Although we have always conceptualized five elements or constituents of countertransference management ability, our most recent study has led us in a slightly different direction. We conducted a large-scale study from therapy supervisors' perspective and conducted an exploratory factor analysis of a revised measure of countertransference management ability. It appears that the five factors we have studied and theorized over the years may be reduced to two overriding factors. They may be labeled (1) Understanding Self and Others and (2) Self Differentiation. The first global factor includes self-insight, empathy, and conceptualizing ability, whereas the second factor includes self-integration and anxiety management. Clinically this makes a great deal of sense, so long as it is clear that these global factors each include elements from the 5-factor model.

Interrelations Among the Elements of the Tripartite Model

I earlier noted that the elements of the tripartite model are interrelated, that is, each connects in clinically important ways with the other and each influences the other. Just how are they interrelated?

The Real Relationship and the Working Alliance

In his theorizing about the real relationship, Ralph Greenson (1967) believed that the real relationship was the fundamental relationship ingredient in the therapist–patient connection. He suggested that the working alliance emerged from the real relationship, and was an artifact of the work. In other words, a real relationship between therapist and patient was the foundation of the therapeutic relationship, and the working alliance that developed did so for the purpose of getting the work done. The nature of the alliance was deeply affected by the real relationship. All of the research that my collaborators have done on these two variables supports this contention in the sense that working alliance and real relationship have been strongly related to one another. Still, they contribute to the process and outcome separately. So they are indeed different variables, but they are also highly interrelated. Clinically, it makes sense that these two relational variables mutually influence one another. That is, the strength of the developing real relationship, as earlier defined, has a great effect on the quality of the developing working alliance. If my patient and I each have a sense of whom the other is fundamentally, if we are genuine with each other, and if our feelings for the realistically perceived other are mostly positive, then it is a good bet that we shall work well together. Similarly, if we work well together, it also makes sense that this working bond will fuel a stronger personal connection. It is unclear, however, if Greenson was right in his inference that the working alliance emerges from the real relationship, and some evidence actually does not support this supposition (Kivlighan, Hill, Gelso, & Baumann, 2016). Rather, what makes the greatest sense is the idea of a deep and mutual influence of the two elements on each other.

As for their differences, when making presentations on the real relationship, I am often asked to clarify just how the two constructs differ. After defining the two constructs, I invite attendees who have had two or more personal therapies to ponder the differences in their relationships. I describe the therapeutic relationship I had with two different therapists. With one of them, we worked well together and the outcome was successful. I trusted him to do his job effectively, and he did. However, our personal connection was kind of nondescript. I did not particularly take to him, and I do not believe he particularly took to me as a person. But he helped me considerably with some anxiety issues with which I was dealing. So we had a sound working alliance, a weak to moderate real relationship, and the work was successful, although narrowly so. With the second, we also had a sound working alliance and a strong personal connection. Despite many differences, in keys ways we were in the same tribe – we fit well with each other, had compatible senses of humor, and liked each other. The work also went well and had a wider impact than did the first treatment. I have not had the experience of a strong real relationship and a weak working alliance, but it is hard to imagine an effective treatment in which the two persons connected as people, but did not work well together.

Transference, Countertransference, and the Working Alliance

Both transference and countertransference have the potential of damaging the working alliance if left unchecked and ununderstood. As for transference, its hindering effects can be seen most clearly in the case of negative transference, e.g., negative reactions to and expectations of the therapist based on projections of early significant relationships. Left uninterpreted and ununderstood, these negative feelings and perceptions can poison and destroy the alliance, and for many or perhaps most patients, such negative feelings do not simply go away. It is imperative that the therapist help the patient look at where the feelings come from and help them gain insight into both the source of the feelings and how the feelings have not been really "earned" by the therapist. There is ample empirical evidence of the negative relationship between ununderstood negative transference and treatment success (Marmarosh, Gelso, Markin, Majors, Mallery, & Choi, 2009; Levy & Scala, 2012), but most therapists have known the personal sting and disruptive influence of the patients' negative transferences. At the same time, such transferences can greatly aid the alliance and progress in therapy if they are understood by the patient. Thus, as has been found, high degrees of negative transference accompanied by high amounts of patient insight tend to produce highly favorable session and treatment outcomes. What this means for the practitioner is that s/he needs to be on the lookout for negative transference, and to face it when it arises. Just how the therapist is to face it depends on many factors, including the therapist's theory of therapy, personal inclinations, sense of what the patient can tolerate, etc. Transference will be discussed in much greater depth in Chapter 4.

I earlier indicated that the hindering effects of transference are clearest in the case of negative reactions. Positive transferences (e.g., positive misperceptions of the therapist that are carryovers from what the patient wished for but did not get in early significant relationships) often have more subtle effects on the working alliance. The patient who experiences me much more favorably than is fitting for me or than I have earned often seems to benefit from this misperception, which has led clinical theorists to suggest that the therapist not address such positive transferences – just let them do their work in the aid of treatment. However, these positive transferences, as Greenson (1967) early noted, are treacherous allies, i.e., they cannot be counted on. They can readily shift to negative reactions. At times, too, they hide negative reactions and if they are not addressed these hidden negative reactions can damage the work. What I have always found effective is that when the patient's positive reactions to me seem off base or unearned by me, I can point out the positivity (without first indicating that it is not fitting), and invite the patient to explore it. This often opens the door to a deeper exploration of what the patient didn't get while growing up and what the patient yearns for now. Such work deepens the working alliance.

As for countertransference and the alliance, generally speaking, countertransference that is unmanaged and is acted out in the treatment tends to weaken the working alliance and hinder the work, as has been indicated by meta-analyses of studies on this topic (Hayes, Gelso, & Hummel, 2011). As discussed earlier, it is deeply important that the therapist seek to understand what s/he feels in the session, about the patient, and about him/herself in the session with this particular patient so that countertransference reactions do not spill over into the work, but instead are used in the service of the work. This statement applies to positive as well as negative countertransference (see Chapter 5).

I have been discussing how transference and countertransference both aid and weaken the working alliance. The reverse is also true. That is, the strength of the working alliance also affects transference and countertransference. When the alliance is strong, this serves as a buffer against the potentially pernicious effects of transference, and facilitates the patient's willingness to look into the transference rather than acting it out in the treatment. In this sense, the good working alliance positively influences transference work, which then ultimately strengthens the alliance. So too with countertransference. A sound alliance diminishes countertransference and also makes it easier for the therapist to understand the countertransference reactions that do occur.

Transference, Countertransference, and the Real Relationship

Given that part of the definition of the real relationship implies that the therapy participants perceive and experience each other in ways that befit the other, it naturally follows that transference and the real relationship are negatively related. In fact, this has been supported by virtually every study that has examined this relationship. The more realistically the participants perceive and experience each other, and the more they are genuinely themselves with each other, the less the amount of transference that emerges. Still, transference and the real relationship can co-exist, as indicated by the following case:

> In my first session following a rather serious surgery, my patient, John, expressed concern by asking "How are you doing buddy?" I replied honestly, "I am doing well, thanks." As I began to pursue how some of his concern was transferentially related to the material with which we had been dealing, John replied, "Well, that may be so, but I also was just concerned about you as a person." As I pondered the expression of concern, it seemed clear to me that his single expression was both very rich with transference and very deeply reflective of the real relationship.
> (Gelso, 2009, p. 257)

Moreover, as I have elsewhere elaborated, transference and the real relationship can co-exist in the same session, and indeed in the very same expression. Still, transference, especially negatively valenced transference, can weaken the real relationship if ununderstood. And if the transference is too negative and occurs without understanding, it can essentially destroy the real relationship. On the other side of things, a strong developing real relationship not only can aid in the resolution of transference, but can also facilitate the emergence of repressed transference so that it can be worked through. In this sense, the real relationship serves as a buffer against feelings that are threatening to the patient and the relationship. It allows for a secure base from which feelings that are frightening to the patient can more safely emerge. In sum, although the transference (especially negative transference) and the real relationship tend to negatively influence each other, the strength of the real relationship can foster the emergence and resolution of transference.

Transference and Countertransference

If we take a totalistic perspective (as discussed earlier), patient transference and therapist countertransference invariably and mutually influence one another. They are part of the same dance, and perhaps the tango is an apt metaphor. Each move made by one partner affects the moves of the other in a synchronized fashion. This synchrony continues throughout the life of the dance. When using the totalistic conception, an extremely high correlation would be expected between patient transference and therapist countertransference.

When we move away from the totalistic definition of transference and countertransference, mutual influence would still be expected, but the relationship would not be as strong. Transference and countertransference would not be as synchronous, and the tango metaphor is no longer fitting. The proper metaphor would be to other dances in which the partners are in synchrony to varying degrees, as many of the moves emanate from the individual participants and are not in response to the other. This partial synchrony may occur for several reasons. First, the therapist may experience countertransference internally, but be able to effectively understand these feelings rather than act them out with the patient. Second, not all countertransference is triggered by the patient. As discussed earlier, some countertransference is to the frame of the treatment. That is, some countertransference is chronic. It is carried with the therapist into the treatment and set into motion by simply being in the therapeutic situation. Additionally, some patient transference is not in response to countertransference, but instead is triggered by the therapist's non-countertransference behavior or by simply being in the room with a therapist. Using our integrative definition, rather than the totalistic definition, one would still expect mutual influence of transference and countertransference, but not as strong. In other words, the relationship between the two would be much lower. There has been little research on this topic, but one study in our therapeutic relationship research program at the University of Maryland does support a modest relationship between patient transference and therapist countertransference (Bhatia & Gelso, 2017), suggesting a degree of mutual influence.

The Lived and Living Relationship

I have been describing the elements as if they can be sharply distinguished. Although this is so at times, more often than not the elements operate in concert. In the living relationship, all the elements happen at the same time, although each may come to the surface, and become figure rather than ground, at different points.

In the lived psychotherapy hour, the participants generally busy themselves playing their designated roles of patient and therapist. The patient is busy telling his or her story, getting in touch with feelings and thoughts, trying to understand the whys and whats of his or her life, working on changing, and responding to the therapist. The therapist, on the other hand, is working to grasp empathically the client's inner experience and behavior, creating a secure base from which the patient may explore emotionally threatening feelings and experiences, trying to make sense of the patient's core issues, and attempting to make responses to the patient that show understanding and are drawn from the therapist's implicit or explicit theory of psychotherapy and change. Things happen quickly in the hour, and the therapist must process much information and material in short periods of time. S/he must be both a good observer of the relationship and a sensitive participant in it. Much of what the therapist does in the hour is essentially the same across theories of therapy, although points of emphasis will surely depend importantly on that theory. The humanistic therapist will focus on the inner experience of the patient and will often reflect back to the patient what the therapist hears; the psychodynamic therapist will tend to also explore inner experience, but will search for underlying patterns and defenses which will then be pointed out to the patient; and the cognitive-behavioral therapist will explore the presenting problem, and guide the patient toward changing dysfunctional cognitions and behaviors.

As the patient and therapist go about this business of therapeutic work, the relationship is happening. The working alliance, real relationship, transference, and countertransference are inevitably in progress, generally as the ground or periphery of the work, but at times at center stage. Throughout the work, effective therapists of all theoretical orientations are paying attention to their own inner experience and outer behavior, even as they are observing and participating in the patient's emotional world. This ongoing dual process of participating and observing is one of the great complexities of the practice of psychotherapy, and both theory and empirical evidence support its importance (Gelso & Hayes, 2007; Hayes, Gelso, & Hummel, 2011).

As I have said, the different components of the relationship shift from figure to ground throughout the work. At times, especially times of stress in the relationship or times of intimate connection, the personal relationship comes to the fore and the work is about that. A strong real or personal relationship can be of great benefit when negative transference reactions are experienced and expressed by the patient. This real relationship serves as a buffer against the potentially damaging feelings in the transference. At other points, the working alliance becomes the main thing, e.g., when there are ruptures in the working alliance, when the therapist does something especially effective in the patient's mind, when the therapist enacts an empathic failure. Like the real relationship, the working alliance can serve as a buffer against negative transference. At certain points (sessions or series of sessions), the work becomes all about the patient's transference based feelings toward the therapist or the therapist's reactions to the patient based on the therapist's unresolved personal conflicts.

Even as the elements are fluid, changing from figure to ground during a treatment or a session, they may manifest simultaneously during even a given expression. An example of this dual manifestation follows:

> The patient was a 41-year-old woman who had been in psychoanalytic psychotherapy with the author for several years. During a given session, she was describing her need to separate emotionally from her provocative father and brother if she was to truly enjoy her sexual relationship with her husband, with whom she had a sound and happy marriage. However, the thought of this necessary separation created anxiety and sadness. She had the wish that the therapist would emotionally embrace her and hold her hand during this process, but then realized that one way of being so embraced that she wished for actually served to maintain the unhealthy connection to her father, i.e., the therapist would then become the provocative father. Another way of being embraced would allow the therapist, as a real person, to join with the patient as the adult she had become in helping her cope with the loss resulting from this necessary separation.
> (Gelso & Hayes, 1998, p. 135)

In this vignette, within the context of a strong working alliance, the patient was able to manifest both an eroticized transference and a strong real relationship in the very same expression. This mixture of transference and real relationship exerted its influence on the therapist's countertransference feelings, as well as on his experience of the real relationship with the patient. The strong working alliance facilitated the exploration of these threatening affects in the patient, and they also aided in the therapist's self-exploration.

As earlier discussed, during the hour the therapist is often unaware of the relationship elements or even of the relationship itself. The focus instead is on the patient's story, inner experience, dynamics, and responding in a way that is both helpful and often drawn from the therapist's theory. This is as it should be, for even in very relationship-oriented work, much of what happens in the hour is not and need not be about the relationship. But the relationship is still there, still unfolding. And at times it becomes so salient that only the therapist's defenses would allow him or her to miss it, even if the therapist does not espouse a relationship-based theory.

References

Andersen, S. M., & Pryzbylinski, E. (2012). Experiments on transference in interpersonal relations: Implications for treatment. *Psychotherapy*, 49(3), 364–369. doi:10.1037/a0029116

Bachelor, A. (1995). Clients' perceptions of the therapeutic alliance: A qualitative analysis. *Journal of Counseling Psychology*, 42, 323–337. doi:10.1037/0022-0167-423.323

Bhatia, A., & Gelso, C. J. (2017). Therapists' perspective on the therapeutic relationship: Examining a tripartite model. *Counselling Psychology Quarterly*, 1–23. doi:10.1080/09515070.2017.1302409

Bordin, E. S. (1979). The generalizability of the psychoanalytic concept of the working alliance. *Psychotherapy: Theory, Research & Practice*, 16(3), 252–260. doi:10.1037/h0085885

Bowlby, J. (1988). *A secure base: Parent–child attachment and healthy human development.* New York, NY: Basic Books.

Eagle, M. N. (2011). *From classical to contemporary psychoanalysis: A critique and integration.* New York, NY: Routledge.

Elliott, R., Bohart, A. C., Watson, J. C., & Greenberg, L. S. (2011). Empathy. In J. C. Norcross, &. J. Lambert (Eds.), *Psychotherapy relationships that work* (2nd ed., pp. 132–152). New York, NY: Oxford.

Farber, B. A. & Doolin, E. M. (2011). Positive regard and affirmation. In J. C. Norcross, &. J. Lambert (Eds.), *Psychotherapy relationships that work* (2nd ed., pp. 168–186). New York, NY: Oxford.

Freud, S. (1912/1953). The dynamics of transference. In J. Strachey (Ed. & Trans.), *Standard edition of the complete works of Sigmund Freud* (Vol. 12, pp. 97–108). London: Hogarth Press. (Original work published in 1912.)

Gelso, C. J. (2009). The real relationship in a postmodern world: Theoretical and empirical explorations. *Psychotherapy Research*, 19(3), 253–264. doi:10.1080/10503300802389242

Gelso, C. J. (2011). *The real relationship in psychotherapy: The hidden foundation of change.* Washington, DC: American Psychological Association.

Gelso, C. J. (2014). A tripartite model of the therapeutic relationship: Theory, research, and practice. *Psychotherapy Research*, 24, 117–131. doi:10.1080/10503307.2013.845920

Gelso, C. J., & Bhatia, A. (2012). Crossing theoretical lines: The role and effect of transference in nonanalytic psychotherapies. *Psychotherapy*, 49(3), 384–390. doi:10.1037/a0028802

Gelso, C. J., & Carter, J. A. (1985). The real relationship in counseling and psychotherapy: Components, consequences, and theoretical antecedents. *The Counseling Psychologist*, 13(2), 155–244. doi:10.1177/0011000085132001

Gelso, C. J., & Carter, J. A. (1994). Components of the psychotherapy relationship: Their interaction and unfolding during treatment. *Journal of Counseling Psychology*, 41(3), 296–306. doi:10.1037/0022-0167.41.3.296

Gelso, C. J., & Hayes, J. A. (1998). *The psychotherapy relationship: Theory, research, and practice.* New York: Wiley.

Gelso, C. J., & Hayes, J. A. (2007). *Countertransference and the therapist's inner experience: Perils and possibilities.* Mahwah, NJ: Erlbaum.

Gelso, C. J., Kivlighan, D. M., Wine, B., Jones, A., & Friedman, S. (1997). Transference, insight, and the course of time-limited psychotherapy. *Journal of Counseling Psychology*, 44(2), 209–217. doi:10.1037/0022-0167.44.2.209

Gelso, C. J., & Samstag, L. W. (2008). A tripartite model of the therapeutic relationship. In S. Brown & R. Lent (Eds), *Handbook of counseling psychology* (4th ed., pp. 267–283). New York: Wiley.

Gelso, C. J., & Silberberg, A. (2016). Strengthening the real relationship: What is a psychotherapist to do? *Practice Innovations*, 1, 154–163. doi:10.1037/pri0000024

Goldfried, M. R., & Davison, G. C. (1976). *Clinical behavior therapy.* New York: Holt, Rinehart & Winston.

Graff, H., & Luborsky, L. (1977). Long-term trends in transference and resistance: A report of a quantitative-analytic method applied to four psychoanalyses. *Journal of the American Psychoanalytic Association*, 25(2), 471–490. doi:10.1177/000306517702500210

Greenberg, L. S. (2002). *Emotion-focused therapy: Coaching clients to work through their feelings.* Washington, DC: American Psychological Association. doi:10.1037/10447-000

Greenson, R. R. (1967). *The technique and practice of psychoanalysis* (Vol. 1). New York: International Universities Press.

Hayes, J. A., Gelso, C. J., & Hummel, A. M. (2011). Managing countertransference. In J. C. Norcross (Ed.), *Psychotherapy relationships that work* (2nd ed., pp. 239–258). New York: Oxford University Press.

Hill, C. E. (1994). What is the therapeutic relationship? *The Counseling Psychologist*, 22 (1), 90–97. doi:10.1177/0011000094221005

Hill, C. E., & Knox, S. (2009). Processing the therapeutic relationship. *Psychotherapy Research*, 19, 13–29. doi:10.1080/10503300802621206

Horvath, A. O., Del Re, A. C., Flukiger, C., & Symonds, D. (2011). Alliance in adult psychotherapy. In J. C. Norcross (Ed.), *Psychotherapy relationships that work* (2nd ed., pp. 25–69). New York: Oxford University Press.

Kivlighan, D. M., Hill, C. E., Gelso, C. J., & Baumann, E. (2016). Working Alliance, real relationship, session quality and client improvement in psychodynamic psychotherapy: A longitudinal actor partner interdependence model. *Journal of Counseling Psychology*, 63, 149–161. doi:10.1037/cou0000134

Kolden, G. G., Klein, M. H., Wang, C., & Austin, S. B. (2011). Congruence/Genuineness. In J. C. Norcross (Ed.), *Psychotherapy relationships that work* (2nd ed., pp. 187–202). New York: Oxford University Press.

Levy, K. N., & Scala, J. W. (2012). Transference, transference interpretations, and transference-focused psychotherapies. *Psychotherapy*, 49(3), 391–403. doi:10.1037/a0029371

Linehan, M. (1993). *Cognitive-behavioral treatment of borderline personality disorder.* New York, NY: Guilford Press.

Marmarosh, C. L., Gelso, C. J., Markin, R. D., Majors, R., Mallery, C., & Choi, J. (2009). The real relationship in psychotherapy: Relationships to adult attachments, working alliance, transference, and therapy outcome. *Journal of Counseling Psychology*, 56(3), 337–350. doi:10.1037/a0015169

McMain, S. & Wiebe, C. (2013). Therapist compassion: A dialectical behavior therapy perspective. In A. Wolf, M. Goldfried, & J. C. Muran (Eds.), *Transforming negative reactions to clients: From frustration to compassion.* (pp. 163–174). Washington, DC: American Psychological Association.

Murdock, N. L. (2013). *Theories of counseling and psychotherapy: A case approach* (3rd ed.). New York, NY: Pearson.

Patton, M. J., Kivlighan, D. M., & Multon, K. D. (1997). The Missouri Psychoanalytic Counseling Research Project: Relation of changes in counseling process to client outcomes. *Journal of Counseling Psychology*, 44(2), 189–208. doi:10.1037/0022-0167.44.2.189

Persons, J. B. (2008). *The case formulation approach to cognitive-behavior therapy*. New York, NY: Guilford Press.

Renik, O. (1999). Analytic interaction: Conceptualizing technique in light of the analyst's irreducible subjectivity. In S. Mitchell, & L. Aron (Eds.), *Relational psychoanalysis: The emergence of a tradition* (pp. 407–424). Hillsdale, NJ: Analytic Press.

Rogers, C. R. (1942). *Counseling and psychotherapy*. Boston, MA: Houghton-Mifflin.

Rogers, C. R. (1951). *Client-centered therapy*. Boston, MA: Houghton-Mifflin.

Rogers, C. R. (1957). The necessary and sufficient conditions of therapeutic personality change. *Journal of Consulting Psychology*, 21(2), 95–103. doi:10.1037/h0045357

Safran, J. D., Muran, J. C., & Eubanks-Carter, C. (2011). Repairing alliance ruptures. *Psychotherapy Relationships That Work*, 224–238. doi:10.1093/acprof:oso/9780199737208.003.0011

Teyber, E. (2006). *Interpersonal process in psychotherapy: A relational approach* (5th ed.). Pacific Grove, CA: Brooks/Cole.

VanWagoner, S. L., Gelso, C. J., Hayes, J. A., & Diemer, R. A. (1991). Countertransference and the reputedly excellent therapist. *Psychotherapy*, 28(3), 411–421. doi:10.1037/0033-3204.28.3.411

Woodhouse, S. S., Schlosser, L. Z., Crook, R. E., Ligiéro, D. P., & Gelso, C. J. (2003). Client attachment to therapist: Relations to transference and client recollections of parental caregiving. *Journal of Counseling Psychology*, 50(4), 395–408. doi:10.1037/0022-0167.50.4.395

Yalom, I. D. (2002). *The gift of therapy: An open letter to a new generation of therapists and their patients*. New York, NY: HarperCollins.

Yontef, G. M., & Jacobs, L. (2011). Gestalt therapy. In R. J. Corsini, & D. Wedding (Eds.), *Current psychotherapies* (9th ed., pp. 342–382). Belmont, CA: Brooks/Cole.

2 The Empathic Way and Benevolent Neutrality

The tripartite model discussed in Chapter 1 reflects a structure of the therapeutic relationship that is theorized as cutting across all theoretical types and forms of psychotherapy. But it certainly does not include all of the key ingredients of effective treatment. We may ask the further question of how in general the therapist should be with the patient. Is there a particular way of being or therapeutic stance that serves to strengthen the real relationship and working alliance, and allows for the resolution of transferences that are problematic? Is there a way of being that facilitates depth of self-exploration and the attainment of understanding and insight in the patient, and thus helps the patient feel better about him or herself?

I believe there is such a way, one that is supported by both years of research and clinical experience. We might call it the empathic way. It is theorized further that this way of being is most powerfully curative when offered in a certain context, that of therapeutic neutrality. This is a certain kind of neutrality, far different from the caricature of the indifferent, bland, passive psychoanalyst that has pervaded the psychotherapy literature in recent decades.

It may seem contradictory to lump these two concepts, the empathic way and therapeutic neutrality, together into a conception of effective psychotherapy. Yet I believe that what at first glance may appear to be strange bedfellows will, upon deeper exploration, be seen as compatible partners. The empathic way facilitates the relational connection afforded by therapist empathy, caring, and affirmation (discussed subsequently) that are, to a degree, transformative in and of themselves. It also provides the safety needed by the patient to move into material that may otherwise feel too threatening and dangerous to the patient. However, therapeutic neutrality on the therapist's part is also needed if the patient is to go further – to dig into what it is that makes him or her tick psychologically, the ways in which s/he has become the architect of his or her own miseries (despite the reality that the roots of those miseries are embedded in early relationships and learnings).

This chapter is based on my work with Dr. Katri Kanninen (Gelso & Kanninen, 2017a, 2017b). Kanninen and I shared the view that an empathic way of being was of fundamental importance to successful treatment, but we were both troubled by what has appeared to be a pattern in recent years of therapists of all persuasions sympathizing too much with their patients, too often taking sides emotionally and verbally with their patients' externalization of their problems, providing too much direct support and guidance, and pulling too much for patients' emotions with the implicit or explicit belief that emotional expression was the panacea for psychopathology. It too often has seemed as if sympathetic listening, often to the extent of supportive agreement with the patient, is seen as constituting empathy and is sufficient in the minds and actions of many therapists. Instead, we offer that the empathic way combined with benevolent neutrality is a fundamental condition for therapeutic change. In the remainder of this chapter, the dual concepts of the empathic way and therapeutic neutrality are explored.

The Empathic Way

The empathic way includes the key therapeutic elements of therapist empathy for the patient, caring of the patient, and affirmation of the patient. Taken together, these elements provide the relational context for successful therapy. Indeed, it is hard to imagine psychotherapy or counseling having a positive and transformative effect on the patient if these ingredients are not present or are present in small amounts. Empirical evidence accumulated over decades does support the importance of these factors in psychotherapies of all orientations (Elliott, Bohart, Watson, & Greenberg, 2011; Farber & Doolin, 2011).

Empathy: What it is

Of all the qualities that therapists can possess, I believe that the single most important may well be empathy. Empirical evidence gathered over a period of more than five decades (e.g., Elliott, Bohart, Watson, & Greenberg, 2011) unequivocally points to the value of therapist empathy. This is an ingredient that therapists of virtually all theoretical persuasions agree upon. Humanistic/experiential therapists and psychoanalytic/psychodynamic therapists have written about it most extensively, but cognitive-behavioral therapists, too, agree on its importance. These persuasions do, however, differ in just how important is empathy, and just what it is important for in treatment.

There are many conceptions of empathy within the field of psychotherapy, and conceptions by therapists often diverge from those of social and developmental psychologists (see Bohart & Greenberg, 1997). In considering just what empathy is, it may be best to look at both humanistic and psychoanalytic thinking. In fact, when one gets beyond terminology and semantics, these often divergent theory clusters are generally in close agreement about the meaning of empathy. As for humanistic thought, I believe that Carl Rogers' early formulations have remained highly significant and have not really been improved upon. Let us look at what Rogers had to say:

> The state of empathy, or being empathic, is to perceive the internal frame of reference of another with accuracy and with the emotional components

and meanings which pertain thereto as if one were the person, but without ever losing the "as if" condition. Thus it means to sense the hurt or the pleasure of another as he senses it and to perceive the cause thereof as he perceives them, but without ever losing that it is *as if* I were hurt or pleased and so forth. If this "as if" quality is lost, then the state is one of identification.

(Rogers, 1959, pp. 210–211)

In his later work, Rogers (1980) seemed to amplify this position, perhaps taking it a step further. He says of empathy that:

It means entering the private perceptual world of the other and becoming thoroughly at home in it. It involves being sensitive, moment by moment, to the changing felt meanings which flow in this other person, to the fear or rage or tenderness or confusion or whatever that he or she is experiencing. It means temporarily living in the other's life, moving about in it, delicately without making judgments; it means sensing meanings of which he or she is scarcely aware, but not trying to uncover totally unconscious feelings, since this would be too threatening.

(p. 142)

To this Rogers added a communication element, in terms of what the therapist was to do with the experience of empathy:

It includes communicating your sensings of the person's world as you look with fresh and unfrightened eyes at elements of which he or she is fearful. It means frequently checking with the person as to the accuracy of your sensings, and being guided by the responses you receive. You are a confident companion to the person in his or her inner world.

(Rogers, 1980, p. 142)

Although psychoanalysts may disagree with humanistic conceptions of empathy in terms of its purpose in and impact upon the treatment process, they fundamentally agree with Rogers' conception, as implied above. Thus, for example, Heinz Kohut, the founder of psychoanalytic self psychology and the psychoanalyst most responsible for making therapist empathy the centerpiece of analytic work, viewed empathy as *vicarious introspection*, by which he means "the capacity to think and feel oneself into the inner life of another person" (Kohut, 1984, p. 82). Stated simply, for the psychoanalytic therapist "empathy entails taking the role of the other and seeing the other from his or her internal frame of reference" (Eagle & Wolitzky, 1997, p. 217).

What can we gather about therapist empathy from the above examination? First, *empathy involves some degree of identification with the patient*, consciously or unconsciously. When the therapist puts him or herself into the patient's shoes, the therapist is so identifying, climbing into the other's self or being and/or taking the other inside. Second, *the identification is partial and vicarious, not complete.* When Rogers refers to the "as if" nature of empathy, he implies that the therapist's self is not lost in the patient, the therapist does not merge with the patient. Instead, the therapist always retains a part of his or her self. If the therapist fails at this, enmeshment results, which reflects a serious countertransference problem. This implies that effective empathy involves an optimum distance, neither total immersion nor total separateness. When Kohut (1971, 1977, 1984) defined empathy as "vicarious introspection," I believe that this is what he was driving at, although the phrase itself (vicarious introspection) may seem maddeningly ambiguous. Vicarious introspection may be seen as using part of oneself to introspect as if you were the patient.

Third, empathy may involve both cognitive understanding and/or to an extent feeling the patient's feelings. Nearly everyone agrees with this cognitive part — that empathy entails the therapist understanding intellectually the patient and how s/he is experiencing in the moment, and over minutes, hours, or sessions. However, there is much disagreement as to whether empathy involves the therapist actually feeling what the patient feels. Some suggest that what the therapist feels is how he or she would feel in the same situation the patient is describing and feeling about. And some describe this kind of thing as "egocentric empathy" (Hoffman, 1984). I would offer that the partial identification does involve at times going beyond thinking and entails actually experiencing or partaking of some of what the patient feels, or at least involves the kind of sensing that goes beyond mere cognitive understanding. After all, when the therapist climbs into the patient's shoes, the therapist should be able to experience what the patient experiences, while at the same time remaining partly separate from the patient.

What Empathy is not

Given some of the ambiguities that surround the concept of empathy, it may be just as important to discuss what empathy is not as it is to discuss what empathy is. Over the years, empathy has been too often linked with the technique or helping skill referred to as reflection of feeling. In fact, the equating of empathy with reflection became so strong that old school client-centered therapists seemed to constantly reflect their clients' feelings, intending to have the client experience the therapist's empathy. This reached such a degree that these therapists were poked fun at and were caricatured as simply parroting back to the patient what the patient had just expressed. This deeply troubled Carl Rogers (see Rogers, 1980), and he made the point repeatedly that empathy and other key therapist conditions for client change were attitudes of the therapist, not skills (such as reflection of feeling).

Although reflecting the patient's overt or subtle feelings back to him or her may reveal empathy on the part of the therapist, and may be experienced as such by the patient, this is certainly not always the case. Sometimes reflecting feelings can be experienced as deeply nonempathic. An example from the experience of one of my therapy supervisees, a gifted young trainee, was reported in Gelso & Kanninen (2017a, p. 338). This trainee's

> reflections of feeling were experienced by her patient as distancing, unhelpful and unempathic. The patient, who was suffering from a borderline personality disorder, needed a relationship with a real person, where there was some give and take. The therapist, who was frightened by the patient's aggressiveness, maintained a superficially safe position by constantly reflecting the patient's feelings, which, however accurate, stirred an even deeper feeling of abandonment in this very troubled patient. As the therapist became freer to share what she felt in the relationship, appropriately relate her own views of the patient's experience, and help the patient see what was underlying this experience, the patient's feeling of being empathically understood strengthened, as did the patient's experience of the therapeutic relationship.

Empathy is also neither sympathy nor subtle agreement with the patient's views and feelings. Of course, one of the first things that therapist-trainees learn is that empathy is not sympathy. Sympathy may be seen as involving feeling *for* the patient, with the implication that the sympathizer is highly identified with the patient. It does not necessarily entail understanding what is going on at various levels in the patient's mind. We know that, although therapy must contain some degree of human sympathy, sympathy is not very helpful in the long run.

What tends to be less readily learned (and taught) is how empathy is also neither subtle agreement nor more subtle forms of sympathy. Expressions like "it must be so hard for you to put up with your boy/girlfriend's outbursts" or more simply "that has to hurt," likely communicate both sympathy and agreement with the patient's hidden or overt complaints about his or her partner. A statement like "it sounds like it is really hard for you to take your boy/girlfriend's outbursts" may reflect accurate understanding (empathy), whereas "it must be so hard for you to put up with your boy/girlfriend's outbursts" is more sympathy in the sense that too much of the therapist's self is involved and is taking sides with the patient.

Finally, empathy should not be conflated with caring or positive regard. One can empathically grasp another without especially caring about that person, and in fact, empathy can be used to manipulate the other for personal gains. Some of the world's greatest salespersons have considerable empathy, and they use this knowledge to promote products.

What empathy is and is not is nicely summarized in one of the most illuminating chapters ever written on the topic. Greenberg and Elliott (1997) tell us that

> the empathic therapist attempts to operate within the internal frame of reference of the client and to remain in empathic contact with the client's

inner world. Empathy involves listening from the inside as if 'I am the other,'.... Empathy is not simply friendly rapport, sympathetic encouraging, listening, or being warm and supportive. Conflation of empathy with these common social responses, essentially forms of rapport, has resulted in one of the major persistent misunderstandings of the nature of empathy in some approaches that claim to be empathic.

(pp. 167–168)

How is Empathy Expressed?

How is empathy expressed in therapeutic settings? As pointed to by Bohart and Greenberg (1997), and many others, empathy can be expressed in many ways. A dynamic interpretation that is close enough to the patient's level of awareness that it stimulates the patient's realization about the meaning of certain actions may be experienced as deep empathy. For example, when the psychodynamic therapist points out that the patient becomes teary when she talks about how her former high school teacher still seems to care about her, while she has been talking about her parents without any hint of affection or love from them, the patient realizes that she has been avoiding a deep feeling of being unloved by her parents. The therapist has, in effect, made a well-timed and accurate interpretation of the patient's defensive avoidance of her feelings of being unloved; and because it is accurate and well-timed, thus producing insight in the patient, it is experienced as deeply empathic. Similarly, the experiential therapist's reflections of the patient's feelings that are on the edge of awareness will be experienced as deeply empathic. Even seemingly avoidant or irrelevant therapist responses may be quite empathic. One of my favorite examples of empathy was presented some years ago by Bozarth (1984). Following a session in which a highly vulnerable patient felt terribly blocked, she began the next session by asking her therapist ..."What have you been doing?" He responded by telling a story, lasting nearly the entire session, about his car. The patient subsequently told the therapist how she appreciated his not pushing her to confront once again her struggles, and how in fact the session helped her identify the core of her problems! The therapist apparently deeply grasped the patient's emotional situation and responded in a way that was therapeutic, although on the surface what he did looked like anything but empathy, at least as seen through traditional lenses.

This view that empathy can be expressed in a wide range of ways is in keeping with Rogers (1980) long-standing view that empathy is an attitude and not a technique. As such, it can be expressed through a range of techniques, not simply reflections of feeling.

Why Does Empathy Help?

Just how and why does empathy produce constructive change in patients? This, of course, is a far-reaching and highly complex question that could take an entire book to address fully (see Bohart & Greenberg, 1997), but here I offer a brief viewpoint. In keeping with psychoanalytic self psychologists, as well as humanistic/experiential therapists, the need to be empathically understood is a fundamental part of humanness, and experiencing it sufficiently early in life fosters the development of a solid and healthy self. Similarly, the lack of what has been termed empathic mirroring from our primary caretakers in our early years leaves us vulnerable and without a sound self or sense of self-worth. The therapist's empathy, expressed in manifold ways, has essentially two functions. First, it partially makes up for this developmental deficiency, the weakened sense of self and self-worth, that the patient has carried with him or her, perhaps throughout life and into the therapist's consulting room. In this sense, empathy is curative in and of itself for some patients and to some degree.

The second way in which the therapist's empathy helps is by allowing the therapist to understand how to respond to the patient. From a psychodynamic or humanistic perspective, it is the therapist's empathy more than anything else that permits the therapist to understand the patient's inner workings from the patient's perspective, which in turn informs the therapist about what to say to the patient and how to say it. From a CBT perspective, the therapist's guidance, suggestions, framing of homework assignments, and other tasks cannot simply come from a cookbook. The CBT therapist's empathic comprehension of the patient from the inside out helps that therapist with the nature and timing of suggestions and assignments. Similarly, empathy allows for the psychodynamic therapist's framing of well-timed and effective interpretations and for the experiential therapist's sensitive expression of what he or she is hearing in the patient's self-exploration.

Caring and Affirmation

Although empathy is of fundamental importance to effective therapy, it is not enough. As I have said, empathy can be used for the benefit of the recipient (the patient) or of the person offering it. Grasping the other person, even when that grasping allows one to sense or experience some of the other's feelings, needs to be accompanied by other feelings if it is to help the patient. If empathy is to produce the enormous benefits of which it is capable, it has to be accompanied by some other ingredients. The beauty of empathy can then become realized. What are these ingredients? Two seem most important: therapist caring for the patient and affirmation of the patient.

The effective therapist cares. The concept of caring is close to Rogers (1957) notion of unconditional positive regard (UPR). Rogers viewed UPR as the therapist's warm acceptance, without judgment, of all aspects of the patient – the good, the bad, and the ugly. As the term UPR implies, there are no conditions for this acceptance, and instead of conditionality, the person is prized for whomever he is. Many critics have had a problem with this concept of unconditionality. Acceptance without conditions seems to many therapists to go too far, and to defy some of the realities of humanness. Perhaps only a parent's positive regard for his or her child can be unconditional. Actually,

Rogers himself acknowledged this problem when he stated in a footnote in his classic 1957 paper on the necessary and sufficient conditions for therapeutic personality change that "The phrase 'unconditional positive regard' may be an unfortunate one, since it sounds like an absolute, an all or nothing dispositional concept ... unconditional positive regard exists as a matter of degree in any relationship" (1957, p. 101).

The term, caring, may better capture this key element of successful therapy. In a word, the therapist cares about the patient and experiences caring feelings for the patient. Rogers (1957) also believed that caring is crucial, stating that the therapist must care in a nonpossessive way for the client as a separate person. He differentiated this kind of caring from a possessive caring, which aimed at taking care of the therapist's own needs.

These caring feelings exist even as the therapist may also experience negative feelings, at times approaching hateful and rageful feelings (Gelso & Pérez-Rojas, 2017; Wolf, Goldfried, & Muran, 2013). For example, such intensely negative feelings are a common occurrence when working with certain patients, e.g., those suffering from borderline personality disorders (see Winnicott's, 1949, classic paper on hate in the countertransference). However, even within the context of such intensely negative feelings, the therapist cares for the patient. And in the most effective work, the therapist cares quite a bit. This is especially so in longer-term work, where the therapist comes to know the patient very deeply.

The concept of therapist caring leads readily to the question of how much of what kind of caring does or should the therapist experience for the patient. In longer-term therapy, and often even in relatively brief work, successful therapy is marked by deeply positive feeling for the patient. That is, the therapist feels love for the patient. The concept of love has been a forbidden topic for a long time in the psychotherapy world, probably because it seems loaded with the potential for serious and deeply damaging acting out of countertransference problems, including sexual acting out on the part of the therapist. I recall some years ago, while attending a meeting of leading psychotherapy scholars who were discussing key ingredients of effective therapy, I brought up the topic of love in psychotherapy. I was being cautioned by my senior colleagues (it was a few decades ago) to avoid this topic because of its dangerous connection to therapist sexual acting out. However, I believed then, as I do now, that the topic of love (and sexuality) in therapy is important and should not be skirted (see Gelso, Pérez-Rojas, & Marmarosh, 2014).

The existential psychoanalyst and intellectual icon of the 1960s, Rollo May, had much to say about the topic of love and sexuality in psychotherapy. He believed that:

> There are four kinds of love in Western tradition. One is *sex*, or what we call lust, libido. The second is *eros*, the drive of love to procreate – the urge, as the Greeks put it, toward higher forms of being and relationship. A third is *philia*, or friendship, brotherly love. The fourth is *agape* or *caritas*

as the Latins called it, the love that is devoted to the welfare of the other, the prototype of which is the love of God for man. Every human experience of authentic love is a blending, in varying proportions, of these four.
(May, 1969, p. 38)

My collaborators and I (Gelso, Pérez-Rojas, & Marmarosh, 2014; Gelso & Pérez-Rojas, 2017) have proposed that this blending also occurs in the patient–therapist relationship. The therapist's experience of philia and agape can have a healing effect on the patient. Thus, when the therapist cares deeply for his or her patient, this likely will have a healthy effect on how the patient perceives, interprets, and behaves in relationships, and also on how the patient feels about him/herself. Within the context of agape or philia, there may also be a healthy sexual element, similar to May's eros, a kind of affectionate caring combined with attraction (see Blum's, 1973, landmark paper on healthy erotic transferences). As we have said,

> because the therapist is experiencing these feelings toward a person that he or she has come to or is coming to know deeply, the feelings and attraction can be mostly reality-based and genuine and thus be part of the real relationship. It may be of greater concern when such feelings are absent in the therapist than when they are present, given the intimate nature of the therapeutic relationship.
> (Gelso et al., 2014, p. 319)

Annie Rogers (1996) hit on the depth of feelings in the therapeutic relationship when she shared that, "The psychotherapy relationship is two-sided, whether we acknowledge it or not ... [It] is an interchange of love, longing, frustration, and anger in the vicissitudes of a real relationship" (p. 319).

Although agape may reflect a sound real relationship, we should not be naïve to the fact that at times it may also be indicative of countertransference conflicts in the therapist. Gelso et al. (2014) use as an example of countertransference the therapist who has unresolved dependency issues, and who feels loving toward a patient who compulsively takes charge. Also, more purely lustful or sexual feelings, depending on their frequency, intensity, and duration, may well point to unresolved conflicts within the therapist. It is crucial that the therapist seek to understand these so as not to act them out on or with the patient.

Although the therapist's loving feelings may be an important and healthy part of the therapeutic relationship, I do not think that such feelings generally need to be shared directly with patients. These feelings preferably form the backdrop of effective therapies, particularly long-term work. They show themselves and have their impact through the therapist's abiding concern for doing what is best for the patient, the therapist's ongoing efforts to empathically grasp the patient's inner and outer worlds, and the therapist's attempts to "look deeply into his or her own inner world to admit sexual and loving feelings to him/herself, and to seek to understand, however imperfectly, their sources, especially the extent to which these feelings are countertransference based" (Gelso et al., 2014, p. 135).

Not doing so may well lead to therapist acting out, usually indirectly (e.g., through being detached, seductive, aggressive), but at times directly, with deeply destructive effects.

The effective therapist affirms. Affirmation has been often lumped with caring, positive regard, warmth, and several other similar concepts. To be sure, these concepts are all closely interrelated, but still there are elements of each that are distinctive. The distinctive feature of affirmation is the therapist's communication to the patient that the patient has a right to experience what s/he experiences, has a right to his or her feelings, and indeed has inner experiences and feelings that are capable of being known and understood by another person – and that they make sense to another. The Norwegian psychoanalyst Killingmo (1995, 2006) has written extensively about affirmation within the psychoanalytic framework. He states that by affirming, the analyst

> breaks the emotional isolation of the patient and conveys to him a feeling of selfhood....To affirm is not to gratify the patient's needs, but to convey acceptance and understanding of the *legitimacy* of the needs. By furnishing an affirmative mode, the analyst does not evaluate the patient's self image, which would have been a narcissistic gratification, but he strengthens the patient's feeling of safety and meaningfulness of his self experience. The essence of affirmation is to *validate* experience.
>
> (1997, p. 157)

In contrast to Killingmo, I suggest that affirmation is indeed gratifying in the sense that it is part of a gratifying general atmosphere of effective psychotherapy. This general atmosphere allows for the softening of patients' defenses and fosters deep exploration of otherwise unapproachable inner experience. Indeed, the empathic way, marked by high degrees of empathy, caring, and affirmation, surrounds the therapeutic relationship with a kind of supportiveness that makes it possible for the patient to look into otherwise too threatening feelings.

Does affirmation imply agreement with the patient? It is important to make a distinction between agreement and affirmation. As shall be explored in detail in the next section, it is important that the therapist not take sides in the patient's inner struggles or interpersonal struggles. Affirmation does not mean that the therapist agrees with the patient *against* others or agrees with one side or another of the patient's intrapsychic struggles. Instead, affirmation says "I understand how you feel," "your feelings makes sense given what you have been describing," and "you have a right to feel what you do, even if it is painful or unkind."

Still, there are situations in which affirmation bespeaks a certain kind of agreement, where the patient's report of wrongdoing to him or her is substantiated by the therapist. This agreement may serve to justify the patient's feelings, to confirm the appropriateness of those feelings. Such justification makes particular sense in the case of trauma experienced by the patient, especially when the patient was not complicit in that trauma. I have found, for example, that affirming that traumatized patients were in fact deeply wronged, were dealt a bad hand, or had injustices perpetrated against them can make them feel less crazy, and can confirm the patient's sense of self and self-cohesion. As an example, Killingmo (1995) uses one of Ingmar Bergman's television plays, *Face to Face* (1976). As described by Killingmo:

> the main character, a woman, Jenny, is lying in a bed in hospital. She is about to recover after taking an overdose. Tomas, her friend, sitting at her bedside, speaks calmly to her while she desperately discloses her deeply ambivalent emotions about her parents and grandparents, oscillating between hatred, love, and ruthless self-accusations and culminating in a state of mute, paralysed gestures. After a while, she suddenly breaks the silence and says in a clear voice: 'Can you imagine shutting up a child who is afraid of the dark, in a wardrobe? Isn't it astonishing?' (...). Tomas, sitting expectantly on his chair, answers in a low-voiced and definitive way: 'Yes, it is astonishing'. With Tomas's answer, Jenny's state of mind alters. The agony is over. Something has been brought to a close.
>
> (pp. 506–507)

Here Tomas affirms Jenny's feelings in the sense of agreeing with her. What was done to her was indeed astonishing. Similarly, when I communicate to my patients who experienced trauma throughout their childhoods that indeed they were mistreated and indeed it was not fair, this serves to remove doubt from their minds and fortifies their sense of self and self-worth. Although I believe that this sort of affirmation is important, I also believe that therapists must be careful not to simply support patient's defensive externalizing, that is, blaming others and absolving their own responsibility. The kind of affirmation that sustains a feeling of justification must only be used when the therapist is sure that, in fact, the patient was traumatized, wrongly treated, and/or dealt a bad hand. Such situations usually occur in childhood, generally at the hands of caretakers; but they can also happen in adulthood, e.g., horrific losses, accidents, instances of rape or abuse, racial discrimination, etc.

So far, I have been focusing on what I term the empathic way (empathy, caring, and affirmation), as offered by the therapist. This way provides the patient with a supportive context that facilitated the exploration of feelings that had been heretofore denied, and in the case of treatments like CBT, facilitates the patient's adherence to the therapist's behavioral guidance. This forms the basic human background of any good psychotherapy. However, to move forward in exploration and understanding, I am suggesting that another ingredient is helpful, if not essential. The therapist must be able to maintain a certain kind of neutrality. Let us now look into this concept that has been so vilified in recent times.

The Role and Importance of Benevolent Neutrality

Probably most persons who seek psychotherapy have a conscious or hidden wish to have their needs to be taken care of and cared about satisfied directly by their therapist. The question of under what conditions and how much to try to satisfy these needs for dependency and affection directly is one I have pondered for a long time. I first wrote about the topic almost four decades ago (Gelso, 1979). My curiosity about this topic stemmed initially from working with a few patients who seemed insatiable. Nothing I could do seemed like enough for them, short of providing my ongoing presence in their lives, and even that would likely have been dismissed as inadequate. (It was at that time that, as a young psychologist, I began to develop an appreciation of Winnicott's, 1949, famous paper on hate in the countertransference!)

This question of whether and when to satisfy patients' dependency and affectional needs directly (by, for example, giving advice, providing structure, expressing caring and affection) led to an examination of the broader topic of therapeutic neutrality and to the related topics of what Freud termed gratification and abstinence. Regarding neutrality, the caricature, and perhaps too often the reality of the detached, unfeeling analyst or therapist was troublesome and seemed to, more than anything, reflect what Ralph Greenson (1967) long ago termed affective atherosclerosis rather than an ultimately helpful therapeutic stance. Yet there seemed to be an important kind of neutrality that should not be thrown out with the bathwater, neutrality that would be helpful, perhaps even necessary, if provided within a context of therapist empathy, caring, and affirmation.

Stemming from this reasoning, Kanninen and I (Gelso & Kanninen, 2017a) have theorized that there are essentially five meanings of helpful neutrality or ways of being neutral. These ways of being effectively neutral seem most pertinent to psychotherapies that seek to foster patient insight, awareness, and understanding, e.g., the psychodynamic/psychoanalytic and humanistic/experiential therapies. I believe that they are also applicable to CBT therapies for the most part.

The Ways of Neutrality

What does it mean to be neutral in a way that helps the patient explore, understand, and grow? As indicated, it is posited that there are five what might be termed ways of being effectively neutral.

Taking, in Part, an Observer Position

Perhaps the most fundamental expression of effective neutrality is reflected in the therapist seeking to observe what is happening in the patient, him/herself, and the relationship. Harry Stack Sullivan wrote brilliantly about the therapist as participant-observer, wherein the therapist oscillates between the roles of deep, subjective involvement in the material presented by the patient and the alternate role of standing back and seeking to understand what is happening in the patient, the therapist, and the treatment. It is hard to imagine effective therapy, at least therapy that lasts for more than a few sessions, in the absence of this dual role. Numerous psychotherapists of course have written extensively about the participant role. In this role, the therapist essentially puts his or her thinking and observing role to the side and becomes immersed in the subjective experience of the patient's life and the treatment. This allows the therapist to feel with the patient, to experience empathy and sympathy, to live in the patient's shoes. It also fosters the therapist actually feeling his/her own feelings. Although essential, this participant role is not enough, for if the therapist lives only in that side of the equation, s/he would be lost in a sea of affect, and would be pulled thoughtlessly into whatever direction the patient set into motion, including too often colluding with the patient's defenses.

The observer side, on the other hand, allows what may be termed the therapist's observing ego to take the forefront. Here the therapist pulls away from subjective immersion and observes what is happening, and reflects on why it is happening. S/he thinks about and seeks to understand what is happening, what the patient's feelings and experiencing are about, and why the therapist feels as s/he does. Along the same lines, the therapist uses his or her conceptualizing skills to formulate an explicit or implicit theory of the patient and the therapeutic relationship. In the literature on countertransference, this conceptualizing element has been highly significant, for it facilitates the therapist coming to grips with his/her own conflicts, as well as understanding how the patient's material is involved in stirring those conflicts.

In taking a conceptualizing, observer position, the therapist must seek a neutral ground upon which to reflect objectively. Naturally, the therapist cannot ever be fully objective. Still, taking the observer position moves him/her more in the direction of that objectivity. Of course, this role, while essential, is certainly insufficient, and in fact if the therapist stayed in the observer position, the treatment would end up being sterile, and could not be transformative.

When should the therapist observe and when should s/he participate? This depends on how the session unfolds, as well as the dynamics of the patient. Also, should the therapist take the observer position during or following a session? Carl Rogers, the founder of client-centered and then person-centered therapy, made clear that he wanted to immerse himself in the experience of the client during the entire session, and he did his thinking about the client and the session afterwards. Others prefer to oscillate between the two poles of observing and experiencing during the hour itself. Although it is my predilection to participate in both roles within the hour, I suspect this is a personal matter, with therapists varying in both when to engage in each role, and how much of each in which to participate.

Refraining from Taking Sides in the Patient's Inner Struggles

Anna Freud framed the psychoanalytic conception of neutrality as taking a position midway or equidistant between the id, ego, and superego of the patient. When we divest this definition of its psychoanalytic language, what

Anna Freud meant was not taking sides with one or another of the pushes and pulls within the patient. As therapists, we are constantly faced with our patient's inner struggles, and it is strikingly easy to take sides, perhaps based on our own wishes and fears as human beings. These struggles often, but not always, have to do with the patient's impulses and the patient's sense of what is right and wrong. For example, in the famous and classic video of Carl Rogers doing therapy with Gloria (Shostrom, 1965), Gloria pushes Carl relentlessly to give her advice on whether it is okay to sleep with men with whom she is not in love. Her body says yes, but another part of her just does not feel right about it. Rogers seeks to understand empathically her inner experience, while steadfastly refusing to tell her which push or pull is best. Gloria's understanding consequently deepens, even in the brief filmed encounter. To my mind, Rogers is being beautifully neutral in his response to Gloria.

As an example from my own work, a patient of mine, Andres, has felt for a long time that he does not love his wife. And yet he does not want to break up the family by separating. He struggles with whether or not it is okay for him to seek romantic satisfaction outside the marriage. Although my internal voice wants him to seek such satisfaction, I recognize that this is my own issue. My job is to help Andres understand where he is coming from, to explore his feelings about what he wants versus what is "right." Which way I am pulled depends much on where my issues are, but it is not my job to help Andres tilt in one direction or another. Of course, there are many times in which the patient's choice seems to represent the patient's acting out of his or her unhealthy conflicts, whereas the other side seems like the healthy choice. Here it is still the therapist's job to foster exploration and understanding, although naturally we need to be pointing out patterns and exploring what they are about.

Not Taking Sides in the Patient's Outer Struggles

Our patients inevitably present us with instances of their struggles with other people in their lives, usually co-workers, bosses, friends, or intimates. In such cases, it is tempting to subtly or not-so-subtly side with the patient. (There are indeed times, however, in which therapists are impelled to side with the other, especially when the patient might be termed a difficult patient, or one who creates much conflict within the countertransference.) Siding with (or against) the patient can be done non-verbally through facial expressions, gestures, and tone of voice, as well as through what may seem like empathic responses but in actuality are subtle agreements with the patient that s/he has been wronged and/or that the other person (or perhaps the institution) is to blame, e.g., "you must really be hurt by the things he says to you," "she sounds abusive," or "why would you put up with that?" This is one of the most frequent clinical errors I see in trainees, who may actually believe they are just demonstrating empathic understanding. One so often sees this kind of "siding with" in therapists when working with patients who are exploring painful feelings tied to what seems to be injurious behavior of a spouse or lover. A case example from Gelso & Kanninen (2017b) clearly demonstrates this problem:

> a 27 year old patient ... came to therapy complaining of her spouse's violent behavior and the effects this had on the kids. A novice therapist quickly reassured/validated her, affirming that the situation sounded terrible and that the patient should stand up for herself and her rights, and leave her abusive husband. There were many facts that the therapist missed: The couple had done well for many years in a non-abusive relationship; the wife was having a career crisis and her husband supported her economically, working three jobs so that the patient could find herself and what she wanted. Only one of the many quarrels during this difficult time culminated in violence, with the husband grabbing her arm and throwing her on the bed. The therapist missed the fact that the patient was having an affair begun through an internet connection. The couple separated at the wife's initiative, but six months later she wanted to return to the relationship. By that time, the husband had sought his personal therapy and was working on his issues. He no longer wanted to return to the relationship.
>
> (p. 333)

The effectively neutral therapist, rather than siding with the patient against the other person, inspects his or her own urge to side with the patient verbally or nonverbally, and where that comes from. The therapist then seeks to help the patient explore her feelings, understand the meaning of his involvement in that relationship, and perhaps help the patient understand his conscious and unconscious wish for the therapist to support the patient's internal reactions against the spouse or lover. In my own practice, when I feel the urge to attack the person who seems to be inflicting pain on my patient, I often ask the patient why I would be feeling this, since the patient's spouse, for example, has done nothing to me. The patient then often explores how she wants me to join with her against the "bad" other in feeling right or in expressing the feelings that she could not express. This usually leads to an exploration of what the patient is avoiding when she attempts to get me to act out, for instance, her anger against the other.

Refraining From Manipulating the Patient into Emotional Expression

Another way of expressing this means of effective neutrality is that the therapist needs to modulate his or her own affect when interacting with the patient so that the therapist does not, in effect, seduce the patient into emotional expression. Regarding this "seduction," I believe it is a good idea to consider how warmth can be used seductively by the therapist – to get the patient to feel what the therapist thinks the patient should feel or does feel down deep. Just listening to the tone of voice of some therapists, and looking at their facial expressions, makes me want to weep about all of what I did not and do not get in my life, all of the pain I feel, and how my mother didn't love me enough! It is one thing to use the gentle, caring therapist voice and exhibit a kind facial expression. But it is another to go so far with these nonverbals that the patient is, in effect, manipulated into feeling. When the patient then shows the desired affect, e.g., cries, it is as if the proud therapist has earned the famed Freudian victory cigar or whatever the counterpart is for therapists of non-psychoanalytic orientations.

The reality is that it is pretty easy to get most people to feel, cry, etc. The problem with pulling or pumping for affect in this way is that it impedes the patient's autonomy and actually does not help much in the final analysis. It does not produce the kind of deeper understanding and awareness that is mutative, or that fosters important change in the patient. Helping the patient understand what stops him or her from expressing feelings, or indeed actually feeling feelings, and what that is about, actually allows feelings to emerge. Thus, emotional expression, which certainly is important, usually accompanies and follows such understanding. This process yields greater change than does simply creating conditions so that the patient expresses feelings. The latter is so often merely cathartic rather than mutative. The following case summary presented in Gelso & Kanninen (2017b) also exemplifies how pulling for affect through the therapist's nonverbal and verbal behavior can be problematic for some patients.

> The patient was a 23 year old woman who sought therapy because of depression and incapacitating social anxiety. She had experienced significant abandonment by both her mother and father at different times in childhood, and, although she felt loved by her parents, she had many memories of feeling alone, anxious, and out of contact. During the first two years of therapy, the amount of therapist affect she could tolerate was minimal. She could hear calmly understanding words, descriptions, and words linking feelings to their causes, but she could not tolerate sympathetic facial expressions or warmth in the therapist's tone of voice. When the therapist responded with much nonverbal or direct verbal warmth, the patient would emotionally withdraw. She was also contemptuous when the therapist showed sadness, which she saw as a sign of weakness. The therapist's supervisor named how the therapist needed to respond emotionally to this patient as "not too much water for the cactus." This began to shift as the patient developed greater emotional strength.
>
> (p. 334)

Helping the patient understand in the way I have suggested does require patience on the part of the therapist. It does not seek a quick fix, but instead reflects an understanding that durable change is usually a slow process. The reader might consider change processes in his or her own life and the time and effort that were required for major changes to take place.

Every supervisee with whom I have worked over a period of nearly five decades has seemed to understand the importance of patience and the gradualness of change a bit more when I have asked them to think of their own growth process!

Following Guidelines about When to Satisfy Directly the Patient's Wishes and Demands

The fifth way of being effectively neutral involves the controversial psychoanalytic concepts of abstinence and gratification. Like the construct of neutrality itself, the concepts of abstinence and gratification have been pretty much relegated to the trash heap in the current psychotherapy and psychoanalysis zeitgeist. However, rather than being mere garbage, I suggest that these concepts have something important to offer if understood as general guidelines rather than rules.

The concept of abstinence and what has been termed the "rule of abstinence" were formulated by Freud in the early part of the 20th century, when he stated that "Analytic treatment should be carried through as far as possible under privation, in a state of abstinence ....Cruel though it may sound, we must see to it that the patient's suffering, to the degree that it is in some way or other effective, does not come to an end prematurely" (Freud, 1919, pp. 162–163). Freud believed that if the therapist gratified the patient's emotional needs in the treatment itself (e.g., by advising, structuring, supporting, sympathizing, and directly expressing caring), the patient would get hooked on the treatment – on the warm, soothing support—and not work to get better. In other words, the patient would give up the need for cure, and instead substitute the need for treatment. There is a great deal of merit to Freud's position, as long as psychotherapy is conducted within a general atmosphere of empathy, caring, and affirmation, as discussed earlier. To be sure, directly gratifying or supporting the patient is likely to have short-term effects, just as being soothed by another has comforting effects; but it is not likely to help the patient do the hard work of making fundamental changes, and may get in the way of work that is needed for growth in the ways Freud worried about. And yet at times and in particular with certain patients, it is helpful, even necessary, to provide certain direct gratifications.

This concept of abstinence seems important if, as noted above, it is thought of as a general guideline rather than a hard-and-fast rule, and if it is used flexibly, taking into account aspects of the patient and the treatment. The notion of abstinence as a guideline raises the questions of under what conditions and to what extent should the therapist provide direct gratification in response to the patient's conscious or unconscious pull or demand for it. To what extent should the therapist offer advice, provide supportive reassurance, seek to soothe the patient so that his or her emotional pain subsides, structure or guide the treatment hour to make things less stressful for the patient, and express affection and caring directly? It should be reiterated that I am suggesting the ongoing provision of an atmosphere of general gratification (i.e., of empathy, caring, and affirmation) as the foundation of any effective psychotherapy.

Rules of Thumb for Gratification

Four rules of thumb seem especially helpful. The first is to use *abstinence as a baseline*. In other words, a wise fundamental approach is to seek to understand the patient and help the patient understand him/herself within the empathic atmosphere earlier described – and to abstain from directly gratifying the pulls for dependency and affection that the patient may manifest. The therapist then deviates from this basic approach only when certain indicators suggest that s/he should do so. The more the patient can progress in exploratory work without advice, reassurance, soothing, direct expressions of caring, and directions in the hour, the better.

When gratifications are offered in response to the patient's pull for them, for example, when the therapist seeks to take care of the patient by offering advice, it is helpful to eventually explore what is behind the patient's pull for advice or guidance. Exploring what is behind this pull needs to be well timed, as doing such exploration too soon may be insulting to the patient and may undercut the very support that the gratification sought to provide. So when the support is given, exploratory work is returned to when the patient is ready for it.

The second rule of thumb is to *differentiate what the patient wants from what the patient needs*. Most conscious or unconscious pulls to be taken care of or cared for by the therapist are from patients who want such responses but do not need them. How can the therapist assess this distinction between want and need? "Need" is evidenced by the therapist's sense or formulation that the patient will experience deterioration or fragmentation if the therapist does not, for example, provide advice and support, or that the working alliance will be seriously, perhaps irreparably, damaged if the therapist does not explicitly express that s/he cares and/or how much s/he cares for the patient. If it seems that the patient will get worse or the alliance will be severely damaged without direct gratification, then gratification is clinically indicated.

Patients' demands or wishes for direct gratification seem to stem from anxiety, and are aimed at reducing or eliminating the unconscious sources of anxiety. These sources may be the patient's internalized critical voice, fears of being insufficient, feelings of being unlovable, etc.

The direct gratification generally makes the patient feel better temporarily, and the patient may want this ardently. However, what the patient may need most is an understanding of what is impelling him or her to want the gratification. The patient also may be helped more by coming to grips with what is stopping him or her from getting this gratification in his or her life outside of treatment. It is likely to be more helpful for the therapist to share with the patient why the therapist cannot provide direct gratification than to actually provide the gratification. Telling the patient why you cannot give the patient what s/he is wanting and/or pulling for also facilitates the patient's perception of the therapist as genuine. An example of this is a person I worked with weekly for six months:

> I looked forward to our sessions, admired the patient's courage, her sense of humor, and who she fundamentally was. However, when this patient pulled at me as she pulled at everyone close to her, to tell her I cared for her, I told her instead that I just did not think this would help her in any enduring way. What seemed most important, I said, was that we explore and work through why she so desperately needed that from everyone and why her getting such expressions of caring felt good for only a few seconds. Despite my nondisclosure of my feelings for this patient, I am certain she rightly perceived me as being quite genuine with her.
> (Gelso, 2011, p. 159)

When I have presented this case example and viewpoint in the past, frequent questions have been, "Why not just tell the patient what you felt?" Why not communicate that you felt deeply for her?" I believe there would be two problems with doing so. First, from all of our interactions, it was clear that the patient would not be able to take in, to internalize, my expressions, just as she had not been able to internalize all of the ways in which I had manifested caring, and just as she had not been able to internalize the caring of others. In addition, to the extent that my direct statement of caring to the patient eased her pain, the therapy would not have helped this patient understand and work through the underlying conflicts and deficits that caused her to endlessly seek and deny others' caring.

The third and fourth guidelines on when to gratify and when to abstain are given as a tandem because they are so interrelated, and each must be understood in the context of the other.

First, *the more severely disturbed the patient, the more appropriate it is to satisfy his or her wishes or pulls for gratification*; and second, *the more emotionally immature the demand, the less wise it is to gratify*. Thus, the key elements in how, what, and how much to directly gratify or support the patient are the degree of disturbance or pathology of the patient in combination with the nature of the pull or demand for gratification. The latter involves the degree of maturity–immaturity of the demand. These two guidelines pertain the moment-to-moment decisions that the therapist must make about when, what, and how much to gratify, along with the general thrust of the therapy around support or gratification.

The patient with more severe psychopathology (e.g., the more severe personality disorders, severe affective disorders, schizophrenic disorders) often clearly needs the therapist's guidance, support, and direct indications of caring. Such patients may be suffering from a profound lack of cohesion, suicide potential, threat of fragmentation, and poor reality testing. These patients tend not to do so well with exploratory work aimed at fostering deep understanding, where the therapist maintains strict neutrality, including refraining from direct gratifications. With these patients, it makes good clinical sense to provide the kinds of supportive gratifications that are ego strengthening. Then, as the patient's inner resources strengthen, the therapist can gradually shift toward more exploratory work involving greater neutrality and abstinence (but, again, always within an empathic context).

Even with the more disturbed patient, the therapist needs to be thoughtful about how much to gratify and just what kinds of direct gratifications are helpful. Levy and Scala (2015) summarize studies suggesting that more troubled patients, e.g., those suffering from borderline personality disorders, can become disorganized and respond negatively to supportive gratifications and positive therapist affect, and may even become more depressed in response to these supportive behaviors. It may be best for the therapist to provide certain direct gratifications when the more severely disturbed patient seems to want them and when such support seems to strengthen the patient's functioning and cohesion.

Generalizations such as those above regarding the need to provide direct gratifications more often to patients who suffer from more severe psychopathologies do not hold up in all circumstances. Even patients with greater strengths will at times experience personal crises or trauma that warrant therapists' support. For example, significant personal losses, health crises, damaging accidents may occur in our patients' lives, and these often call for sympathy as well as empathy. The classical psychoanalyst, Ralph Greenson (1967), gives examples of patients who suffered horrific losses (e.g., a mother's loss of a child) to which their analysts responded with neutrality and abstinence. Neutrality and abstinence in such cases make a mockery of the therapeutic process and of course damage the therapeutic relationship. In the case of such personal crises or trauma, it is best to put exploratory work to the side momentarily, and support patients in their grief, to the point of letting patients hear and see your regrets and sorrow for their losses.

Taking only the patient's level of psychopathology into consideration when deciding when to gratify, although important, is insufficient. Also crucial is how much gratification is to be given (e.g., how much the patient should be taken care of), along with the level of maturity of the patient's conscious or unconscious demands or pulls for gratification. The patient's pulls for support and gratification that reflect dependency and affectional needs vary on a continuum of maturity. More immature demands are more likely rooted in early, often severe, childhood deprivations, including trauma. Thus, the needs these pulls reflect were created in early relationships and carried into the present, including relationships in and outside of therapy.

This continuum of maturity–immaturity of demands for direct gratification may be clarified by some examples. The wish to be held in the lap of the therapist is on the immature side of the continuum, and it is powerfully reflective of very early and profound deprivations. On the other hand, the patient's wish to have his or her hand held during a time of a profound loss or pain is not so immature. Indeed, it may be situated on the mature side of the continuum. Still, the demands/pulls for physical gratification from one's therapist are generally more immature than the demands for verbal gratification, since these physical demands are more likely rooted developmentally in preverbal experiences. To continue these examples, a patient's request for an extra appointment during a crisis may well be mature, and certainly more mature than requests for extra sessions or extended sessions regularly. Finally, the wish to be consoled when experiencing a crisis, especially when the crisis is not of the patient's making, likely reflects emotional maturity.

Again, the more psychologically immature the demand/pull for gratification from the patient, the less helpful it is to gratify. Such demands are more likely to be made by more profoundly troubled patients. For these patients, deep direct gratifications of more primitive, immature needs can create fragmentation, rather than helping the patient heal (see Levy & Scala, 2015). I recall when I was a young psychologist a rather chilling case presentation made by an experienced psychodynamic therapist working with a deeply troubled woman. The patient's pulls for gratification were intense and reflected very early and profound deprivations. During a series of sessions, the therapist cradled the patient in her lap, intending to care for the greatly hurt child in the patient. After a period of this, and driven by the patient's wish to merge with the all-good therapist/mother, the patient began parking outside the therapist's home on a regular basis, eventually becoming floridly psychotic. She was subsequently hospitalized. It certainly is possible that the therapist's cradling the patient was a response to deterioration that was on an unstoppable course, and that the patient would have had a psychotic break regardless of what the therapist did. However, in listening to the details of the case, it seemed to the case consultant and conferees more likely that the patient was suffering from a stable borderline personality disorder, and the therapist's gratification of the patient's primitive pulls/demands actually fostered the malignant regression resulting in psychosis.

On the other hand, when the patient is suffering from more severe problems and is consciously or unconsciously pulling for more mature direct gratification, it is generally more helpful to provide the support. For example, when my borderline patient is floundering in sessions and pulling for guidance and structure, it is wise to provide the needed structure and guidance, with the aim of helping strengthen the patient psychologically. More exploratory rather than supportive work can be done following such strengthening.

References

Blum, H. P. (1973). The concept of erotized transference. *Journal of the American Psychoanalytic Association*, 21(1), 61–76. doi:10.1177/000306517302100104

Bohart, A. C., & Greenberg, L. S. (1997). *Empathy reconsidered: New directions in psychotherapy* (1st ed.). Washington, DC: American Psychological Association. doi:10.1037/10226–018

Bozarth, J. D. (1984). Beyond reflection: Emergent modes of empathy. In R. F. Levant, & J. M. Shlien (Eds.), *Client-centered therapy and the person-centered approach: New* directions in theory, research, and practice (59–75). Westport, CT: Praeger Publishers/ Greenwood Publishing Group.

Eagle, M., & Wolitzky, D. L. (1997). Empathy: A psychoanalytic perspective. In A. C. Bohart, & L. S. Greenberg (Eds). *Empathy reconsidered: New directions in psychotherapy* (217–244). Washington, DC: American Psychological Association. doi:10.1037/10226-009

Elliott, R., Bohart, A. C., Watson, J. C., & Greenberg, L. S. (2011). Empathy. *Psychotherapy*, 48(1), 43–49. doi:10.1037/a0022187

Farber, B. A., & Doolin, E. M. (2011). Positive regard. *Psychotherapy*, 48(1), 58–64. doi:10.1037/a0022141

Freud, S. (1955). Lines of Advance in Psychoanalysis. In J. Strachey (Ed. & Trans.), *Standard edition of the complete psychological works of Sigmund Freud* (Vol. 17, pp. 135–144. London, England: Hogarth Press. (Original work published in 1919.)

Gelso, C. J. (1979). Gratification: A pivotal point in psychotherapy. *Psychotherapy: Theory, Research & Practice*, 16(3), 276–281. doi:10.1037/h0085889

Gelso, C. J. (2011). *The real relationship in psychotherapy: The hidden foundation of change.* Washington, DC: American Psychological Association. doi:10.1037/12349-000

Gelso, C. J., & Kanninen, K. M. (2017a). Neutrality revisited: On the value of being neutral within an empathic atmosphere. *Journal of Psychotherapy Integration*, 27, 330–341. doi:10.1037/int0000072

Gelso, C. J., & Kanninen, K. M. (2017b). Understandings and misunderstandings about neutrality in an empathic context. *Journal of Psychotherapy Integration*, 27, 359–364. doi:10.1037/int000098

Gelso, C. J., & Pérez-Rojas, A. E. (2017). Inner experience and the good therapist. In L. G. Castonguay, & C. E. Hill (Eds.), *How and why are some therapists better than others? Understanding therapist effects.* (pp. 101–116). Washington, DC: American Psychological Association.

Gelso, C. J., Pérez-Rojas, A. E., & Marmarosh, C. (2014). Love and sexuality in the therapeutic relationship. *Journal of Clinical Psychology*, 70(2), 123–134. doi:10.1002/jclp.22064

Gelso, C. J., & Silberberg, A. (2016). Strengthening the real relationship: What is a psychotherapist to do? *Practice Innovations*, 1(3), 154–163. doi:10.1037/pri0000024

Greenberg, L. S., & Elliott, R. (1997). Varieties of empathic responding. In A. C. Bohart, & L. S. Greenberg (Eds). *Empathy reconsidered: New directions in psychotherapy* (pp. 167–186). Washington, DC: American Psychological Association. doi:10.1037/10226-007

Greenson, R. R. (1967). *The technique and practice of psychoanalysis.* London: Hogarth Press.

Hoffman, M. L. (1984). Interaction of affect and cognition in empathy. In C. E. Izard, J. Kagan, & R. B. Zajonc (Eds.), *Emotions, cognition, and behavior* (pp. 103–131). New York, NY: Cambridge University Press.

Killingmo, B. (1995). Affirmation in psychoanalysis. *The International Journal of Psychoanalysis*, 76(3), 503–518.

Killingmo, B. (2006). A plea for affirmation relating to states of unmentalised affects. *Scandinavian Psychoanalytic Review*, 29(1), 13–21. doi:10.1080/01062301.2006.10592775

Kohut, H. (1971). *The analysis of the self: A systematic approach to the psychoanalytic treatment of narcissistic personality disorders.* New York: International Universities Press.

Kohut, H. (1977). *The restoration of the self.* New York: International Universities Press.

Kohut, H. (1984) *How does analysis cure?* Chicago: University of Chicago Press.
Levy, K. N., & Scala, J. W. (2015). Integrated treatment for personality disorders: A commentary. *Journal of Psychotherapy Integration*, 25(1), 49. doi:10.1037/a0038771
May, R. (1969). *Existential psychology* (2nd ed). New York: Random House.
Rogers, A. G. (1996). *A shining affliction: A story of harm and healing in psychotherapy.* New York: Viking.
Rogers, C. R. (1957). The necessary and sufficient conditions of therapeutic personality change. *Journal of Consulting Psychology*, 21, 95–103. doi:10.1037/h0045357
Rogers, C. R. (1959). A theory of therapy, personality, and interpersonal relationships: as developed in the client-centered framework. In S. Koch (Ed.), *Psychology: A study of a science (Vol. 3).* New York: McGraw Hall.
Rogers, C. R. (1980). *A way of being.* Boston: Houghton Mifflin.
Shostrom, E. L. (1965). *Three approaches to psychotherapy. Vol. I.* Santa Ana, CA: Psychological Films.
Winnicott, D. W. (1949). Hate in the counter-transference. *The International Journal of Psychoanalysis (30)*, 69–75.
Wolf, A. W., Goldfried, M. R., & Muran, J. C. (2013). *Transforming negative reactions to clients: From frustration to compassion.* Washington, DC: American Psychological Association. doi:10.1037/13940-000

3 Building a Real Relationship and Forging a Working Alliance
What Is a Therapist to Do?

The real relationship and the working alliance work in concert and are highly interrelated. Together they form the bedrock of the psychotherapy relationship in all theoretical approaches to treatment. As I have said in Chapter 1, the real relationship may be conceptualized as the foundation of the relationship, since it represents the fundamental connection between patient and therapist, the person-to-person relationship. If the real relationship is the foundation, the working alliance is best viewed as the catalyst, in the sense that in most cases and to a high degree, the success of therapy, and indeed the very continuation of it, depends on a sound working connection or working collaboration between the participants. It is hard to imagine therapy continuing for long if the patient and/or the therapist felt they worked together poorly, i.e., had a poor working alliance.

In his seminal theoretical writing on the real relationship and the working alliance, Greenson (1967) viewed the real relationship as being omnipresent right from the first moment of contact between therapist and patient. The working alliance was seen as emerging subsequently from the real relationship as the work moved forward. In this sense, Greenson believed that the working alliance was an artifact of psychotherapy, that it existed solely to get the work done. Recent research (e.g. Kivlighan, Hill, Gelso, & Baumann, 2016) has not supported Greenson's proposition that the working alliance emerges from the real relationship. Instead, these researchers found that both appear to emerge simultaneously. This certainly fits with clinical experience. Both begin to form at the beginning of the work, and they do so in a way that is highly interrelated but still separate. Furthermore, each contributes some to the treatment process and outcome in and of itself, while also being interdependent. There is substantial empirical support for this notion (see summary by Gelso, 2014).

The strength of the real relationship and, in particular, the working alliance that is needed for therapy to move forward effectively depends upon many factors. One such factor, in particular, stands out: the kind of therapy and the demands it places on the patient. The three major theoretical orientations examined in this book make different demands on the patient, and they require different degrees of strength of the working alliance and the real relationship. For example, person-centered therapy demands that the patient be able to work well with the generally reflective posture of the therapist, along with the relative absence of therapist-provided guidance and structure. This is very difficult for some patients, and for these a strong working alliance and real relationship are needed. Similarly, the demands of classical psychoanalysis are powerful. It requires the patient to free associate, which can be quite threatening emotionally. The patient must also face the intensity that is created by multiple sessions each week over many months and years. Classical analysis, too, requires that the patient reveal all in a climate in which the analyst is highly interested but not highly supportive. These ingredients require considerable psychological strength in the patient, along with a very sound working alliance. In CBT, on the other hand, the patient has to be able to follow the homework assignments suggested by the therapist. This is probably less emotionally demanding (if the assignments are arranged properly), and because of that, CBT may not require as strong a working alliance to be successful. Still, it surely does require a sound working alliance that encourages the patient to stick to what may feel like difficult assignments.

I have been discussing how different therapies make different demands on patients and how the strengths of these demands also differ for the various approaches to treatment. In addition, it is important to consider that different patients need or want differing ingredients from their therapists if the working alliance is to be strong. Within the three general theoretical orientations discussed in this book, for some patients a more supportive approach is needed if the alliance is to be strong, whereas for other patients, different approaches strengthen the alliance. I shall have more to say about this a bit later in this chapter.

The key question addressed in this chapter is *what can the therapist do to form, maintain, and strengthen the real relationship and the working alliance*? Although these two ingredients are highly interrelated, it appears that the answers to this question are somewhat different for each of them. Below I address this question for the real relationship and working alliance separately.

The Development and Strengthening of the Real Relationship

It will be recalled that the real relationship is defined as *the personal relationship between therapist and patient marked by the extent to which these participants are genuine with one another and perceive each other in ways that are accurate and fitting*. The real relationship is the person-to-person, non-work element that is present in each and every relationship.

The definition offered in the above paragraph implies that the real relationship has two basic qualities: genuineness and realism. Genuineness refers to the quality of being real and non-phony in the relationship. Realism, on the other hand, pertains to experiencing and perceiving the other in ways that fit the other, rather than these perceptions being based on the perceiver/experiencer's issues. The most important aspect of the real relationship in psychotherapy is its strength, which is determined by two ingredients: *magnitude* of the real relationship (just how much real relationship exists in the overall relationship) and what we term *valence* (the extent to which the participants' feelings and attitudes toward one another are positive vs. negative). Generally speaking, the greater the magnitude and the more positive the valence of the real relationship, the stronger it will be, and the more beneficial will be its impact on the work. In psychotherapy, the strength of the real relationship varies in each dyad and may also vary within the same dyad across treatment and even within each session.

When considering the strength of the real relationship, it is important to differentiate between two qualities that are too often conflated: strength and salience. Strength is what we have already described, whereas salience has to do with the extent to which the real relationship stands out or is center stage in the work. When we think about what a therapist can do to affect the real relationship, the salience aspect is relatively easy to affect. If you want greater salience of the real relationship, you can simply be more open and disclosing. This is what the psychoanalyst, Renik (1999), refers to when he recommends that therapists "play with their cards face up." If the therapist plays with his/her cards face up, the real relationship will be at center stage. It will be salient. The problem with this is that salience does not necessarily add to the strength of the real relationship, and in some cases it can diminish strength, e.g., when the therapist's self-disclosures reveal a person that the patient does not take to. In this sense, while playing with your cards face up makes the real relationship take center stage (salient), it does not strengthen, and may indeed weaken, the real relationship. Whether or not salience does strengthen the real relationship depends on several factors, which we shall discuss subsequently.

Strengthening the Real Relationship: The Negative Case

From one perspective, as discussed by Gelso and Silberberg (2016), there really is nothing the therapist can do to strengthen the real relationship. To deliberately try to strengthen it is to weaken it, just as planning spontaneity negates spontaneity. If the patient does not take to the therapist as a person, so be it. The therapist must simply be him/herself and let the chips fall as they may. The strength of the real relationship is determined, in part at least, by whether the therapist and patient are in the same "tribe," whether they click as human beings. That is, are the two similar enough in important ways to foster the kind of liking and attraction on the patient's part that is key to a strong real relationship? Do they share a certain sense of humor? Do they have similar tastes on matters that are important to them? Do they mesh in terms of at least some key personality dimensions? It is important to note that being in the same tribe does not mean that therapist and patient are interchangeable. They may be different in many ways, but be in the same tribe on one or more fundamentally important dimensions. An example is a patient with whom I had worked in long-term therapy spanning more than a decade:

Sally was different from me in many ways. Our interests were vastly different; our senses of humor did not jibe; and some of our values, including religious views, were far apart. However, she, like I, was highly relational. Relationships mattered deeply to her, as they do to me, and she worked very hard to stay connected emotionally with others. She deeply enjoyed and profited from the process of looking inward in psychotherapy. In terms of her relational orientation and introspective nature, we were very much in the same tribe. Our person-to-person connection was very strong, despite major differences in aspects of our tastes and values.

It is also true that as the therapist comes to know the patient, the therapist will have a growing appreciation for the person of the patient. And this will solidify their personal bond, despite their differences.

So the real relationship forms and unfolds on its own, without the deliberate effort of the therapist. It traverses an ineluctable path based on personal qualities of therapist and patient. The inevitability of the formation and development of the real relationship, however, is only part of the story; for, in another sense, as Silberberg and I (Gelso & Silberberg, 2017) have explored, there are some things the therapist indeed can do to develop and strengthen this element of the overall therapeutic relationship.

What the Therapist Can Do to Strengthen the Real Relationship: The Positive Case

The ingredients I shall describe below are highly interrelated, as the reader will see. Also, they contribute to both the strength of the personal or real relationship and the working alliance. Here, though, I focus on their impact on the real relationship. Subsequently I discuss factors that influence the development of the working alliance.

Being empathic. As discussed in Chapter 2, empathy entails a partial, vicarious identification with the patient, or what the pioneer of psychoanalytic self psychology, Heinz Kohut, called vicarious introspection. The therapist climbs into the patient's shoes and introspects into the patient's mind, as if s/he were the patient. This allows the therapist to grasp, emotionally and cognitively, what is on and in the patient's mind and in the patient's inner experience. In so grasping, the therapist can experience, at least to an extent, what the patient experiences. Although debatable, I believe that in close relationships in which there are high degrees of empathy, the therapist can actually partake of some of the patient's feelings, actually feeling them. Decades of research supports the view that therapist empathy is a key part of effective psychotherapy (see the review and meta-analysis by Elliott, Bohart, Watson, & Greenberg, 2011).

Why does the therapist's empathy strengthen the real relationship? For the therapist, empathy allows him or her to understand the patient, as they really are, often in a way that is quite profound. Being known in this way is intimate, and this sense of intimacy in both therapist and patient fosters a strong personal bond between the two. It also fosters a good working connection, which shall be discussed when the working alliance is examined. The therapist's empathy also facilitates the development of empathy in the patient, and this empathy quite naturally connects to the person of the therapist. Thus, despite the fact that the therapist is not sharing with the patient in the same way or to the same extent that the patient is sharing, the patient comes to develop a healthy interest in the therapist, one that goes beyond transference, and comes to know the therapist as a person based on all of the ways the therapist shows whom he or she is, e.g., sense of humor, nonverbal behavior, things the therapist does share, office décor, what the therapist attends to in the patient. In sum, the therapist's empathic understanding of the patient fosters a connection within the real relationship and also fosters the patient's empathy and empathic understanding of the therapist, which further strengthens the real relationship.

Providing consistency and constancy. At the most fundamental level, the patient needs to be able to trust that the therapist will show up for each session and be on time. I recall a patient who feared and half expected his therapist to have forgotten their appointment each time he visited the therapist's home office. This reflected a deep vulnerability within this patient, as the therapist always showed up and nearly always was on time. In this case, the therapist's constancy allowed the personal connection between patient and therapist to deepen, and provided the holding environment that permitted the patient to move forward in the treatment.

Also in terms of constancy, it is important that the therapist will be dependably the same person from session to session. The therapist does not need to be identical in mood and responsiveness from session to session, for this would be inhuman. But there does need to be a sense that the patient can count on the therapist to be about the same each session. I recall a therapist-trainee who changed dramatically in her approach during one session in the early phase of a psychotherapy. The therapist had been reliably exploratory with the patient, displaying an inquiring attitude aimed at fostering self-understanding in the patient. In this particular session, however, the therapist became very active, both confronting the patient aggressively and pushing for change. The patient was quite shaken, and even communicated his anxiety and a feeling of mistrust for the therapist as a person. The patient noted that the therapist was being very different with him, which made him uncomfortable. In the following session, the therapist sought to explore the patient's mistrust in terms of the patient's core issues (rather than her own conflicts that provoked her aggression in the session), but this only deepened the rupture in the personal relationship. The patient terminated treatment by not returning for subsequent sessions.

Consistency is also reflected in the therapist's theoretical approach to treatment. Does the therapist possess a reasonably coherent approach to treatment, or is s/he continually changing approaches to meet what seems to make sense in the moment? Although therapist spontaneity can be at times helpful, continually changing approaches, including theoretical approaches, is more impulsive than helpful. This makes it hard for the patient to trust the therapist as a person, and it saps the strength of the real relationship. I should underscore here that this willy-nilly approach is certainly not what is meant by psychotherapy integration, a more reasoned and effective way of integrating different theoretical views.

A type of consistency that is particularly important is that between the therapist's verbal and nonverbal behavior. When there is a disconnect between these two forms of communication, the real relationship as perceived by the patient is sure to suffer. Consider the therapist whose words communicate caring and interest, but whose voice tone is flat, who looks away from the patient, and who moreover appears bored. It is hard to feel a sense of personal trust and safety, as well as a personal bond, with the therapist under these conditions.

Managing countertransference. As presented in Chapter 1, the definition of countertransference used in this book is that proposed by Gelso and Hayes (2007): *the therapist's reaction to the patient based on the therapist's own unresolved conflicts and vulnerabilities.* Countertransference can occur at a behavioral, affective, and/or cognitive level. That is, the therapist can act it out behaviorally in the treatment, and/or can experience it internally in the form of feelings or thoughts. In addition, although the locus of countertransference is the therapist's conflicts and vulnerabilities, the trigger for it is often something the patient says or does. In other cases, the very frame of psychotherapy is the trigger. In such cases, simply doing therapy sets off a chronic countertransference reaction in the therapist. For example, in some therapists, doing therapy sets in motion an excessive need to be helpful and supportive, which can ultimately hinder the patient's progress.

Countertransference can be for better or worse, a benefit or a hindrance. Whether it helps or hinders depends, to a large degree, on how effectively the therapist manages his or her countertransference. Furthermore, the extent to which countertransference is effectively managed has been found to be consistently related to the success or failure of psychotherapy sessions and of the treatment itself, as revealed in the meta-analysis by Hayes, Gelso, and Hummel (2011).

Countertransference and its management will be discussed in depth in Chapter 5. In the present section, the point of interest is how and why countertransference management relates to the strength of the real relationship. To clarify this connection, we must look at the elements of countertransference management. In the most recent study of our countertransference research program, my collaborators and I (Pérez-Rojas, Palma, Bhatia, Jackson, Norwood, Hayes, & Gelso, 2017) found that a key factor in managing one's countertransference effectively may be labeled understanding self and others. Thus, the therapist's interest in and ability to understand him/herself, as well as the patient, allows for controlling and using countertransference reactions in the service of the work and the patient, rather than acting it out on the patient. This understanding facilitates the therapist's separation of his or her own issues from the patient's issues, thus allowing the therapist to see the patient more clearly. In turn, separating what are the patient's issues from what are the therapist's issues facilitates the therapist's empathy for the patient. This process deepens the personal connection between therapist and patient. At poorer levels of countertransference management, the patient may be confused about where the therapist is coming from, and certainly would not feel a secure personal attachment to the therapist, which naturally is a significant part of the real relationship.

Playing with your cards face up. I have suggested that the therapist's playing with his/her cards face up, or self-disclosure as it is commonly referred to, does not necessarily strengthen the real relationship. Instead, self-disclosure is a measure of the salience of the real relationship – the extent to which the real relationship takes center stage in the treatment. That being said, there is evidence that the therapist's self-disclosure does relate, at least moderately, to the strength of the real relationship (e.g., Ain & Gelso, 2008, 2011). Interestingly, we do not find high degrees of therapist self-disclosure in our researches. So therapists naturally are careful about how much to play with their cards face up, as Hill and Knox (2003) have suggested. And within this low to moderate amount of self-disclosure, there is a tendency for self-disclosure to strengthen the relationship. (For the statistically sensitive reader, the correlation coefficients between amount of therapist self-disclosure and the strength of the real relationship, from both patients' and therapists' perspectives, tends to be between .30 and .40.)

The point here is that the therapist's sharing aspects of him/herself, and revealing what s/he is experiencing in the treatment, does tend to strengthen the real relationship. When the therapist reveals him/herself, the patient is able to see directly what the therapist is about, and who the person of the therapist is. Because most therapists are probably wise in how, what, and how much they reveal about themselves in the hour, these revelations also likely make the therapist more likeable and safer as a person to the patient. It is important to note that, although there is a tendency for the amount of therapist self-disclosure to relate to the strength of the real relationship, just what is revealed is of critical import. In one of our studies, for example, an unpublished "finding" was that one of our patient participants complained that her therapist talked too much about himself, especially the fact that he got his doctorate from Yale! Thus, a key factor in just how self-disclosure affects the real relationship is just what is revealed, and the timing of when it is revealed, as well as its direct relevance to the patient. Probably the best suggestion to therapists is that they be thoughtful about how much to self-disclose, as well as to make sure their disclosures are for the sake of the patient rather than themselves, and are connected to what the patient is exploring (see Greenberg, 2002; Hill & Knox, 2003).

Many gifted therapists disclose very little about themselves and still are able to form very strong real relationships with their patients. What allows for a strong real relationship in the face of little or no direct self-disclosure? I would suggest that clarification by the therapist of why s/he is not disclosing greatly helps the work, and also strengthens the real relationship. At a minimum, telling the patient why you are not disclosing prevents the kind of rupture in the real relationship that can seriously hinder the therapeutic relationship, and thus the success of the treatment. A case example present in Chapter 2 bears repeating. The patient was a university senior, whom I shall call Jane. I had seen her for six months in weekly sessions:

> I looked forward to our sessions, admired the patient's courage, her sense of humor, and who she fundamentally was. However, when this patient pulled at me as she pulled at everyone close to her, to tell her I cared for her, I told her instead that I just did not think this would help her in any enduring way. What seemed most important, I said, was that we explore and work through why she so desperately needed that from everyone and why her getting such expressions of caring felt good for only a few seconds. Despite my nondisclosure of my feelings for this patient, I am certain she rightly perceived me as being quite genuine with her.
> (Gelso, 2011, p. 159)

I should add that I had communicated in many ways caring for Jane, and I often asked her what made her doubt that I cared, in light of my behavior with her. We explored her feelings deeply, and explored the many experiences in childhood that greatly diminished her sense of self and self-esteem. Telling the patient why you will not tell them what you feel, why you will not self-disclose, can serve to deepen the real relationship, that is, when you do have a good reason clinically not to do so.

Building and Strengthening the Real Relationship: A Case Example

A case example may be helpful to demonstrate the building of a real relationship through the ingredients we have been discussing (empathy, constancy and consistency, countertransference management, self-disclosure). The case I shall be describing is a patient who suffered from the lack of a sense of self and self-esteem. Cara had what may be described as narcissistic injuries or a narcissistic personality disorder (see Levy, 2012). Persons with these kinds of problems have difficulties forming close relationships in which the other person is experienced as a separate self. The other is experienced as what may be termed a self-object in which they are part of the patient's self, and are internalized with the aim of mirroring the patient's greatness (as in the grandiose narcissist) and/or strengthening a highly depleted sense of self (as in what may be termed a depleted narcissist). In either case, the other is not appreciated as a separate person. Given this, the patient is unable to form a strong real relationship with the therapist, and naturally the therapist has difficulty forming a real relationship with the patient. In such cases, it is vital that the therapist empathically grasp the patient's deep suffering, maintain him/herself as a separate person, provide the security that comes from constancy and consistency, and share aspects of him/herself through well-timed and appropriate self-disclosures. These ingredients provided by the therapist help the patient and therapist develop a real relationship with each other and facilitate the gradual building in the patient of a sense of self and self-esteem. Ayelet Silberberg, a psychodynamic psychotherapist who conducted once-a-week sessions with the patient, treated the case described below. The case was described in Gelso and Silberberg (2016, pp. 161–162) and the following description adds subsequent material to the published case:

> Cara was a 29-year-old, White, heterosexual woman who was experiencing intense depression and hopelessness following the dissolution of a romantic relationship a few months prior to entering treatment. The client described feelings of emptiness and worthlessness without the significant other whom she described as "powerful." The client often expressed frustration that though there had been some progress in her depressive symptoms, she did not feel as if her problems had been solved. At this point, I had been seeing Cara for seven sessions, and I felt difficulty connecting with her. I sensed the RR was low in valence and in magnitude. That is, although I felt as if she was being genuine with me, and was not hiding her true feelings or withholding her reactions, I also felt difficulty empathizing with her. I examined my own reactions and came to the conclusion that I was not acting countertransferentially out of my own unresolved conflicts, so it was likely that I was seeing her realistically. However, I did not feel similarly realistically seen by Cara. In fact, her tendency to reject reflections of pain or other difficult emotions, and to react flatly to validation or positive support, made me often feel as though I didn't really matter in the room. I recognized this, as well her idealization of her former partner, as a clue that she might have a poor sense of self that would make it difficult for her to differentiate herself, and thus, connect with, other people in a genuine way.
>
> Though this conceptualization guided my work with Cara, I never shared it with her in a direct way. Still, I realized that sharing my experience of her might be a way to increase my own genuineness within the relationship and give her the opportunity to see me and our work together in a more realistic way. I also hoped that telling her what I thought and felt about her and the work would add differentiating structure into the relationship, or in other words, would help her see me and herself as two separate beings sharing a relationship but experiencing it in different, yet related, ways. In our next session, I told Cara that I sometimes feel like she is not sure who she really is deep inside, and that she used her partner as a reflection of her worth and identity. I explained how this could create feelings of deep depression in the wake of the partner's romantic rejection, and how this would contribute to feelings of worthlessness and even more identity confusion. Cara, for the first time, acknowledged that what I had

said resonated with her (she felt realistically seen by me), and shared that the sense of emptiness had been with her since she was a child. She took ownership of my conceptualization by assigning her own word "value," to describe what she felt was missing in her inner experience ("I never felt like I had real value, and I don't even know what that value would be"). I reflected back to her that it must be painful to experience such an emptiness and lack of value for so long, and she accepted and took in my reflections in a way she had not done before. As a result, I also felt genuinely appreciated and realistically seen in the relationship.

For the rest of the session and over the next few weeks, we discussed and explored her struggles in this new framework, and Cara was able to move in the direction of curiosity about her lack of sense of self. (In our work, I noticed an interesting absence of explicit transference that made it difficult to address. I suspected that as psychotherapy progresses, transference-based reactions in the client would emerge; see Gill's, 1982, classic work on transference resistance.) There was a strong working alliance element at play in this exchange, because she saw me as an expert and agreed on the direction of our work together, but the RR was also strengthened and became more salient as a result of my disclosure. She was more able to see me separately and distinctly from herself, while feeling understood in ways she hadn't before, and I was also able to feel like I mattered to her in a realistic and genuine way.

Over the course of the next months of our work together, our sessions centered on ways that Cara's lack of a concrete self was manifested in different areas of her life. She realized that she tended to strive and define herself by achieving external goals; however achieving the goals never gave her a sense of fulfillment so she was constantly setting new, more difficult goals. She recognized that she had longed for a significant other to validate and support her for many years; however, she also became aware that she was not interested in meeting those needs in others. In exploring her recent romantic relationship, she was able to characterize her feelings toward her significant other as "almost worship" and could see the ways in which she had trouble differentiating between herself and her partner. Throughout the sessions, Cara was able to articulate a desire for internal worth and concrete feelings of identity, which would be separate from others around her, as well as separate from external goals.

Though fully developing a sense of self is a long process in psychotherapy, it was clear that in these beginning stages Cara was starting to develop an ability to tap into her own pain and inner experience, while recognizing feelings of emptiness that had been with her since childhood. At the same time, she could see me and my role in helping her reach these insights, and valued my presence and our relationship. As she worked toward developing a sense of self, the real relationship was increasing in both valence and magnitude because I was able to more readily access and connect with her feelings of pain, regret, and loss, and feel compassionately toward her. This allowed me to intentionally become more genuine and increase the realness with which Cara was viewing me and our relationship. Cara was able to take in what I was offering, and I felt genuinely valued, which increased my positive feelings toward her. Additionally, as she became more self-aware and psychologically minded, and developed a stronger sense of self, it strengthened my sense of both of us being members of the same tribe and I felt closer to her as a person. As the real relationship increased, our work together also became more meaningful, and the real relationship and Cara's personal development enhanced each other.

Over the course of our work together, Cara's depressive symptoms lessened substantially. She no longer experienced suicidal thoughts and was not taking time off of work due to overwhelming sadness and hopelessness. She had also started to expand her social network in ways that helped her feel more supported, though she remained aware of her tendencies to judge others, as well as herself, on shallow issues of self-presentation, hobbies, and fashion sense. After 17 sessions together, Cara took a new job that made it more difficult for her to attend our sessions, and decided to discontinue our work based on her sense that her depression was under control. In our final session, Cara said "I know there is more work to be done about my sense of who I really am, and I know there are issues that I am avoiding, like things with my mom, but I think it would be better for me to set that aside at the moment and continue on with my life." I felt disappointed that our work was ending in what felt, to me, like a transition period that would allow for deeper, more meaningful change, but I was also impressed at Cara's self-awareness and ability to articulate the gravity of the work that remained to be explored. I expressed this to her, but I respected the boundary she had set. In terms of the RR, the work with Cara was stopped short before her sense of self was developed enough to give me the feeling of being fully and accurately seen. However, the relationship was evolved enough for both of us to feel free in expressing our genuine feelings about the work and our feelings about ending.

(Ayelet Silberberg, Personal Communication, March 31, 2017)

Forging a Working Alliance

Although the real relationship is deeply important to the success or failure of treatment, it often takes a back seat to the working alliance. Simply put, it is hard to imagine successful treatment in the absence of a sound working alliance. The work can proceed and even have a modicum of success in the absence of a sound real relationship, but if the patient and therapist cannot form a working union, the necessary work of therapy will not get done. There is a huge amount of empirical support for the importance of the working alliance (e.g., see review by Horvath, Del Re, Flukiger, & Symonds, 2011), but this same research indicates only a modest relationship between alliance and treatment outcome. However, clinical experience and common sense suggest that the empirical findings actually underestimate the importance of the working alliance. When one considers the enormous complexity of the therapeutic relationship, all the variables related to it, and the interaction of all those variables in their influence on treatment, the correlation of any one variable is rarely, if ever, very strong statistically. To lose sight of this statistical inevitability is tantamount to losing one's observing capacity and one's intellect when seeking to understand the therapeutic relationship. How can psychotherapy possibly work effectively if the participants cannot work well together effectively? That it can is just about inconceivable.

In Chapter 1, I noted that the working alliance is that part of the total therapeutic relationship that pertains directly to the work connection between therapist and patient. I employed Gelso and Carter's (1994) definition of the working alliance as *the alignment or joining together of the patient's reasonable self or ego with the therapist's analyzing or therapizing self or ego for the purpose of the work, of accomplishing the work of psychotherapy*. This joining together affects and is affected by a working bond that the participants form, an explicit or implicit agreement on the goals of the work, and an explicit or implicit agreement on the tasks that are needed to meet those goals (see Bordin, 1979). Although the working alliance is naturally a bipersonal concept in that it involves the contributions of both the therapist and the patient, my focus here will be on what the therapist can do to build and strengthen the working alliance.

A Paradox in Alliance Formation and Preservation

As implied above, the working alliance has everything to do with the collaboration between therapist and patient, and the therapist's most fundamental job is to foster this collaboration. And the second most important job may be to preserve the alliance that has been formed in the face of inevitable obstacles.

A basic paradox in the therapist's fostering and preserving the working alliance is that, although doing so is perhaps the therapist's most important task, the therapist cannot do so by just being a "good guy," by being consistently kind, sympathetic, and understanding. Freud once commented that there is sadism involved in all good analytic work. What did Freud mean by this rather remarkable statement? What he meant was that all good analysts have to help their analysands deal with and experience painful feelings and realities, and in this sense they inflict pain. I would add that this is the case in all psychotherapies. The therapist has to sensitively help the patient move forward in facing, understanding, and addressing his or her core issues and problems, and doing so involves pain. So the therapist cannot foster and preserve a sound working alliance by simply going along with the patient's story, by sympathetically hearing the patient's externalizing reports of how s/he has been wronged by others, and by uttering the ubiquitous "that must be hard" response to the patient's suffering. Rather, the good alliance is fostered and preserved by helping the patient face the fact that, although the core issues were likely determined by early relationships in which others (e.g., parents) created wounds in the patient's psyche, the patient is now internally and externally behaving in ways that are maladaptive. Of course, the therapist's timing in this process is key, as it is in so many aspects of doing psychotherapy of any theoretical orientation. The therapist must help the patient face the internal music so to speak when the patient is ready to hear and deal with what the therapist wants him/her to face.

Helping the patient face the complex and perhaps painful issues that must be faced requires the therapist to have a good conceptual sense of what those issues are and an empathic attunement to the patient's inner experience. When the therapist does this job effectively, the working alliance is usually strengthened. Still, because the therapist's empathic and conceptual grasp of the patient is imperfect, it is inevitable that the therapist will at times and to an extent fail in his/her effort to help the patient move forward, and make mistakes in the timing of interpretations and suggestions to the patient. These inevitable "failures," including empathic failures, will cause ruptures in the working alliance, ruptures that cannot be avoided, given the human frailties of the therapist, as well as the vulnerabilities of the patient. Even when the therapist does the job of helping the patient face his/her core issues, however, the act of doing so will cause ruptures in the alliance, as clinically described and empirically examined over more than two decades of research by Safran and Muran (Safran & Muran, 2000; Safran, Muran, & Eubanks-Carter, 2011).

Safran and his collaborators (2011) define an alliance rupture as "a tension or breakdown in the collaborative relationship between patient and therapist" (p. 224). Earlier these investigators explored two types of markers of ruptures. One marker (called a withdrawal marker) is that the patient withdraws from the relationship or topic in one way or another, e.g., denial of feelings, minimal responses to therapist explorations, shifting the topic, intellectualization, storytelling, and talking about others rather than the self. The other kind of patient marker that an alliance rupture has occurred (called a confrontation marker) is that the patient confronts the therapist and/or complains about the therapist as a person, the therapist's competence, the activities of therapy, actually being in therapy, the parameters of therapy (e.g., the 50 minute limit, the inconvenience of the meeting time), and the slow or limited progress of therapy. It is important that the therapist pay close attention to the appearance of these markers and help the patient explore ruptures in the alliance.

Working with Ruptures

Given the near inevitability of alliance ruptures, it is important that therapists understand how to work with them so that the treatment may be advanced rather than destroyed. Indeed, there is evidence that not only does the repair of ruptures benefit the work, but that treatments in which there are ruptures that are repaired may be superior in effectiveness to treatments in which there are no known ruptures (Horvath et al., 2011; Safran et al., 2011). Thus, the existence of ruptures may be seen as a good thing, as signifying that the therapist is doing his or her work, so long as the rupture gets repaired.

How might we go about the business of repairing ruptures in the working alliance? First and probably foremost, we therapists need to be on the lookout for ruptures. As indicated, the clues or markers tend to involve the patient's withdrawal in one way or another and/or the patient's negativity about the therapist, the treatment, etc. When we see these markers, it is important that the patient be aided in exploring what the rupture was about. At times, the markers may be quite subtle. A case example was a 44-year-old woman, Aditi, whom I had seen for about two years in weekly psychoanalytic therapy:

> The work had gone well, and I believed we had gotten to the core of Aditi's issues that had caused considerable depression and despair in her life. She not only had gained considerable understanding of the roots of her depression and the internal experiences that fostered depression, but she had worked through many of those experiences and had been depression-free for a few months. So constructive change had occurred and had stabilized. At this point, my patients usually directly or indirectly bring up the idea of ending treatment or they talk about going deeper and further. Aditi did neither. After a few months in which the treatment progress seemed to have stopped, but during which the gains were maintained, I decided to broach the topic of ending. I pointed out the gains and how they had stabilized, and I wondered aloud if it was time to set an ending date (approximately three months hence). Aditi's response was really a nonresponse. She said, "well, maybe" and changed the subject. Her mood also changed slightly, and her voice became a bit flat. These changes were subtle. The session came to an end. The next session began with Aditi engaging in storytelling. After several minutes I wondered aloud how she felt about my bringing up ending during our last session. At this point, she explored her hurt feelings, and was eventually able to relate these to experiences in her early life of being pushed away by significant others. The transference was obvious, but I did not explore the feelings as transference at that point. Rather, I told her that I was not trying to end our work, and in fact enjoyed our work. I clarified more fully why I had brought up ending. This seemed to repair the rupture, and we then began to explore the transference reactions, providing new material around separation and loss.

Repairing ruptures may require that the therapist do something that is more active than helping the patient explore what s/he is experiencing. For example, the patient may confront the therapist about how the therapist's approach will help the patient. This has occurred frequently with my therapist-trainees, and it has occurred in my own work, too. Here it is important that the therapist actually have a theory, a refined notion of how his or her approach fosters change in patients, and then explore with the patient how that sounds to him/her, whether that is agreeable to him/her. When the time is right, the material involved in the patient's confrontation may be examined, as it often connects to core themes in the patient's life.

At still other times, a rupture is best addressed with an apology (see Rhodes, Hill, Thompson, & Elliott, 1994). When the rupture is caused by a mistake on the therapist's part, not acknowledging it will signify to many patients a lack of respect. Naturally, the simple apology ought to be followed by some exploration on the therapist's part of the patient's reactions and, when the time is right, the relevance of those reactions to the core issues that the treatment revolves around. At times an empathic error will be connected to the patient's defensive obfuscation of what s/he is seemingly trying to communicate. That is, the patient will be very unclear in his/her communication to the therapist, perhaps due to a defensive wish not to understand or be understood. In such cases, although a simple apology may be helpful, it is important that the therapist also explore what is getting in the way of the patient's clarity.

In sum, the therapist needs to be sensitive to the occurrence of ruptures, and s/he needs to sensitively explore what the rupture is about. Repairing the rupture may involve the therapist clarifying where s/he was coming from, apologizing, and exploring the patient's feelings around the rupture. When the time is right, it is also important to explore the relation of the rupture, as well as the patient's way of dealing with the rupture, to the patient's core issues. However, to the extent that the rupture is fundamentally the responsibility of the therapist, it is important that the therapist not simply place the root of the rupture on the patient and his/her conflicts.

How to Foster and Preserve the Working Alliance

Grasp what is alliance building for the patient. Perhaps the most important way of fostering a sound working alliance is for the therapist to grasp what actions are alliance building for particular patients. Experience suggests that different patients need different qualities in the relationship in order to experience a sound working alliance. In this respect, a classic qualitative study by Bachelor (1995) is telling. When a sample of clients at a university consultation service was asked what they viewed as a good client–therapist working relationship, their responses readily grouped into three clusters. Bachelor labeled the first type as *nurturant*. The nurturant working relationship was characterized by the therapist being respectful, nonjudgmental, attentive, and understanding. This cluster seemed very similar to Carl Rogers' conception of the ideal therapist-offered relationship. The relationship was similar to that with a caring friend and confidante. It bears a close resemblance to many humanistic therapies.

The second cluster of clients perceived the good working relationship as involving primarily therapist facilitated *self-understanding or insight*. Therapist activities that were pointed to by this cluster of clients as enhancing the good working relationship were interpretation, exploration, uncovering covert meanings and unverbalized feeling states, and pointing out and integrating past and present connections that have previously been unconscious. This cluster seems to reflect a more psychodynamic approach to treatment. The third cluster, the smallest one, centered on *client–therapist collaboration*. Clients in this cluster wanted a collaborative relationship in which they and their therapist worked together and the client very actively contributed to setting the agenda and solving problems.

In essence, the Bachelor study underscores how therapist stances and activities are differentially alliance fostering for different clients. Over a period of more than two decades, I have taught an advanced psychotherapy seminar to doctoral students from the University of Maryland's counseling psychology program, and in each class I have asked students to talk about what would be alliance fostering in their own personal therapies. It has been illuminating to see that in just about every group, the three clusters found by Bachelor appeared. The take-home message for therapists is that they need to develop a sense of what is alliance-fostering for each of their patients and, to a reasonable extent, bend their own approach to fit the needs of given patients. I should add, though, that for nearly all clients in the Bachelor study, the conditions similar to those discussed in Chapter 2 as part of the empathic way were seen as important. Thus, these conditions (empathy, caring, affirmation) may be seen as fundamental and cutting across approaches. The take-home message is that in order to foster and preserve the working alliance, therapists need to provide these conditions and, beyond this, provide their patients with one or another of the types of alliances that Bachelor found clients to prefer.

Actually be competent. The second way of fostering and preserving the working alliance almost goes without saying. The therapist needs to be highly competent in whatever approach s/he is taking. Whatever theoretical approach the therapist adopts needs to be played out with skill and sufficient expertise. Naturally, mistakes and empathic failures are inevitable, but, in general, the patient will be much more likely to feel s/he can work effectively with a therapist who in fact is highly competent or expert. Competence or expertise pertains to both technical matters and relational matters (see Hill, Spiegel, Hoffman, Kivlighan, and Gelso, 2017). The former has to do with the effective use of techniques and interventions during sessions, whereas relational competence or expertise pertains to the therapist's ability to form and maintain relationships. These two forms of expertise are of course highly related, but they are not the same. Both are important for the development and preservation of the working alliance. In terms of Bordin's (1979) conception of the working alliance, not only does a working alliance require that the patient and therapist agree on the tasks that patient will need to do in order to reach the goals of the treatment, but that the therapist effectively implement these tasks and the techniques that will foster them.

Although of course humility is a way of being which most of us value and aspire to, in forming a working alliance, it is helpful to communicate competence and expertise. For example, I have had many attorneys as patients over the years. This is an occupational group that places a premium on reasoning ability and knowledge. I have learned that it is okay to show them that I know some things and can think logically. Of course, this is a slippery slope, as it is equally important that the therapist not show off and get caught in competitive games with the patient. I am reminded of how utterly competent and expert the humble and nondirective Carl Rogers was in his cases. He communicated that "I cannot possibly help you by giving you advice and answers because doing so would not be helpful." He showed that he knew what he was doing in his nondirectiveness.

Empathically understand the patient and communicate empathy. A key way of demonstrating effectiveness and fostering the working alliance is for the therapist to empathically understand the patient and communicate empathy. Earlier I discussed how therapist empathy strengthens the real relationship. It also fosters the working alliance. Being able to climb into the patient's inner world, grasp that world, and communicate it to the patient nonjudgmentally will tend to create within the patient a sense that this therapist is indeed competent, that the therapist gets the patient, and, in turn, that the patient can work productively with the therapist. Because being so understood tends to feel so good, the patient's motivation to work with the therapist will be strengthened.

As I did in Chapter 2, I must caution the reader not to conflate empathic understanding with either sympathetic agreement or the technique labeled reflection of feeling. Depending on the context and how it is said, expressions like "I can understand how you feel" or "I would feel that way too" can be experienced by the patient as sympathetic agreement rather than empathy. Also, reflecting what the patient feels can be experienced as unempathic, whereas a wide range of other responses (e.g., interpretations, questions, or even talking about seemingly irrelevant things) can be experienced as empathic. In other words, the therapist can climb into the patient's inner world in myriad and nonobvious ways.

Be attentive to ruptures and work to repair them. The concept of ruptures in the working alliance has been discussed above. So I shall just summarize here that (1) ruptures are essentially inevitable; (2) ruptures are sometimes obvious, but are often more subtle and nonobvious; (3) it is wise to be on the lookout for ruptures in the alliance; (4) in keeping with the work of Jeremy Safran and Christopher Muran over several years, ruptures are often signified by patient's withdrawal behaviors and/or confrontation or complaining related to the work; (5) it is important for the therapist to attend to and address ruptures; (6) when ruptures are caused by therapist mistakes or errors, an apology is usually wise, accompanied by exploration; and (7) when ruptures are addressed and worked through, the working alliance is usually further strengthened.

Maintain patience and curiosity. We are an action-oriented society in which things are expected to happen fast, and a premium is placed on active problem-solving. One of the ways in which this is manifested in the psychotherapy field in the United States is through the enormous emphasis over the past several decades on brief and time-limited therapies. Agencies such as university counseling centers and mental health clinics seem to be doing briefer and briefer work. The belief that change happens quickly is fostered by books written on brief approaches. Cases are often presented in texts that further this view. Therapist-trainees who read these texts internalize this view of speedy change brought about by the exceptional use of therapeutic techniques. The message is: "if you take this or that approach using these techniques really effectively, dramatic change can happen quickly." I often hear case presentations in my psychotherapy classes in which trainees talk about how the patient (who often is dealing with long-standing difficulties) is *only gradually* opening up and changing... after four or five sessions. The implication is that opening up and changing after a few sessions represents slow change! By way of contrast, when I have asked trainees and colleagues how long it took them to make important changes internally and behaviorally in their own lives, almost to a person they have talked in terms of years rather than weeks or months. Although we long ago discovered empirically that some changes certainly can indeed happen quickly (e.g., Gelso & Johnson, 1983), it is equally true that significant changes in long-standing or pervasive patterns and conflicts take time, often years, to emerge.

In the rush to produce quick change, a priceless commodity has too often been forgotten about: patience. I would offer, in fact, that patience might be the most neglected therapist quality in our field. Deeper and more pervasive changes take time, and patients cannot be pushed beyond what they are ready for. Inner resistances cannot simply be broken by magical techniques. Instead, the therapist's presence and patience is a vital part of the strengthening and preservation of the working alliance.

When therapist-trainees lament the slow pace of change, I usually ask them why they would expect long-standing patterns to give way to a few sessions or months of therapy, and invite them to examine their own active strivings and fears surrounding their passive sides. I have come to believe that our own passive sides are one of our most feared qualities, and that this fear is a serious impediment to therapists' willingness to allow the work to unfold naturally and at the pace that the patient needs.

Regarding the sister quality of curiosity, the ability to be interested in understanding what the patient is about, what defenses are operating and why, or for the CBT therapist, what reinforcers are controlling the unwanted behaviors, is a major alliance builder. Taken together, therapist patience and curiosity naturally make the patient feel understood and like the other is deeply interested in what makes them tick. These feelings serve to solidify a strong working alliance.

Help move the session forward. One of the key tasks of the therapist is to facilitate therapeutic movement in the psychotherapy hour. At first glance, this suggestion may seem contradictory with my call for patience and curiosity. And it is certainly true that, generally speaking, directing the session is neither alliance building nor effective. However, it is important and alliance building for the therapist to pay attention to the patient's drifting away from productive exploration, telling stories, "talking about" things in a distant or impersonal way, and avoiding key material. In such cases, it is the therapist's job to help the patient examine what is happening and why it is happening, or at least to help bring the patient back to exploring therapeutic material. This is so even when the unproductive material represents the patient's style of relating. In such cases, it is at times important to accept the storytelling mode, rather than try to actively stop it, but still help the patient to go beyond it and into more productive material. An example is the case of Sandra, a 48-year-old woman, who was a university professor, and with whom I worked for four years in weekly therapy that would be seen as successful by any yardstick:

> Sandra was a storyteller. She described personal events in her life in great detail, and left to her own way, she almost never looked inward. In the first few months of our work, it became clear that this was an ingrained way of being with Sandra, and to push her to work through this pattern would damage our working alliance and moreover be ineffective. Sandra at times would say teasingly that she does not like that "touchy, feely stuff." My approach with her throughout the therapy was to patiently listen to her reports of her experiences and those of close family members. As she reported, Sandra certainly had feelings, e.g., anger toward her sister and mother, deep affection for her younger brother, love for her husband. Still, these feelings were almost always "talked about" when Sandra was in her storytelling mode, rather than presented as something to be worked on in herself. The approach that worked with her, and helped preserve our working alliance, was for me to listen to her stories for perhaps half the session, asking questions about the events she related, at times reflecting feelings that seemed relevant, and being interested in her life. Then at some point, I would stop Sandra and ask how things were going between her and her. At times, I would say, a bit teasingly, that "I know you do not like that touchy, feely stuff, but I have to do my job," and I would proceed to help her look inward. In the latter part of our work together, Sandra often talked about how much it helped her to look inward, to explore that "touchy, feely stuff." When interacting with her family members, she would often even talk with them about how important it was to look at their inner feelings. I am convinced that our working alliance would have suffered, perhaps been irreparably damaged, had I not accepted her storytelling mode and confronted her with its defensive function. At the same time, it would also have been unproductive and naturally damaged the working alliance had I simply allowed the session to drift into storytelling for the entire time.

If the reader has gotten the impression that building and preserving the working alliance requires much the same activities on the therapist's part as conducting good therapy, I would not argue against that. The work of therapy builds the alliance and the alliance fosters the work of therapy. The two go hand in hand.

References

Ain, S. C., & Gelso, C. J. (2008). *Chipping away at the blank screen: Self disclosure, the real relationship, and therapy outcome.* Poster presented at the annual convention of the North American Society for Psychotherapy Research, New Haven, CT.

Ain, S. C., & Gelso, C. J. (2011). *Client and therapist perceptions of the real relationship and therapist self-disclosure: A study of psychotherapy dyads.* Paper presented at the 2011 Convention of the North American Society for Psychotherapy Research, Banff, Canada.

Bachelor, A. (1995). Clients' perceptions of the therapeutic alliance: A qualitative analysis. *Journal of Counseling Psychology, 42,* 323–337.

Bordin, E. S. (1979). The generalizability of the psychoanalytic concept of the working alliance. *Psychotherapy: Theory, Research, and Practice, 16,* 252–260. doi:10.1037/h0085885

Elliott, R., Bohart, A. C., Watson, J. C., & Greenberg, L. S. (2011). Empathy. *Psychotherapy, 48*(1), 43–49.

Gelso, C. J. (2011). *The real relationship in psychotherapy: The hidden foundation of change.* Washington DC: American Psychological Association.

Gelso, C. J. (2014). A tripartite model of the therapeutic relationship: Theory, research, and practice. *Psychotherapy Research, 24*(2), 117.

Gelso, C. J., & Carter, J. A. (1994). Components of the psychotherapy relationship: Their interaction and unfolding during treatment. *Journal of Counseling Psychology, 41*(3), 296–306. doi:10.1037/0022-0167.41.3.296

Gelso, C. J., & Hayes, J. A. (2007). *Countertransference and the therapist's inner experience: Perils and possibilities.* Mahwah, NJ: Erlbaum.

Gelso, C. J., & Johnson, D. H. (1983). *Explorations in time-limited counseling and psychotherapy.* New York: Teachers College Press.

Gelso, C. J., & Silberberg, A. (2016). Strengthening the real relationship: What is a psychotherapist to do? *Practice Innovations, 1*(3), 154–163. doi:10.1037/pri0000024

Gill, M. M.(1982). *Analysis of transference, Vol 1: Theory and technique.* Madison, NJ: International Universities Press.

Greenberg, L. S. (2002). Integrating an emotion-focused approach to treatment into psychotherapy integration. *Journal of Psychotherapy Integration, 12*(2), 154. doi:10.1037/1053-0479.12.2.154

Greenson, R. R. (1967). *The technique and practice of psychoanalysis* (Vol. 1). New York: International Universities Press.

Hayes, J. A., Gelso, C. J., & Hummel, A. M. (2011). Managing countertransference. *Psychotherapy, 48*(1). 88–97. doi:10.1037/a0022182

Hill, C.E., & Knox, S. (2009). Processing the therapeutic relationship. *Psychotherapy Research, 19,* 13–29. doi:10.1080/10503300802621206

Hill, C. E., & Knox, S. (2003). Therapist self-disclosure: Research-based suggestions for practitioners. *Journal of Clinical Psychology, 59*(5), 529–539. doi:10.1002/jclp.10157

Hill, C., Spiegel, S. B., Hoffman, M. A., Kivlighan, D. M., & Gelso, C. J. (2017). Therapist expertise in psychotherapy revisited. *The Counseling Psychologist, 45*(1), 7–53. doi:10.1177/0011000016641192

Horvath, A. O., Del Re, A. C., Flukiger, C., & Symonds, D. (2011). Alliance in adult psychotherapy. In J. C. Norcross (Ed.), *Psychotherapy relationships that work* (2nd ed., pp. 25–69). New York: Oxford University Press.

Kivlighan Jr.D. M., Hill, C. E., Gelso, C. J., & Baumann, E. (2016). Working alliance, real relationship, session quality, and client improvement in psychodynamic psychotherapy: A longitudinal actor partner interdependence model. *Journal of Counseling Psychology*, 63(2), 149–161. doi:10.1037/cou0000134

Levy, K. N. (2012). Subtypes, dimensions, levels, and mental states in narcissism and narcissistic personality disorder. *Clinical Psychology: In Session*, 68, 886–897. doi:10:1002/jclp.21893

Pérez-Rojas, A., Palma, B., Bhatia, A., Jackson, J., Norwood, E., Hayes, J., & Gelso, C. (2017a). The development and initial validation of the Countertransference Management Scale. *Psychotherapy*, 54, 307–319.

Renik, O. (1999). Getting real in analysis. *Journal of Analytical Psychology*, 44(2), 167–187. doi:10.1111/1465-5922.00082

Rhodes, R. H., Hill, C. E., Thompson, B. J., & Elliott, R. (1994). Client retrospective recall of resolved and unresolved misunderstanding events. *Journal of Counseling Psychology*, 41(4), 473–483. doi:10.1037/0022-0167.41.4.473

Safran, J. D., & Muran, J. C. (2000). *Negotiating the therapeutic alliance: A relational treatment guide*. New York: Guilford Press.

Silberberg, Ayelet. Personal Communication, March 31, 2017

Safran, J. D., Muran, J. C., & Eubanks-Carter, C. (2011). Repairing alliance ruptures. In J. C. Norcross (Ed.), *Psychotherapy relationships that work* (2nd ed., pp. 224–238). New York: Oxford University Press.

4 Detecting and Working with Transference

In this chapter, I am going to build on the summary of transference presented in Chapter 1. Although there will be some repetition with Chapter 1, here I seek to look further into how transference may be dealt with generally, as well as within the three major theoretical approaches to treatment that I highlight in the book.

As I have said, the concept of transference is indelibly rooted in psychoanalysis, and many view this construct as one of Sigmund Freud's greatest discoveries, residing next to his discovery of unconscious processes in importance. Freud pondered deeply and wrote eloquently about transference throughout his long career, but some of his earliest papers provided the core of his views of this complex phenomenon (Freud, 1905/1953, 1914/1959). In the 1905 paper, for example, after explaining why his neglect of transference in the case of Dora (one of his most famous cases) resulted in a failed treatment, Freud had this to say about the meaning of transference:

> What are transferences? They are new editions or facsimiles of the impulses and phantasies which are aroused and made conscious during the progress of analysis; but they have this peculiarity, which is characteristic of their species, that they replace some earlier person by the person of the physician. To put it another way: a whole series of psychological experiences are revived, not as belonging to the past, but as applying to the person of the physician at the present moment. Some of the transferences have a content which differs from that of their model in no respect whatsoever except for the substitution. These then – to keep the same metaphor – are merely new impressions or reprints. Others are more ingeniously constructed; their content has been subjected to a moderating influence – to *sublimation,* as I call it – and they may even become conscious, by cleverly taking advantage of some real peculiarity in the physician's person or circumstances and attaching themselves to that. These, then, will no longer be new impressions, but revised editions.
>
> (Freud, 1905/1953, p. 116)

Although there has been an enormous amount of writing about transference over more than a century within and outside of psychoanalysis, it has been my contention that this basic conception continues to have merit. Still, within both psychoanalysis and its many variants, there have been a range of views and considerable debate about what constitutes transference.

Conceptions and Definitions of Transference

As Jeffrey Hayes and I had noted in our earlier book about the therapeutic relationship (Gelso & Hayes, 1998), one may view conceptions of transference as residing within three basic clusters: the classical conception, the interpersonal view, and the relational perspective.

The *classical conception* sees transference as springing from the Oedipus complex during the phallic stage of development, which is most prominent from around ages 4–7. If the inevitable conflicts faced by the child during this stage are not sufficiently resolved during that time and again during adolescence, when Oedipal issues re-emerge, conflicts in adult life result. These unresolved difficulties manifest, in particular, in close relationships. The heterosexual male, for example, may have conflicts in relationships with women, gravitating toward women who are similar to his mother in important ways or the opposite of mother in those ways. The women toward whom the person is attracted, like the mother, are likely also unavailable or unattainable in important ways. The conflicts may also involve competition with other men. Although the Oedipus complex is somewhat different for women (and also often referred to as the Electra complex), the same fundamental issues are involved: attraction to the father and rivalry with the mother. Such problems are also expected in gay patients, although the attractions and competitions are, of course, connected to different genders than is the case for heterosexual patients. In terms of transference, the unresolved conflicts stemming from the phallic phase and the Oedipus complex emerge in the psychotherapy relationship, as the patient experiences the therapist and behaves toward the therapist in ways similar to what s/he experienced with one or both parents or parent-surrogates during that stage. In an important sense, the unresolved issues form a template through which the patient experiences the therapist and behaves toward him or her. In other words, the therapist's reality in the patient's eyes is distorted due to the unresolved conflicts in the patient. For example, the therapist may be seen as punishing, seductive, omnipotent, exceedingly appealing or unappealing, etc. in ways that the therapist has not "earned" and that are tied to unresolved Oedipal issues.

The *interpersonal view* conceives of transference as a repetition of past conflicts with significant others, such that attitudes, feelings, and behaviors tied to those earlier relationships are displaced onto the therapist. This definition is broader than the classical perspective in the sense that transference is seen as springing from significant relationships, not just the Oedipal triangle; the source is significant relationships, not just the patient's parents and parent surrogates; and the time of the origin of transference is much broader than just the years of the phallic stage and the Oedipus complex. The origin may occur at any period in the patient's childhood. One important feature of the interpersonal perspective is that transference is seen as having a partly realistic basis in the sense that it may have been appropriate at an earlier point in time. For example, the child may have developed a cautious and self-protective view of relationships because of actual psychological dangers in his/her relationship with excessively punitive parents. The problem becomes that this view is then carried over to present relationships in which it is not fitting. Or perhaps the opposite view may be carried into the present, where significant others are seen/experienced as unrealistically trustworthy. This template is then carried into the therapeutic relationship, where it is intensified because of the nature and purpose of the psychotherapy. The interpersonal view stems from the work of the early interpersonalists and neo-analytic theoreticians such as Sullivan (1954) and Fromm-Reichmann (1950).

The third and most recent cluster I refer to as the *intersubjective-relational perspective*. This viewpoint about transference emerged from a combination of post-modern philosophy, psychoanalytic self psychology (e.g., Kohut, 1984), the interpersonal perspective, and relational psychoanalysis (e.g., Mitchell, 1988, 1995). Advocates of the intersubjective-relational perspective view their approach as representing a two-person conception, rather than the one-person perspective of the approaches that preceded them. In the one-person perspective, transference resides in the patient, and any good therapist would provide the conditions for that transference to emerge. Thus, the patient's transference would be essentially the same with any therapist. Within the two-person perspective, however, both patient and therapist contribute to the transference. That is, the transference is co-constructed, and both therapist and patient explore and examine what they have co-constructed. In the extreme, within this position, there exists no core of the patient, no reality that is to be understood. There is only co-constructed reality.

Each of these three fundamental viewpoints has its problems. The classical perspective is limited by its restricted view of transference as emerging from the unresolved Oedipus conflict. The interpersonal view, while moving beyond the restrictions of the classical view, is still a one-person psychology. The relational perspective, while focusing on the mutual input of both therapist and patient, implies that there are no core issues within the patient that s/he carries with him or her into relationships, that emerge in the transference in psychotherapy, and that need to be addressed. There is only co-construction. This is a hard pill to swallow, both logically and empirically. Although there is certainly co-construction within the transference, there are also obviously core issues within the patient that emerge in the therapy in the form of transference. This viewpoint has ample support empirically, for example, in the numerous studies of the core conflictual relationship theme existing within patients and manifesting as transference in therapeutic relationships (see, for example, Luborsky & Crits-Christoph, 1998). An additional difficulty is that from the relational perspective, transference is often seen as all of the patient's reactions to and about the therapist. From a scientific viewpoint, this position is difficult to defend. If all reactions are transference, and there are no reactions that are not transference, then the construct, transference, becomes scientifically meaningless. A construct is only meaningful when it has boundaries – when we can determine what it is not, as well as what it is.

An Integrative Conception of Transference

The conception of transference that I have advocated (Gelso & Bhatia, 2012; Gelso & Hayes, 1998) seeks to integrate what I believe are the most defensible and meaningful aspects of the three approaches that have been summarized. As a working definition, we may define transference as *the patient's experience and perceptions of the therapist that are shaped by the patient's psychological structures and past, involving carryover from earlier significant relationships and displacement onto the therapist of feelings, attitudes, and behaviors belonging rightfully to those earlier relationships*. A controversial and fundamental issue in any conception of transference has to do with the idea of distortion. Particularly in the intersubjective-relational perspective, the notion of the patient having perceptions of the therapist that are distortions representing figures from the patient's past tends to be eschewed. All perceptions are co-constructed by therapist and patient, and the idea that the patient is distorting the therapist misses the point of this co-creation. This position is hard to defend clinically, logically, and empirically. Not only is there sound evidence that patients possess core issues that would lead to very similar transferences with different therapists (Levy & Scala, 2012; Luborsky & Crits-Christoph, 1998), but, indeed, the fundamental idea of transference has to do with that portion of the patient's experiences and perceptions that are carried from the past into the present. Totally devoid of such displacement, it is hard to see how the process can be called transference at all. Indeed, distortion may be seen as the heart of transference, so long as it is understood that this distortion may be extremely subtle and complex, or in Freud's terms, may represent revised editions rather than simple reprints. The patient may experience the therapist as, and try to make the therapist into, a figure the patient needed but never had (e.g., the good father or mother); the patient may idealize the therapist, making him/her into the all-powerful parent who was needed but unavailable during critical periods of childhood; the patient's projections onto the therapist may be a complex mixture of good and bad elements of, for example, mother and father; and the patient may steadfastly (consciously or unconsciously) resist the development, emergence, or awareness of transference. Or s/he may develop distortions precipitated by the therapist's actual behavior.

An example of the transference being precipitated by the actual behavior of the therapist is the case I like to refer to as The Tired Therapist. The therapist, who continually dozed off in sessions with the patient, stirred significant paternal transference in this patient. The patient was flooded with memories of his father picking up the newspaper when the patient wished to talk with him. There was, of course, a realistic part of the patient's angry and hurt reactions; but the part of those reactions that went beyond this realism was indeed a carryover of the patient's father, who could not spend more than a few seconds listening to whatever the patient wanted to communicate over the course of the patient's entire childhood. The therapist communicated an apology and revealed that he always got drowsy right after lunch, when the session occurred. This helped assuage the patient's pain, but the experiences still stirred many transference memories and experiences in the patient.

The case of The Tired Therapist highlights how co-construction could occur at the same time that distortion occurs. Indeed, there is no doubt that there is almost always co-construction when transference occurs, but, as proposed, there also must be distortion. The process of transference distortion may be nicely explained by the Piagetian notions of assimilation and accommodation. John Bowlby (1988) drew on this developmental psychology theory when he viewed assimilation as the patient wrapping new information into an existing mental scheme, whereas in accommodation, the pre-existing scheme is modified to take into account the new information. Transference represents a predominance of assimilation. All patient reactions may be seen as a combination of transference and realistic perception, or assimilation and accommodation.

Rules of Thumb about Transference

In seeking to understand the fundamentals of transference, I have found it useful to spell out five rules-of-thumb:

1

To one degree or another, transference is always an error. This rule-of-thumb pertains to distortion as we have discussed it. Although there is almost always an element of accuracy or realism in transference reactions, and despite the fact that transferences are generally a function of the therapist's as well as the patient's behavior (co-constructed), there is always a core of transference, ipso facto, that represents a misperception or uncalled-for expectation of the therapist that is a carryover from early significant relationships.

2

Transference may be positive or negative. The transference reactions that patients have to their therapists may be positively or negatively valenced, or they may be a mixture of the two. That is, the patient may perceive or experience the therapist in positive ways that do not accurately capture the therapist's feelings and behavior or in negative ways that do not fit. An example of negative transference is the patient's experiencing a therapist who is warm and empathic as subtly critical and demeaning in a way that is reflective of the patient's early and ongoing relationship with her mother. A positive transference example, on the other hand, might be reflected in the patient's experience of his warm and empathic therapist as a perfect pillar of warmth and empathy, unlike the patient's mother. Generally speaking, because therapists are typically positive, caring, and empathic toward their patients in reality, it is more difficult to detect positive transference than negative transference. That is, it can be hard to differentiate positive transference from realistic positive reactions toward an actually positive therapist.

3
The emergence of transference is facilitated by the therapist's neutrality and ambiguity. If the therapist does not take positions for or against the different voices in the patient's inner world or in the patient's struggles with significant others, the transference inclinations of the patient are more likely to emerge. Similarly, if the therapist refrains from presenting a clear picture of his or her personal feelings, attitudes, and life, transferences are more likely to take shape and emerge, or at least come into view in a way that is understandable as transference. The idea behind this guideline is similar to the assumption that underlies all projective testing: present the subject with an ambiguous, neutral stimulus, and the subject's reactions and interpretations to and of it are likely to reflect his or her inner, less conscious world. Transference is likely to exist no matter what the therapist does, but it is more likely to emerge into the open, and be less "contaminated" by the therapist's values, beliefs, wishes, and being as this therapist maintains some degree of neutrality and ambiguity. Note that this does not imply that therapists are supposed to be highly neutral and ambiguous, only that these qualities will facilitate transference coming into the open in a way that is understandable and interpretable. Whether or not this is desirable depends on the therapist's theoretical inclinations and the patient's dynamics.

4
Transference is not conscious. This is one of the trickier of the guidelines. Transference-based feelings and thoughts are very often fully conscious. The patient does have transference-based reactions to and expectations of the therapist. However, the fact that these reactions and expectations are transferential is typically not conscious, although they may reside close to consciousness. For example, the patient who expects her therapist to forget their appointment session after session, feels diminished by this, and feels angry toward the therapist (who had never forgotten) may be quite aware of these expectations and feelings. But she is not aware that they represent a projection of her feelings about herself being forgettable tied to the fact that her mother paid so little attention to her. The feelings about the mother may also be conscious, but, again, the fact that the patient's expectations of the therapist are a projection are not. Indeed, helping the patient see the connection and come to understand, emotionally as well as intellectually, that her expectations of her therapist are transferential is a major step toward the resolution of this transference and changing the patient's destructive behavior in intimate relationships.

5
Transferences are most likely to occur in areas of greatest unresolved conflict with significant others earlier in one's life. As I shall amplify in

the subsequent "Why Transference" section, transference is not the same as the behavioral concept of stimulus generalization, that is, reactions to the therapist based on experiences with similar figures or situations in the patient's life. Instead, transference is best seen as driven by unresolved conflicts and issues early in the patient's life, and, in part, as an attempt to resolve those conflicts in the present or avoid re-experiencing the emotional pain associated with these conflicts. For example, when the patient has many unresolved conflicts around her relationship with her father, feeling that he never admired or perhaps even noticed her, she is more likely to have feelings toward and projections onto her male therapist related to these unresolved conflicts. She may experience the therapist as a father figure who thinks the world of her (a "resolution" of the painful situation with her actual father). Or she may believe that the therapist does not care for or even notice her (avoidance of re-experiencing what she felt with her father by projecting those feelings onto the therapist – painful but not as deeply hurtful). In this sense, rather than being a simple stimulus generalization, transference is best seen as motivated and resistant to extinction. Indeed, if these transferences were a simple stimulus generalization, they would disappear if the therapist just pointed them out, and noted that s/he was not like the patient's father. Although such pointing out may be one step in the resolution of the transference, such resolution usually takes many sessions, and interpretations such as the therapist's must be offered repeatedly. In sum, because transference is motivated and based on early unresolved conflict, it tends to be difficult to modify or work through. This is one of those clinical facts that becomes clear with experience. Inexperienced therapists generally must practice for some time before it fully hits home.

Although I have given examples of transference that is gender-linked (e.g., the female patient who has unresolved issues with her father transferring these father issues onto her *male* therapist), experience suggests that transference is not gender specific. For example, the female patient may transfer father issues onto her female therapist, or the male therapist may become the good mother in the transference. Transferences that cross gender lines seem to happen more frequently later in treatment, as less rational material comes to the surface and into the open.

Transference as a Universal Phenomenon

Research evidence supports the assertion that there is transference, as defined above, in all psychotherapies, regardless of the theoretical orientation of the therapist and the inclinations of the patient. Going a big step beyond this, I also propose that there is transference in all human relationships, both in and out of psychotherapy. This is similar to Freud (1959/1912) position, although he did add that transference gets magnified and intensified in psychoanalysis because, essentially, the analysis is set up to accentuate and bring into the open these transferences.

What is the warrant for my broad assertion about transference? A review of empirical studies by Bhatia and me (Gelso & Bhatia, 2012) clearly points to the existence of transference beyond the confines of traditional psychoanalysis and psychodynamically based therapy. Although there is not sufficient data to conduct a sound statistical meta-analysis, virtually all studies pointed to in Bhatia's and my review supported the existence of transference in non-dynamic therapies. After reviewing the empirical evidence, we concluded that

> consistent findings from several laboratories support the assertion that transference indeed happens in nonanalytic therapies, and it does not happen much less than in analytic therapies. The content of transference is essentially the same in nonanalytic and analytic therapy, and transference does not appear to be an artifact of the analytic therapist. That is, it is not simply created by the therapist's belief in its existence. Lastly, transference is likely to show itself, perhaps increasingly, whether or not the therapist attends to it.
>
> (p. 387)

In addition, the social psychological research program conducted by Susan Andersen and her students over many years (see Andersen & Przybylinski, 2012) leaves little doubt of the existence and importance of transference in essentially all human relationships. For example, after reviewing the accumulated social psychological evidence for the existence of transference in everyday life, Andersen and Przybylinski concluded that:

> Our theoretical framework and the accumulated evidence strongly suggest that mundane, everyday encounters involve more than meets the eye, and that transference occurs throughout interpersonal life in everyday perception and behavior. Prior relationships can and do play out in present ones. As one example, qualities of a new person that are similar in some way to a significant other, even when subtle or minimal in that resemblance, can trigger processes of transference, through which the past can reemerge in the present.
>
> (p. 181)

What are the implications of these findings for the psychotherapist? First, it is helpful for the therapist, regardless of theoretical orientation, to be on the lookout for the patient's transferences in his or her life outside of therapy. The transference displacements that occur in intimate relationships, in particular, seem important to work through so that the patient is better able to take the other for whom the other is rather than being seen through the transference lenses of past relationships. As for transference in therapy, the relevance of transference work may be best captured by Schaeffer (2007), a practicing therapist who received her doctoral training in a cognitive-behavioral training program. Schaeffer says that phenomena such as transference (and countertransference, too; see Chapter 5) were hardly mentioned in her training; but once she began to practice, these phenomena began to loom large. Schaeffer tells us that

...there is no question that *all* therapists and clients transfer functions and roles they or others played in the past to each other. There is no question that *nonanalytic* therapists must identify transference and countertransference as soon as possible. There is no question that they must diagnose them accurately and give serious consideration to interpreting them to appropriate clients so that, rather than be controlled by them, they can control them and benefit from the major contribution they can make to variables responsible for positive outcome....Otherwise, the double-edged swords of transference and countertransference will cut their way through what is working and enable variables responsible for negative outcome to gain a stronghold.

(p. xi)

In the remainder of this chapter, I shall explore transference-related topics that are central to the work of both psychodynamic and non-dynamic therapies. I focus on why transference happens, how to identify transference, and what to do about transference from different theoretical perspectives.

The Why of it All

Perhaps the first question to be asked by the clinician/theoretician is, "why does transference happen to begin with?" And speaking to its resistance to extinction, we might ask, "what makes humans maintain their perceptions and experiences of others in the face of contrary evidence?" If transference is indeed the universal construct that I have suggested it is, then there must be something about humans that creates the proclivity to engage in transference reactions, to experience others in ways that reflect earlier significant relationships.

Over the decades, there have been several answers to our question of "why transference?" This is a question that occupied Freud for many years, and he offered three primary reasons. First, humans have a basic and conservative tendency to repeat (e.g., repetition compulsions). We are hard-wired to do so, and our early learnings in deeply significant early relationships live on throughout life. Second, and perhaps more clinically meaningful, humans have a tendency to seek satisfactions of which they had been deprived.

> As an example of this phenomenon, my female patient who suffered from the lack of healthy mothering, and a profound lack of empathy from a mother who by all accounts was emotionally barren, experienced me as the good, embracing mother, and in a certain sense, created that in me (which she eventually was able to understand and work through). She was receiving in the present what she had been deprived of so painfully throughout childhood. Had I simply been the good, gratifying mother in the therapy, this would have been of limited help. Instead, we were able to explore the painful deprivations, which ultimately allowed her to learn to be her own good mother, to take care of herself in an empathic way,

although the scars of those early years would never completely go away. Her growing understanding also allowed her to obtain healthy nurturance in her close relationships, rather than seeking what others could not possibly give her and then feeling deeply disappointed.

The third reason Freud offered for the existence and enactment of transference (Freud, 1959/1912; 1914/1958) was to allow the patient to avoid painful or traumatizing memories of childhood. In this sense, transference is a reflection of the patient's unconscious attempt to *not* remember the deeply hurtful past. A brief example from my practice is:

> My patient felt sure that I could give her solutions to her life problems, which in fact were profound. She felt I knew the solutions but was withholding them from her, and because of this harbored a deep anger toward me. During one session, this patient angrily criticized me and pleaded for me to "tell her." In fact, she wanted what I could not possibly give her, and I pointed out the bitterness in her plea and how her feelings likely echoed feelings from long ago. The patient responded by tearfully sharing how she felt she never got her fair share from her parents and of how she was never taken care of. This brief interaction early in our work was one crucial step toward helping the patient eventually come to terms with what she was so desperately avoiding: her deep hurt and sense of deprivation throughout childhood. In this example, the patient's anger toward me cloaked and kept from awareness the deep source of this transference projection. The problem with this pattern was that the patient carried it into all of her close relationships, thus preventing her from having successful intimacy. So, the transference allowed her to hide from her pain, but the price of it was too great, as is typically the case when transferences allow patients to hide from early trauma.

A fourth reason for why transference happens is similar to the first, which I called the conservative human tendency to repeat. The fourth reason is that transference represents a familiar way of dealing with stressful situations. The patient experiences, perceives, and responds to the therapist in ways s/he learned to respond to significant others early in life. These ways helped the patient survive difficult experiences in early life. They protected the patient from dangers that presented themselves in the patient's interpersonal life. So naturally they became embedded in the patient's response repertoire. The problem is that in the patient's current life, while the old patterns may keep him or her protected, they also entrap him or her. That is, in wrapping the past into the present, they cloud the patient's perceptions and experience of here-and-now relationships, and foster responses to others that are not facilitative of healthy or effective relationships. These transferences occur in the patient's life outside of therapy, and I believe they are, more than any other single factor, responsible for the patient's failures in both love and work. Within the therapeutic relationship, these tendencies are naturally revived and magnified. Understanding them and helping the patient see how the tendencies operate within as well as outside of therapy can be of immense benefit. Indeed, helping the patient change these basic interpersonal patterns (how the patient experiences/perceives significant others' treatment of him/her, how the patient responds to these perceptions of others) may be the most fundamental personality change of which psychotherapy is possible.

Finally, a fifth reason for transference, first uncovered by Weiss and Sampson (e.g., 1986), is that it represents the patient's attempt to test a pathogenic belief about how s/he will be responded to, with the hope that the therapist will disconfirm this belief. In carrying over the past into the present, the patient expects a negative or unhealthy response from the therapist but, at the same time, hopes that this will not happen, that the expectation will be disconfirmed. When the therapist responds therapeutically by empathically comprehending the patient's transference expectation, not being critical, or not enacting defensively or negatively, the patient's negative expectancy is disconfirmed and at least a step is taken toward self-understanding and the resolution of transference, as well as its enactment outside of the therapy office. The patient also begins to remember more of his or her hidden feelings from the past and see how they became part of his or her expectations of the therapist and others in close relationships.

In sum, there are many roots to the question of "why transference." Which one of these or cluster of these is predominant may differ from patient to patient, and it is the therapist's job to try to grasp the patient's unique transference dynamics. How and the extent to which this is done will depend on the personal and theoretical proclivities of the psychotherapist.

How to Identify Transference

Although few practicing psychotherapists currently would view themselves as classically psychoanalytic, I have found the five markers of transference suggested by the classical analyst, Ralph Greenson, extremely useful to this day. In fact, they seem to transcend any particular theory and may be seen as universal. Before discussing these markers, however, it may be helpful to reiterate that the particulars of transference and its enactment are never simply a manifestation of the patient's inner world. Instead, they are co-constructed by therapist and patient. Thus, although the core transference theme (which may be called the core conflictual relationship theme, the cyclical maladaptive pattern, the central issue, etc.) will naturally be the same because it is part of the patient's psyche, the specific ways in which transference shows itself is contributed to by the person of the therapist and the therapist's specific interactions with the patient. The markers provided by Greenson follow.

Inappropriateness

Although whether or not a reaction is inappropriate is often arguable, when the case data indicate that the patient's reactions to the therapist are not realistic and clearly do not fit the situation, including the therapist's behavior, transference is the likely culprit. For example, early in the work, a patient says to her therapist, "You seem very kind and understanding, but when I look into your eyes, I feel there is a cold bitch inside." At the therapist's invitation, the patient then explored her thoughts and associations around this perception. She soon began many hours of exploration in this long and successful treatment about her mother, whom she felt to have an enormous amount of hidden aggression. The patient's reaction very clearly did not fit who this therapist was or what this therapist felt toward the patient.

Before drawing conclusions about how realistic versus appropriate is the patient's reaction to the therapist, it is important to determine the extent to which the therapist's behavior justifies this reaction. If, for example, the therapist is not attending properly to the patient (e.g., answering phone calls during sessions, dozing off in session, being late for sessions, not listening to the patient), it is unlikely that the patient's annoyed reaction is transferential. On the other hand, if the patient becomes furious or is unable to continue exploring after a therapist lapse, there may be transference added to the realistic wound caused by the therapist's inattention. A case similar to that of The Tired Therapist, as described earlier, may exemplify the inappropriateness marker:

> The therapist had not been feeling well during this particular session, and had had a poor night's sleep. During a part of the session, he had trouble taking in what the patient was describing, and his attention wandered. The patient noticed this and was unable to continue exploration. He felt too angry and wounded, and felt that the therapist was bored with him and uncaring, indeed only faking interest in him. This was not the case, and in fact the therapist liked the patient and always looked forward to their sessions. For the patient, the therapist's empathic failure revived deep wounds around his relationship with his father, who seemed chronically unable to pay attention to the patient's feelings and thoughts, and the patient reacted to the therapist in the same way he did toward his father. Transference was added to a realistic empathic failure on the therapist's part and a realistic hurt in the patient.

Of the five markers of transference, inappropriateness may be seen as the most fundamental. All of the other markers also involve inappropriateness in one way or another.

Intensity or Lack of Emotion

Both highly intense reactions to the therapist (assuming that these are not "earned" by the therapist) and non-reactions or emotional flatness toward the therapeutic relationship are potential markers of transference. As for intensity, the reactions may be positive, negative, or both. The patient may feel intensely loving, intensely fearful, intensely anxious, hateful, etc. toward the therapist in a way that does not fit the therapist's behavior or the therapeutic relationship. One of my patients, for example, was intensely grateful for any normal act of kindness or understanding on my part. Although a part of me enjoyed this, it was clear that the patient was making attributions that I had not deserved. As this therapy unfolded, it became clear that in a part of the transference relationship, I was the good mother, that is, the mother that was almost the opposite of what the patient experienced.

> On the negative side was the patient who saw me early in our work as the knowing but ungiving parent. She was sure I knew the solution to her problems, but was withholding them. This patient had intense and chronic feelings of deep anger toward me. During one session in which she angrily criticized and pleaded with me to "tell her," I pointed out the bitterness in her request and how her feelings must echo something from long ago. She tearfully shared how she never felt she got her share from her parents, and how she was never taken care of. This particular interaction was a critical step in the patient's coming to understand both her transference and her reactions in relationships outside of treatment, and toward working through the conflicts underlying these reactions.

A general rule of thumb in working with intensely negative transference reactions in particular is that it is important to help the patient understand early on that the reactions to the therapist are coming from somewhere else in the patient's life, i.e., are not earned by the therapist. This is a delicate matter because it must be done in a way that does not deny the patient's feelings or their legitimacy. However, if the patient does not come to see that his/her perceptions of the therapist are not earned by the therapist, and that these seem to come from another time and place, the danger is that the working alliance will be severely damaged and the entire treatment will be endangered.

Lack of emotions toward the therapist may be just as indicative of transference as are intense emotions. In this case, what we have may be termed a resistance to transference or a transference resistance. For some patients, it is important to keep feelings toward the therapist out of the room and out of consciousness. The patient may want to keep the relationship rational and may fear that emotions will hinder the work. What to do about this depends on how well the patient is progressing in the absence of the overt expression of transference reactions, the therapist's theoretical orientation, the patient's general dynamics and psychological strengths, the possible duration of the treatment, etc.

> An example of lack of emotions in the therapeutic relationship is a patient I worked with in weekly therapy for three years. This 50-year-old professor grew considerably in the therapy, as she came to understand how strong her inner critic was, how that was related to her internalization of her critical father, and how helpful it was to explore her feelings rather

than simply trying to unemotionally solve problems. By the end of treatment, this patient, who had suffered from severe depression with suicidal ideation, was symptom-free, no longer depressed, and doing well in her marriage and work. At no point in this work did she express feelings toward me other than polite cooperativeness. During our termination phase, upon my inquiry, she shared that I was a doctor to her and our relationship was businesslike. She had pleasant and appreciative feelings toward me, but no intensity of any kind. My approach during treatment was to accept this and not push for hidden transference, which I did believe was there. The patient did very well in treatment, and there seemed no need to open up another level of repression that was likely involved in the transference.

In cases in which the treatment is not progressing or is at a standstill and the therapist has evidence for transference resistance, gentle prodding on the therapist's part may be needed to help bring it to consciousness; for example, the patient who presents as pleasant and neutral toward his therapist, which disguises mistrust and fear of abandonment. This mistrust and fear fits the central relationship theme in his life, but he is unable to explore it in a way that goes beyond subtle blame of others in his life. He remains alone and lonely. Treatment is at a standstill until the therapist helps the patient see the mistrust and fear in the consulting room that has not been earned by the therapist and they begin to explore where that comes from.

Hidden Ambivalence

Perhaps it goes without saying that all human relationships are punctuated by some degree of ambivalence. What is often a marker to transference is repressed ambivalence wherein one side of the ambivalence is repressed and the other side is acted out. For example, the patient suffering from borderline personality disorder may oscillate between conscious idealization of the therapist and conscious depreciation. The flip side of these extreme states (primitive rage and primitive idealization) may be repressed while the other side is experienced and acted out. Or the patient may experience and enact very positive, loving feelings toward the therapist that serve to cover repressed anger. Both the expressed and the repressed feelings represent the transference, not just the repressed feelings. In the example just given, the loving feelings may represent the patient's way of winning the rejecting parent over, while the repressed anger may reflect the patient's feelings about being rejected. In this situation, the therapist is put in the role of the rejecting parent.

The repressed side of the ambivalence may also show itself in the patient's reactions to others. For example, the patient may express continued anger toward authority figures, while reacting uniformly positively to the therapist. To the extent that this hidden ambivalence is playing out in the therapy and, more importantly, is hindering the patient's life outside of therapy, it is important to be explored in treatment.

Capriciousness

Many years ago, Glover (1955) wrote about "floating transferences" to capture transferences that were highly changeable from one session or cluster of sessions to the next. This capriciousness seems to more often occur early in the work, especially when the therapy is intensive (more than one session per week). Such capriciousness seems more characteristic of patients with certain personality disorders, e.g., borderline or histrionic personalities.

When the patient's perceptions of and reactions to the therapist are highly fluid, seemingly changing, at times dramatically, from one moment to the next, transference is likely. Greenson (1967) gives the rather extreme example of this with his patient who, during the course of four consecutive sessions, changed from (a) being in love with her analyst, who was perceived as an idealistic dreamer, to (b) feeling overwhelmed by guilt because her love made her neglect her child, to (c) feeling that the analyst was cold and disdainful, to (d) experiencing the analyst as endearingly clumsy in his work.

Tenacity

Capriciousness is most likely to occur early in treatment. However, if the work continues beyond a few sessions or a few months, a more stable transference pattern is likely to appear. This pattern or template may take myriad forms, reflecting the infinite ways in which human beings may perceive or experience others in intimate relationships and those relationships involving one person helping another. The therapist may be experienced as the all-good mother and/or father, the nurturing parent the patient never had, the potentially damaging authority figure, the critical mother or father, etc. This pattern tends to be held to by the patient with tenacity. Simply telling the patient that his or her perceptions of the therapist are incorrect will essentially never resolve the transference pattern or template. For example, I have noticed that less experienced therapists are typically very uncomfortable with what might be termed idealizing transferences. In these transferences, the therapist is essentially experienced as all-knowing and all-giving; and, as Heinz Kohut discovered (Kohut, 1971, 1977), such transferences are most often exhibited by patients with certain disorders of the self that involve damaged self-esteem or narcissism. Idealizing transferences in these patients are there for a reason, and this makes such transferences tenacious. I have often noticed that therapy trainees, and some experienced therapists too, will clarify to such patients that they are not perfect, but rather just normal human beings with frailties like all human beings. Attempts by therapists at "humanizing" themselves are most often met with further idealizations by the patient, e.g., "ah, you are so wonderfully modest." So, the attempt at de-idealization results in further idealization.

The tenaciousness of transference reactions is not limited to a few kinds of disorders, e.g., narcissistic personality disorders. And this tenacity in the patient's transference pattern or template is generally one of the clearest indications that the patterns are indeed transferential. Given this tenacity, how is the therapist to help the patient resolve the transference pattern or template? These fundamentally important questions will be addressed subsequently in this chapter.

Look for the Core Theme

The discussion of tenacity leads to perhaps the most useful method of recognizing when patient reactions represent transference. That is, in nearly every patient I have seen directly or through psychotherapy supervision of doctoral trainees, there is a core conflictual relationship theme in their intimate relationships that will emerge in the therapy. This core relational theme will invariably reveal what the key transference pattern will be. For example, the patient may be disbelieving that her intimates will truly care for her and that she can lean on them when needed. This theme may be present consistently in close relationships. Childhood exploration reveals that this patient was, in fact, a burden to her mother, who gave birth to her when she was 17 years old. The patient has no memory of the mother ever holding or embracing her. So, this early and ongoing experience with mother forms the nucleus of what she expects from others and how she feels toward others who are close to her, and it surely will show up as the key transference theme in her therapy. It may show up directly, or it may be cleverly disguised. For example, the patient may be excessively appreciative of her therapist's empathic concern, showering praise on the therapist for a level of empathy and caring that is not at all remarkable. The patient's excessive appreciation may belie a deeper mistrust of the therapist and an expectation that the therapist's empathy may go away at any moment. Thus, the patient's appreciation is both a genuine reflection of her getting something in her therapy that she did not expect or, indeed, deserve. And, as well, it serves to hide her expectation that the therapist will stop caring at any moment or really does not care.

At times, it appears that there is no transference theme, but a look into the patient's childhood will suggest a hidden theme. For example, a therapy supervisee of mine, who had not previously been accustomed to looking for the transference theme, presented a case in which she could not detect transference. The patient, a 22-year-old male, Filipino college senior, shared little of any depth with the therapist, a 28-year-old female, Hispanic doctoral student who is generally highly nurturing and caring. The patient's responses to this therapist were often abrupt, terse, and dismissive. Still, while the therapist felt annoyed with this behavior, she also experienced a deep sense of caring and a wish to take care of the patient. In this sense, she felt very motherly, while at the same time, her mothering behaviors were dismissed or pushed away. A look into the patient's background revealed a situation in which he received little mothering and had a father who was severely critical of the patient for any nurturance he might seek or his mother might offer. The therapist had the impression that this young man yearned for mothering but felt anxious about this yearning and deeply mistrusting of the nurturance he did receive, as one would expect. So, it appeared that the transference theme was a resistance to a maternal transference, an unconscious craving for the good mother and an attendant fear of this craving and an expectation that good mothering would not happen. Thus, the patient pushed away the therapist's therapeutic nurturance. The transference, in other words, was well hidden beneath a bitingly dismissive way of being with the therapist.

In sum, if the therapist looks into the patient's background, a core relational theme will appear and will be suggestive of the transference pattern or template. The therapist's inspection of his or her own feelings with the patient, when combined with an examination of the patient's early years, will help illuminate that pattern or theme.

What to do About Transference

How are transference reactions best dealt with by the therapist? Although it seems that transference is common to all forms of therapy, there is no agreed-upon way of working with it. In this section, I describe how transference is seen and worked with in the three dominant theoretical orientations examined throughout this book, and I offer some suggestions about what might be addressed.

The Psychodynamic Way

There are innumerable approaches to psychotherapy that fall under the psychodynamic umbrella. On one end of the psychodynamic continuum, there is classical psychoanalysis, in which psychoanalysts meet with their patients, called analysands, usually 3–5 times a week for several years. Even within this general approach, there exist several different main theories, often clustered into drive theory, ego analysis, object relations theory, and psychoanalytic self psychology. Typically, the analysand reclines on a couch, free associates, presents dreams, etc; and the analyst focuses on listening and offering well-timed interpretation when called for.

At the other end of the continuum are approaches that might be considered psychodynamically informed psychotherapies. Here one or more psychodynamic theories are used to understand the patient, while the therapist employs a range of techniques to help the patient develop understanding and behavior change. In between these two ends of psychodynamic continuum is a wide array of treatments based on a number of specific psychodynamic theories. However, there is a tie that binds these theories and approaches. As Summers and Barber (2010) suggest, the essence of psychodynamic therapy is the "exploration of current conflicts and relationships in order to understand how they relate to the past, the search for recurring patterns, and a focus on the therapeutic relationship to see how conflicts are repeated" (p. 10).

It is easy to see from this general definition how central transference is to dynamic therapies. That is, when the therapist seeks to understand how patterns develop in which past conflicts are repeated in the present and in the therapeutic relationship, in a general sense the therapist is helping the patient understand transference. Thus, we have what has often been referred to as the triangle of insight, wherein the patient's past, present extra-therapy life, and the therapeutic relationship are connected in order to develop understanding and change. And it is the therapeutic relationship that is often most alive, the place in which problems show themselves directly and immediately in terms of the patient's experience and perceptions of the therapist and his/her reactions to the patient. This display of the patient's conflicts within the therapeutic relationship is the essence of transference. And transference in this sense is the essence of psychodynamic psychotherapy.

The effective psychodynamic therapist possesses what has long been termed an analytic attitude (see review by Schafer, 1983). That is, the therapist maintains a stance of curiosity, believing that everything is worth exploration and understanding. There is no rush to change the patient, and certainly no judgment is called for; instead, the good dynamic therapist aims to be curious and to foster the patient's curiosity. From the understanding created by this curiosity emerge the seeds of change. The analytic attitude needs to be ever-present, including as regards to the therapeutic relationship in general, and the transference in particular. I believe that it is this analytic attitude, coupled with empathy, that allows for the patient's awareness and expression of threatening feelings and thoughts, especially as these have to do with the therapist, i.e., the transferences.

Does what I have stated above suggest that transference must be a key element of all psychodynamic therapies if they are to be successful? Although transference has been posited to be a part of all psychotherapy in the sense that it is in the background or foreground of the therapeutic relationship, part of the patient's conscious expression or unconscious life, it is not a necessity that it be explored as transference in all dynamic therapy. Often the analytic therapist is able to help the patient explore his or her inner life as it relates to the patient's past and present life and relationships, and this exploration, which includes working through of inner conflicts in the present, can happen effectively in the absence of transference exploration. I have participated in and observed (through colleagues' and students' case presentations, and through therapy supervision) many therapeutic relationships, especially in brief dynamic therapies, in which there were strong working alliances and real relationships, and the available transferences (those that were conscious and shared) were positive. In many of these instances, little exploration of the patient's transference experiences of the therapist needed to be done, particularly in the sense of the patient's transference reactions needing to be connected to their source, e.g., early unresolved conflicts. Still, even in these cases, in effective psychodynamic therapy, discussion of the here-and-now therapeutic relationship is helpful. Such exploration can include the patient's feelings about the therapist and therapy in the here-and-now, as well as the therapist's feelings when appropriate, without the connection to the early conflictual relationships that fueled these feelings. In the majority of cases treated by dynamic therapy, however, sensitive and well-timed exploration of the triangle of insight is a key element.

The Cognitive-Behavioral Way

Although historically CBT was technique focused, and in its early days minimized the importance of the relational factors in the psychotherapy dyad, over the years this persuasion has paid increasing attention to the therapeutic relationship. Currently popular (and effective) CBT approaches virtually all seem to incorporate a sound therapeutic relationship as a necessary, although not sufficient, element of effective treatment. In particular, the modern CBT therapist does indeed pay attention to the working alliance and the real relationship elements of the therapeutic relationship (see, for example, Goldfried & Davila, 2005; Lejuez, Hopko, Levine, Gholkar, & Collins, 2005; Linehan, 1993; Persons, 2008; Tsai et al., 2008; Wolfe, 2005). Still, transference is rarely addressed in CBT, and when transference phenomena are addressed, terms other than transference are usually used to capture what is happening in the therapeutic dyad.

Ironically, transference was indeed addressed in some of the earlier treatments of CBT. For example, Goldfried and Davison (1976), two highly influential CBT theorists, actually used the term, transference, and discussed how it can be helpfully incorporated into CBT treatments. Following Sullivan's (1954) interpersonal psychodynamic theory, Goldfried and Davison suggested that the patient learns certain attitudes in early interactions with parents, and these learnings then serve as prototypes for his or her reactions in similar situations later in life. The therapeutic relationship is one such situation in which the patient plays out these earlier prototypes. In this sense, the patient's reactions to the therapist are similar to his or her reactions to significant others in present life, and both are a reflection of the prototypes. It follows that the patient's transference to the therapist is a great example of how the patient reacts to significant others – an important sample of behavior that the CBT therapist can work on and with. Rather than exploring the early roots of this behavior, however, the CBT therapist would "provide direct feedback, primarily to help the client realize how his maladaptive behavior manifests itself" (p.57). In other words, transference behavior is used as a sample of maladaptive behavior toward which the CBT therapist brings the patient's attention. This is seen as a first step toward changing that behavior.

Moving to the current scene, Persons (2008) provides an excellent model of transference, conceptualized in learning terms, and how it might be used to the benefit of CBT treatment. The patient, Adele, was not progressing in therapy, in Persons' view. She was destabilized after losing her job and regressed to her pattern of moving from crisis to crisis. Persons says that:

> We had discussed her setback and agreed that she needed more intensive treatment. She agreed to begin meeting twice weekly. One reason she needed so much treatment was that she had no support network.
>
> Adele failed to follow through with our plan to meet more often. On the first week of the new plan, she called after the first session to cancel her second session of the week. When I called to urge her to reschedule, she agreed it was a good idea but said she felt so overwhelmed by her problems that she was having trouble scheduling the appointment. However, she agreed to try to sort out a time she could come and said she would call to let me know if she could meet. She did not.
>
> I felt frustrated and let down. As I thought about the situation, I realized that Adele's behavior with me fit a pattern that occurred outside the therapy as well. Because she had grown up in an abusive environment, Adele had learned to say whatever was needed to placate powerful others on whom she depended when they wanted her to do things she didn't want to do or feel able to do. She had learned to give these people enough of what she wanted (I'll try to work it out) to placate them while simultaneously getting what she wanted. She had learned not to ask directly for what she wanted because when she did she was often attacked or abandoned or both. Thus, her behavior with me had been reinforced in the abusive environment in which she grew up. However, in her current environment, her behavior was maladaptive. In fact, it caused what she feared. That is, her behavior was alienating me even though I was one of the few supportive people in her life. In learning theory terms, Adele's behavior was extinguishing my efforts to help her.
>
> Although my interaction with Adele was frustrating (the bad news), the good news is that it helped me flesh out my conceptualization of her case. In particular, it helped me understand why Adele had not support network! Also, conceptualizing her behavior as a consequence of her learning history and an example of her problems more generally, not just with me, reduced my frustration with it.
>
> (p. 173)

Here we have seen how Persons has conceptualized her patient, Adele, around transference, although Persons uses learning terminology rather than the term, transference. Persons also tells the reader how she uses the transference (or the patient's enactment of her learning history in the treatment itself) to guide her interventions with Adele:

> The conceptualization gave me some information about the ideas (distinction between abusive people and others) and skills (assertiveness and reinforcing those who offered help) I needed to teach Adele to help her to build a support network. In addition to using those technical interventions, I could also use my interactions with her to intervene. One way of doing this is to verbalize the consequences of her behavior in the moment it

occurs. I might say to her, "When you do this it really gives me a good feeling and I want to help you more" or "When you do that it demoralizes me and gives me less energy to help you."

(p. 173)

Observation of the current scene in CBT, as well as the past, suggests that too many CBT therapists pay no attention to transference, even when it endangers the treatment. The strand of thinking in CBT beginning with Goldfried and Davison (1976) and continuing in the current scene needs to become a basic part of CBT training if this approach is to actualize its potential. Schaeffer (2007) tells us that there is no question that nonanalytic therapies such as CBT must identify transference as early as possible if they are to prevent treatment failures and maximize their potential. I cannot argue with Schaeffer's viewpoint, regardless of the terminology used to depict transference.

Finally, Goldfried himself recently exemplified how transference may be used in CBT. He provided this brief case example:

> The case that can illustrate transference was a 35-year-old female accountant, who continually apologized for things during the initial assessment sessions with the therapist. Her presenting problem was excessive stress and anxiety, typically precipitated on an ongoing basis by a critical supervisor at work, as well as her long-term interaction with her critical, guilt-instilling mother. Once the therapist felt he had established a sufficiently strong therapeutic bond with the client, he was able to point out to her the frequency of her apologies in the therapy sessions, inquiring whether or not this was the kind of thing that was related to her problems in the rest of her life. This occurred during an actual apology to the therapist, which allowed for an in-session (in-vivo?) exploration and re-evaluation of the client's interpersonal concerns that were driving her apologies (e.g., wanting to please others, excessive concern about their view of her, etc.). Not only did the therapy involve pointing out how she was more concerned about pleasing others rather than honestly and non-defensively expressing what she thought, felt and wanted, but also how this behavioral pattern did not get her what she wanted to begin with. Nor did it facilitate her feeling good about herself. Thus the therapy involved not only a focus on what was going on in the relationship with the therapist, but also illustrated how this was a sample of what was going on in her life. Thus the therapy interaction functioned as information that she was able to use in her life at work and in personal relationships to help her become her own person.
>
> (Marvin Goldfried, Personal communication, April 30, 2017)

The Humanistic Way

The humanistic/experiential psychotherapies are split in their views of the importance of transference. For those therapists who identify with the

Rogerian person-centered tradition and the emotion-focused therapy approach, two highly prominent forms of humanistic therapy, transference is rarely addressed or considered to be a significant phenomenon. This view began with Rogers himself (Rogers, 1951, 1957), who acknowledged the existence of transference attitudes in the client, but did not believe they needed to be dealt with directly. If the therapist simply conducted effective person-centered therapy that entailed being empathic, unconditionally accepting the client, and being genuine, transference attitudes would essentially dissipate. Nothing needed to be done directly to the transference or because of the transference attitudes.

More recently, Bohart (2005) has clarified the modern person-centered position. He notes that the key in determining if a phenomenon is transference is "whether or not we attend to the *discrepancies* between what is new and different in the present from our past experience and use that to learn and to adjust our perceptions" (p. 130). Bohart goes on to say that clients often persist in their "misreading" of the therapist, not because they are enacting transference but because they mistrust themselves and their own inner voice. Thus, their ability to listen to corrective information from others and from their own inner experiencing has been compromised. This sounds very compatible with the conception of transference delineated earlier in this chapter. However, the solution is not to point out the client's misperceptions. Instead, as clients come to listen to their own feelings and to trust these feelings as well as the therapist, they are able to correct the misreadings. What allows this is the person-centered process of therapist empathy, unconditional positive regard or acceptance, and genuineness. This position is essentially a slight elaboration of Rogers' views.

Emotion-focused therapists have been silent on the topic of transference, and have largely shared the person-centered position I have just described. However, one of the leading EFT theoreticians, Rhonda Goldman, has further clarified the EFT position as follows:

> The therapist is seen as having an active presence with respect to the client.
>
> In short, the client may have a variety of experiences, feelings, fantasies, attitudes, protective impulses throughout the sessions that the therapist attempts to help the client explore, emotionally deepen, and perhaps transform. These are not, however, interpreted as products of early childhood experiences with significant others or necessarily repetitions of responses originating in earlier childhood that do not appropriately fit present circumstances. Perhaps important here is that the therapist is not guided by attempts to understand motives behind behavior or discern relational patterns, but rather acts primarily in a more understanding, exploratory mode. The therapist does not view relationships as indiscriminate, non-selective repetitions of the past. EFT therapists do assume that how you act with me may be as much a function of your responding

to me, as it is a response to past relational experience. In other words, the therapist's role is strongly considered. I know that I do not respond the same with each person and that the therapist assumes that s/he may engender different responses in different people.

(Rhonda Goldman, personal communication, July 21, 2017)

A problem for person-centered and EFT therapists may occur when the patient's transference is negative to the point of damaging the treatment if it is not dealt with more directly, as transference. This most commonly occurs with patients suffering from borderline personality disorders and other severe disorders. Here it is important to help the patient see rather quickly that s/he may be coming from another time and place when experiencing highly negative expectations of and feelings toward the therapist. If such transferences are not understood as such early on, the patient is likely to break off treatment. To simply explore emotions or reflect feelings is likely not enough (see Levy & Scala's, 2012, review of research on this topic).

For gestalt therapists, transference is seen much differently, and it is viewed as an important, even crucial, part of treatment (see Joyce & Sills, 2014; Yontef, 1991). Like Goldman, and the relational-intersubjective psychoanalysts discussed earlier in the chapter, the gestalt therapist views transference as a co-construction, contributed to by both therapist and patient. Thus, the gestaltist considers his or her own role in whatever transference occurs, and how his/her contributions meld with the patient's transference template to create the specific transference that is happening. The transference is then explored in the immediate present, in the here-and-now, through facilitating the patient's expression of his/her feelings, using imagination to help the patient realize who is being projected into the therapist, and perhaps through inviting the patient to be that projection in the moment. For example, if the patient feels the therapist is being ungiving, the gestalt therapist helps the patient explore this feeling, imagine who the therapist is reminding the patient of (e.g., mother when the patient was seven years old), talks to that person as a seven-year-old, perhaps using what is referred to as the empty-chair technique. For the gestaltist, all therapeutic action occurs in the here-and-now, so the transference is brought into the present. This approach is similar to psychodynamic therapy, but in gestalt therapy there is a greater tendency to clarify and modify the transferences quickly. One can hear echoes of Fritz Perls telling his patient, "I am not your father. Stop treating me as your father. Put your father in that chair and talk to him now."

Although this is changing, especially in the earlier days of gestalt therapy, e.g., the 1960s and 1970s, there appeared to be a naïve belief that transferences could be corrected quickly through therapist directives, reflecting a lack of appreciation of the tenacity of the transference template. It is important that the gestalt therapist appreciate that transferences are motivated and require time and therapist patience in order to be worked through.

Things to Keep in Mind About Transference

However transference is dealt with in the different theoretical approaches to therapy, there are some key points to be mindful of about transference.

The Present is the Thing – Even When it is the Past

We see time and time again in psychotherapy that all of the therapeutic action – all that is mutative – occurs in the here-and-now, in the immediate present. Here the humanistic concept of experiencing merges with the psychodynamic concept of integrative insight (when intellectual understanding and emotional awareness come together). Change happens when the patient experiences a new and felt awareness in the moment. This is so even when the patient is exploring the near or distant past. That is, if the patient merely talks about the past without experiencing that past that is being talked about, rarely if ever does change happen. However, when the past is felt in the here-and-now, what may be referred to as the present past, change can happen.

The here-and-now may be about the therapeutic relationship, perhaps the real relationship or working alliance, but to the point of this chapter it may be about transference. When the patient is exploring his or her feelings about and experiences with parent figures in childhood as these may be connected to the therapeutic relationship, it is important that this be done in a way that is immediate – such that the feelings in the past are to an extent re-lived in the moment of the therapeutic relationship.

For example, when the patient talks about his relationship with his father in childhood in a way that shows that the patient understands cognitively how that relationship caused him to doubt himself in virtually all significant aspects of his life, this does not make him doubt himself less. And it does not resolve transference feelings. However, when this patient re-lives in the moment hurtful experiences with this father, re-lives the pain, and feels how that made him then and now doubt himself, this tends to produce change. And part of what is changed is the patient's transference template that he uses in intimate relationships, including psychotherapy. Thus, the therapist is more likely seen for whom he is rather than as the critical doubting father. I should add that the change during any single session or segment ordinarily is not great, as I have seen few profound feeling-changing moments in psychotherapy; but experiencing in the moment, including when the experiencing is of long-ago events and feelings, helps the patient take a step toward the deeper transformation that s/he and her/his therapist seek, including a transformation or resolution of the transference template.

Intellectual Exploration is Sterile – Usually

If exploration in the present is to be mutative, generally it has to be feelingful exploration. That is, the patient cannot simply talk about what is happening in the moment. Fritz Perls derisively referred to this feelingless "talking about" as mind-fucking and underscored how it does not help. In order for change to happen, the patient must experience or feel what is being talked about.

Does intellectual exploration and understanding ever help, or is it completely sterile? Here is where I believe gestalt therapy, starting with its founder, Fritz Perls, went wrong. Sometimes and in certain ways, intellectual insight does help in psychotherapy. Regarding transference, the patient can intellectually grasp that her experience and perceptions of her therapist are not quite correct, and she can intellectually understand that the past is being carried into the present. And this intellectual understanding can serve as a roadmap to further exploration and eventual integrative understanding – affective awareness coupled with intellectual insight. More generally, intellectual insight can help the patient feel less crazy – can allow him or her to see, if only intellectually, that what is going on with him or her, including in the therapeutic relationship, makes some sense, given his or her past.

Transference is Most Important to Explore When it is Negative

Research has taught us that therapies that do not focus on transference tend to be successful, just as do therapies that place a premium on understanding and interpreting transference to patients. The findings have accumulated over the decades to the point that they are essentially inarguable. However, regardless of one's theoretical orientation, it seems equally inarguable that the therapist needs to learn about and be able to identify transference when it is happening, and, as well, learn ways of working with it, especially when it is negative. Thus, when the patient initially or subsequently sees his or her therapist through a negative transference template, ignoring that will likely often lead to the patient breaking off treatment and/or having an unsatisfactory therapeutic experience.

Just how the therapist specifically conceptualizes transference (there are many ways of doing so), and just what approaches the therapist uses to treat transference may not especially matter. What is important is that the therapist help his or her patient come to understand that, at least to a significant extent, the patient's perceptions of the therapist and what the therapist feels are not accurate, and likely come from different times, places, and relationships. Certainly, there is co-construction, and it is important that the therapist know and share this; but there is also the patient's contribution, one that the patient carries with him or her into other significant relationships. If the patient does not see this (and, of course, if the therapist does not see it), but instead continues to experience the transference template, it is hard to see how therapy can be successful. Again, this is especially so when the transference is negative – when the patient projects negative feelings onto the therapist and him/herself carries negative feelings from early relationships into the therapy relationship.

I have noted repeatedly that the transference perception is not earned by the therapist, but instead is a carryover from the past to the present. There are exceptions to this assertion. At times, and with particular patients, the therapist does indeed have feelings created in him or her by the patient. Thus, for example, the patient may create anger, even rage, in the therapist through subtle or more blatant behaviors such as contempt, dismissiveness, arrogance, etc. These feelings that are created may be very similar to, or even duplicate, what the patient felt with his or her caretakers. Here it is important that the therapist be able to observe and admit his or her own feelings, but also understand how they were created by the patient. Of course, the therapist must also understand his or her own issues and vulnerabilities that make him or her susceptible to these feelings. Often referred to as projective identification on the patient's part, this process can destroy the therapy if the therapist is unaware of the dynamic involved and/or if s/he acts out his anger, rage, etc. in the treatment, against the patient, or if the therapist denies to him/herself these feelings (which will likely assure that they are acted out!).

There is a question about whether positive transferences should be addressed in treatment. Many psychoanalysts believe that such transferences cover more negative transferences, which must be unearthed. Although positive transferences may at times serve to hide negative transferences, experience suggests that most often these positive transferences tend to meld with the realistically positive reactions to the therapist, and these reactions (both transference and realistic ones) can help fortify the working alliance. It is certainly appropriate for the therapist to ask the patient about what s/he is feeling toward the therapist when the transference seems positive, but in my view, it does not especially help to explore how these positive reactions are rooted in past conflict and pain. Instead, it is best to simply accept the positive transference and let it work for the therapy, that is, unless the therapist suspects that the patient's positive reactions are hiding important negative reactions.

In discussing positive transference, it is important to differentiate it from what may be termed idealizing transferences. In the latter, the therapist is not just experienced in a positive way that goes beyond the therapist's realistically positive behavior, the therapist is experienced as if s/he were omnipotent and omniscient. The patient experiences the therapist as extraordinary, brilliant, giving just the right amount, always on the money in his/her comments and interpretations, etc. As the founder of psychoanalytic self psychology, Heinz Kohut (1971, 1977), so brilliantly articulated, such idealizing transferences are common among patients with certain kinds of narcissistic personality disorders. These patients have an incomplete self, poor self-esteem, a sense of depletion, and the lack of parental figures who were sufficiently strong during early childhood, when the patients needed this strength in their parents. These patients unconsciously look for figures in their lives to idealize, and through identifying with such figures, they gain the strength they lack. They need their idealizations. In therapy, it is important to allow these idealizations, which can be very uncomfortable for the therapist. It does no good to try to dissuade the idealizations, as the patient who idealizes will be found to cling to them. When the therapist, in effect, says "stop idealizing me, I am just an ordinary human being with many flaws," the patient's reply, again in effect, is, "Oh, you are so wonderfully modest." Gradually, though, over months or years, the idealization will dissipate, and the patient gains his/her own strength and simultaneously sees that the therapist is not perfect. Trying to explore these idealizing transferences before the patient is strong enough to give them up is usually a futile effort. They need to be accepted as the therapist explores the patient's dynamics, provides empathy, acceptance, and genuineness, or modifies behavior through cognitive-behavioral suggestions, depending on his or her theoretical inclinations.

How Transference Affects the Patient's Life should be Kept at Center Stage

Although it may be hard to accept, it is wise to keep in mind that our relationship with our patients is not what ultimately matters most in psychotherapy. It is the patient's life outside of therapy that is the bottom line, and any good therapy must ultimately pay most attention to that extra-therapy behavior. It follows that the key to whether any phenomenon should be addressed by the psychotherapist is whether, and the extent to which, that phenomenon is affecting the patient's life outside of therapy. So, if the patient's transference does not seem relevant to life outside of therapy, and is not hindering the patient in the quest for meaning and satisfaction, it should not be of concern to the therapist. The one glaring exception to this assertion is if and when the transference is hindering treatment, as discussed above.

In contrast to what was discussed in the last section, if a positive transference is indeed hindering the patient's life outside of treatment, it needs to be explored. For example, if this positive transference allows the patient to avoid understanding and needed change outside of treatment because the patient is getting everything s/he wants and needs in the treatment itself, this transference needs to be explored.

I am reminded of a workshop on masochism that was offered by the great psychoanalytic psychotherapist, Esther Menaker. To the psychoanalytic audience's great surprise, Esther claimed that she rarely focused much on transference! She developed a positive relationship with most of the patients with whom she worked, and this positive relationship, presumably a combination of positive transference and the real relationship, allowed her to work effectively with these patients who suffered from masochistic pathologies. In these particular cases, the transference did not hinder the therapy and it did not affect life outside of treatment. However, if the transference did have these effects, there was no doubt that Menaker would have it in her sights.

References

Andersen, S. M., & Przybylinski, E. (2012). Experiments on transference in interpersonal relations: Implications for treatment. *Psychotherapy*, 49(3), 370.

Bohart, A. C. (2005). Evidence-based psychotherapy means evidence-informed, not evidence driven. *Journal of Contemporary Psychotherapy*, 35(1), 39–53.

Bowlby, J. (1988). *A secure base: Clinical applications of attachment theory*. London, England: Routledge.
Freud, S. (1959) Recollection, repetition and working-through. In E. Jones (Ed.), & J. Riviere (Trans.), *Sigmund Freud: Collected papers* (Vol. 2, pp. 366–376). New York, NY: Basic Books. (Original work published in 1914.)
Freud, S. (1958). The dynamics of transference. In J. Strachey (Ed.), *The standard edition of the complete works of Sigmund Freud* (Vol. 12, pp. 97–108). London, England: Hogarth. (Original work published in 1912.)
Freud, S. (1959). Fragment of an analysis of a case of hysteria. In E. Jones (Ed.), & J. Riviere (Trans.), *Sigmund Freud: Collected papers* (Vol. 3, pp. 13–146) New York, NY: Basic Books. (Original work published in 1905.)
Fromm-Reichmann, F. (1950). *Principles of intensive psychotherapy*. Chicago, IL: University of Chicago Press.
Gelso, C. J., & Bhatia, A. (2012). Crossing theoretical lines: The role and effect of transference in nonanalytic psychotherapies. *Psychotherapy*, 49(3), 384.
Gelso, C. J., & Hayes, J. A. (1998). *The psychotherapy relationship: Theory, research, and practice*. New York, NY: Wiley.
Glover, E. (1955). Psycho-analysis. *British Medical Journal*, 1(4926), 1392.
Goldfried, M. R., & Davila, J. (2005). The role of relationship and technique in therapeutic change. *Psychotherapy: Theory, Research, Practice, Training*, 42(4), 421.
Goldfried, M. R., & Davison, G. C. (1976). *Clinical behavior therapy*. New York, NY: Holt, Rinehart, & Winston.
Greenson, R. R. (1967). *The technique and practice of psychoanalysis*. (Vol. 1). New York, NY: International Universities Press.
Joyce, P., & Sills, C. (2014). *Skills in Gestalt counselling & psychotherapy*. Sage.
Kohut, H. (1971). *The analysis of the self*. NY: International Universities Press.
Kohut, H. (1977). *The restoration of the self*. NY: International Universities Press.
Kohut, H. (1984). *How does analysis cure?*NY: International Universities Press.
Lejuez, C. W., Hopko, D. R., Levine, S., Gholkar, R., & Collins, L. M. (2005). The therapeutic alliance in behavior therapy. *Psychotherapy: Theory, Research, Practice, Training*, 42(4), 456.
Levy, K. N., & Scala, J. (2012). Transference, transference interpretations, and transference focused psychotherapies. *Psychotherapy*, 49(3), 391.
Linehan, M. L. (1993). *Cognitive-behavioral treatment of borderline personality disorder*. New York, NY: Guilford.
Luborsky, L., & Crits-Christoph, P. (1990). *Understanding transference*. New York, NY: Basic Books.
Luborsky, L., & Crits-Christoph, P. (1998). *Understanding transference: The core conflictual relationship theme method*. Washington, DC: American Psychological Association. http://dx.doi.org/10.1037/10250-000
Mitchell, S. (1988). *Relational concepts in psychoanalysis*. Cambridge, MA: Harvard University Press.
Mitchell, S. (1995). *Hope and dread in psychoanalysis*. NY: Basic Books.
Persons, J. (2008). *The case formulation approach to cognitive-behavior therapy*. NY: Gulford.
Rogers, C. R. (1951). *Client-centered therapy*. Boston, MA: Houghton- Mifflin.
Schaeffer, J. A. (2007). *Transference and countertransference in non-analytic therapy: Double edged swords*. New York, NY: University Press of America.
Schafer, R. (1983). *The analytic attitude*. NY: Basic Books.
Sullivan, H. S. (1954). *The psychiatric interview*. New York, NY: Norton.

Summers, R., & Barber, J. (2010). *Psychodynamic therapy: A guide to evidence-based practice.* NY: Gulford.
Tsai, M., Kohlenberg, R. J., Kanter, J. W., Kohlenberg, B. S., Follette, W. C., & Callaghan, G. M. (2008). *A guide to functional analytic psychotherapy: Awareness, courage, love and behaviorism.* New York: Springer.
Weiss, J., Sampson, H., & Mount Zion Psychotherapy Research Group. (1986). *The psychoanalytic process.* NY: Gulford.
Wolfe, B. E. (2005). *Understanding and treating anxiety disorders.* Washington, DC: American Psychological Association. doi:10.1037/11198-000
Yontef, G. M. (1991). Recent trends in Gestalt therapy in the United States and what we need to learn from them. *British Gestalt Journal*, 1(1), 5–20.

5 Know Thyself, Manage Thyself

In the present chapter, I address the topic of the psychotherapist's inner experience during the treatment hour and how that inner experience is and should be understood and expressed. An important part of the therapist's experience may be captured by the term countertransference, which is explored in depth in the chapter. However, not all of the therapist's inner experience and reactions tied to that experience ought to be placed under the umbrella of countertransference. Such non-countertransference experience is also extremely important to the therapeutic endeavor, and I delve into that, as well.

No one theoretical orientation owns the exclusive rights to countertransference! Therapists of all theoretical orientations experience countertransference, and inner experiences that are not countertransferential, as well. And it is about equally important that therapists of all orientations pay attention to countertransference and other inner experiences, and seek to use them in the service of the work. A key part of this chapter is the exploration of what the therapist is to do about his or her inner experience. I examine how therapists can work with and manage their countertransferential and non-countertransferential experience so that it benefits rather than hinders the therapeutic encounter.

History and Definitions

The concept of countertransference has a long and complicated history in psychoanalysis and psychotherapy. Like so many of our basic concepts, this one was first addressed by Freud. He claimed unequivocally that therapists need to examine and understand themselves deeply, and use this understanding the help their patients (Freud, 1959/1912). At the same time, Freud promoted the view that countertransference was a negative and needed to be done away with. For example, he suggested that:

> We have begun to consider the "counter-transference," which arises in the physician as a result of the patient's influence on his [the physician's] unconscious feelings, and have nearly come to the point of requiring the physician

to recognize and overcome this counter-transference in himself. Now that a larger number of people have come to practice psycho-analysis and mutually exchange their experiences, we have noticed that every analyst's achievement is limited by what his own complexes and resistances permit, and consequently we require that he should begin his practice with a self-analysis and should extend and deepen this constantly while making his observations of his patients. Anyone who cannot succeed in this self-analysis may without more ado, regard himself as unable to treat neurotics by analysis.

(Freud, 1959/1910, p. 289)

So Freud is telling us that if we cannot succeed in self-analysis to the point of working through our issues, we should not be doing psychoanalysis (or, by extension, psychotherapy). Nothing of value can come from the therapist's unresolved conflicts. Then Freud further states that, "I cannot recommend my colleagues emphatically enough to take as a model of psycho-analytic treatment the surgeon who puts aside all his feelings, including that of human sympathy, and concentrates his mind on one single purpose, that of performing the operation as skillfully as possible" (p. 327).

In these two quotes, we see that the therapist should not experience countertransference-based feelings, but instead be healthy enough not to have them. In fact, the good analytic therapist should not be feeling much at all, but just understand the patient and his/her unconscious in order to provide insight. These views had the effect of chasing the concept of countertransference into the psychotherapeutic and scientific underground. Because "having countertransference" was harmful, it had to be avoided. For several decades, the concept was not studied empirically and received only minimal attention theoretically.

This pejorative conception of countertransference began to shift, especially beginning in the 1950s, with the work of analysts who broadened the conception of countertransference as pertaining not only to the therapist's unresolved neurotic conflicts (see history by Stefana, 2017), but to feelings that were expectable, non-neurotic reactions to patients' behavior. This broadened conception emerged importantly as therapists worked more with patients suffering from borderline personality disorders and other severe disturbances. Such patients seemed regularly to stir intense emotional reactions in their therapists that were not simply a result of therapists' unresolved conflicts. As a broader conception of countertransference became theoretically popular, so did the view that countertransference could be an aid, as well as a hindrance, to psychotherapeutic work. In recent decades, countertransference has come out of hiding. It has been given much more attention theoretically, and has been vigorously studied (see review by Hayes, Gelso, Kivlighan, & Goldberg, in press).

Differing Conceptualizations

Over the years, there have been four main conceptions of countertransference (Gelso & Hayes, 2007; Epstein & Feiner, 1988). The earliest and still influential conception has been referred to as *the classical definition*. Countertransference is seen as, essentially, the therapist's transference to the patient' transference. That is, it is the therapist's reactions to the patient's material that is based on the therapist's own unresolved conflicts, originating in early life. An example of this is the therapist who responds to the patient's maternal transference pull (to be taken care of by the good mother) by being excessively supportive tied to his or her experience of not having been nurtured by his/her own mother and a resultant fear of not being nurturing enough as a human being and as a parent. Here, the therapist's unresolved conflict around not having been mothered and being nurturing enough him/herself is activated by the patient's projection into him or her of the needed nurturing parent. The result is the therapist taking care of the patient too much, to the detriment of the patient's growth. It should be noted that the result can be the opposite, i.e., the therapist being rejecting of the patient in response to the transference pull. Both being too nurturant and being too cool and distant may stem from the same unresolved conflict in the therapist.

A second conception of countertransference gained ascendancy around the middle of the 20th century, partly as a reaction to the perceived narrowness of the classical position and partly as a response to the differing kinds of psychopathologies being treated by psychoanalysts as discussed above. This second conception may be referred to as *the totalist view*. In this conception, countertransference is seen as essentially all of the therapist's emotional reactions, attitudes and feelings toward the patient. All such reactions are worth studying, and all could benefit the work of therapy if the therapist succeeded in understanding his or her reactions to the patient. Such reactions were often stimulated by the patient and were an inevitable reaction to what the patient was pulling for. If the therapist could grasp his or her reactions, s/he could get a glimpse of not only how the patient affected others in his or her life outside of therapy, but also of how the patient was treated as a child.

This totalist view allowed the field to embrace countertransference as not only a danger to treatment, but as a potential ally. Whereas it managed to transcend the narrowness of the classical conception, the totalist position introduces another set of problems. First and foremost, if all reactions represent countertransference, the construct has no boundaries, and it is meaningless scientifically, and clinically as well. We could simply use the term "therapist reactions," as the term countertransference adds nothing different or new to that. For a definition to be meaningful clinically and theoretically, it must have boundaries, that is, we must know what the thing is not, as well as what it is. A second problem with the totalist position is that in so often seeing the patient as the cause, it tends to look away from the therapist's contribution. It tends to lead the therapist to look to the patient's dynamics as the culprit or the cause of the therapist's reactions, and to not look into the therapist's own unresolved issues as being fundamentally important. In fact, as I shall discuss shortly, countertransference reactions are best viewed as therapist reactions based on their own issues but precipitated by the patient's behavior.

A third conception of countertransference may be termed *the complementary view*. Here countertransference is seen as a complement or counterpart to the patient's style of relating or transference. Like the totalistic view, the complementary conception sees the therapist's internal countertransference reactions as inevitable responses to the patient's behavior. In fact, the essence of the complementary view is the belief that patient and therapist do an inevitable dance, with each exerting a pull or influence on the other. This dance is best captured by Heinrich Racker's (1957, 1968) "law of tallion" which states that every positive transference is met with a positive countertransference and every negative transference is met with a negative countertransference. These complementary reactions are internal, and do not need to be acted on or out by the therapist. Indeed, the therapist's job is to understand his or her internal countertransference reactions and where they are coming from in order to not act them out, but instead to better understand the patient's inner world.

The complementary conception excels in demonstrating the deeply interpersonal nature of countertransference and the dance in which therapists and patients engage. Although originating within psychoanalysis, this view has been naturally agreeable to interpersonalists who are not particularly psychoanalytic in their orientation, and the complementary position can be readily understood in non-analytic terms. A shortcoming is that, like the totalist position, it tends to situate the countertransference problem in the patient. After all, it is the patient's pull to which the therapist responds in kind.

The fourth major conception of countertransference is *the intersubjective-relational view*. Just as was described in Chapter 4 on transference, this perspective emerged from a combination of post-modern philosophy, psychoanalytic self psychology (e.g., Kohut, 1984), the interpersonal perspective, and relational psychoanalysis (e.g., Mitchell, 1988, 1997). Like the complementary view, the relational perspective focuses on the two-person nature of countertransference. Indeed, for the relational therapist, all conceptualizations must be of a two-person nature. Patient and therapist together co-construct countertransference and it is this co-construction that must be grasped. A key limitation of this perspective is that it often seems forgotten that both therapist and patient have a mind-body-self that precedes therapy and would have core elements that are the same across different relationships. In the resoluteness of its two-person position, the intersubjective-relational approach may tend to overlook the therapist's unresolved issues as fundamentally driving countertransference reactions.

An Integrative Perspective on Countertransference

In seeking to provide a conception of countertransference that transcends the difficulties with each of the four positions described above, Jeff Hayes and I (Gelso & Hayes, 2007) viewed countertransference as situated within the therapist, but also often precipitated by the patient's behavior. Thus, although countertransference belongs to the therapist fundamentally, understanding it requires us to think in terms of both therapist and patient, and is thus rooted in a two-person psychology. It also worth repeating that because countertransference is relevant to all approaches to psychotherapy, the most useful conceptions of it are applicable to all approaches.

A definition that seeks to be applicable to all approaches is *the therapist's internal and/or external reactions to the patient shaped by the therapist's past and present unresolved conflicts and vulnerabilities*. This definition transcends the narrowness of the classical position in that countertransference is seen as a response to more than the patient's transference. It can be a response to nontransference material, as well. Also, the definition places boundaries around the concept of countertransference, unlike the totalist position, which views countertransference as consisting of all of the therapist's emotional responses to the patient. Finally, the locus of responsibility for countertransference is seen as residing in the therapist, even though the patient's behavior may serve as the precipitant. Our conception thus views countertransference reactions as not simply inevitable responses to the patient's behavior (complementary conception) or as only a two-person dance in which countertransference is purely a result of co-construction (the relational perspective).

The Countertransference Interaction Hypothesis

Although I have emphasized that the therapist's countertransference is rooted in his or her unresolved conflicts and vulnerabilities, it is also true that there is usually a patient trigger for countertransference reactions. Over the years, researchers have generally been unsuccessful in finding therapist qualities or patient behaviors that created countertransference reactions. However, we have seen that countertransference is more likely a function of the patient's behavior interacting with qualities of the therapist. For example, in one study drawing upon John Bowlby's theory of infant and adult attachment (Mohr, Gelso, & Hill, 2005), it was found that client's attachment patterns were not, in themselves, related to counselors' countertransference reactions. However, when clients' and counselors' attachment patterns were both examined, interesting findings emerged. Dismissing counselors (in terms of attachment styles) tended to enact hostile, critical, and rejecting countertransference reactions with clients who had preoccupied attachment styles. On the other hand, counselors with a preoccupied style of attachment more often were hostile, critical and rejecting with clients who had dismissing attachment styles. And when the therapist had an avoidant attachment style and the client had a preoccupied style, the therapist more likely exhibited distancing countertransference behavior.

This study points to the importance of therapists paying close attention to how their own qualities mesh with or rub against particular patient qualities. This interaction is what often matters most. There are certainly exceptions to this that have to do with what the therapist carries with him or her into sessions with all clients, and we shall discuss this shortly.

Countertransference versus Non-countertransference Reactions

As I have said at the beginning of this chapter, not all therapist reactions ought to be viewed at countertransference ones. If countertransference cannot be differentiated from other reactions, then the concept itself is scientifically and clinically meaningless. A reasonable way of differentiating the concept is to view those reactions that stem from the therapist's unresolved conflicts as representing countertransference, and those that are non-conflict based as something other than countertransference. These can best be viewed simply as the therapist's emotional, cognitive, or behavioral reactions. They are tremendously important to the therapeutic relationship, just as important as countertransference; but they do not stem from the therapist's problems. Still, these non-countertransference reactions may or may not be shared with the patient. Whether or not the therapist should express his or her feelings to the patient directly depends on many factors, and naturally must be driven by the extent to which such sharing would be helpful to the work, rather than relieving or otherwise gratifying to the therapist.

Non-countertransference reactions have often been viewed as typical and expectable reactions of the therapist to what the patient is expressing verbally and non-verbally. For example, if the therapist experiences anger toward the patient in response to meanness on the patient's part toward the therapist, this seems like a normal, expectable reaction. Some theoreticians prefer to view such reactions as a sub-category of countertransference, a sort of Type B countertransference, whereas what I have been describing as countertransference is seen as Type A countertransference. The famous psychoanalyst, Donald Winnicott (1949), for example, posited *objective countertransference* as the therapist's natural, non-conflictual love and hate reactions to the patient's personality and behavior. His conception would fit with what I am calling Type B countertransference. The question that may be posed about this division is why call such average, expectable behavior on the therapist's part countertransference in the first place.

In fact, over nearly five decades of doing psychotherapy and supervising therapist trainees, what I have seen is that therapist emotional reactions to patients most often represent a mixture of conflict-based and non-conflictual feelings. What may seem at first glance like an average, expectable emotional reaction to the patient is only part of the story. Another part of such reactions is indeed based on the therapist's current or past unresolved conflicts and vulnerabilities. An example of this mixture is based on the work of one of my supervisees in our University of Maryland Psychotherapy Clinic and Research Laboratory. The trainee was in the fourth year of her doctoral program in counseling psychology, and the second year of an externship at this psychodynamic clinic. She had the following to say about her reactions to a patient who was very difficult for her.

> The client is a 32-year-old principal of a Catholic school who is working on issues surrounding a need for control, a pervasive and intense critical

voice, and anti-dependence. Her critical voice often comes out in session, and she pulls for feelings of inadequacy in me. She is often implicitly disappointed with me, and I tend to leave session thinking I did a poor job. While I believe she would pull these feelings from most therapists, I'm also aware that I have a particular vulnerability toward her personality. Attending Catholic school from Kindergarten to 6th grade, I was surrounded by female superiors who my client very closely resembles (i.e., very critical and irritable). One night during our work together, I had a dream uniting my client and Catholic school history:

I'm roaming the halls of my old elementary school as an adult, and reminiscing on all of the memories throughout my time there. As I pass the teacher's lounge, my client and I exchange glances. I approach her and we start talking. I'm aware that I'm trying to be pleasant, but she remains irritable. It feels odd that we're having a similar exchange that I've had many times before as a child with my teachers, and I think about how perfectly she fits in here.

After I had this dream, I realized that my client brings out that appeasing child who wanted to impress her teachers. Similarly to her, I find myself seducing her with too many "mmhmm's" and colluding to make things comfortable for the both of us. Thus, my countertransference is both a reaction to my client's testy and disapproving personality, and to my own unresolved issues around mollifying and impressing this type of person.

(Kathryn Kline, personal communication)

Another case example, reported by Hayes et al. (2011), clarifies further how what may appear to be a purely non-countertransference reaction, includes countertransference as I have defined it. The therapist was a trainee in her fourth practicum, and I was her supervisor. By any yardstick, she was an outstanding trainee.

> In the early part of her treatment with a 20-year-old male patient, she experienced continued strong irritation, and she reacted to the patient in a controlled, muted, and metallic manner. For his part, the patient was an angry, obsessional young man suffering from many borderline features. He negated the therapist's attempt to help him understand how his conflicts might be contributing to his ongoing problems with women, and he denied that the treatment could have any impact. Also, he usually negated the therapist's observations about what he might be feeling.
>
> (p. 243)

It seems clear that this therapist's emotional reactions were average, expectable ones toward an angry and deprecating patient. At the same time, a closer look revealed how the therapist's unresolved conflicts played into her reactions.

> [Her] unresolved anxieties about not being good enough, about fearing that she could not take care of others sufficiently, and about some

transference-based fears of her supervisor's evaluation of her were clearly implicated in her irritation and her muted reaction to the patient. As she came to understand these dynamics, her irritation toward the patient lessened, and she empathically grasped the terrifying emotions that were underlying much of his negativity.

(p. 243)

Some Key Considerations

In seeking to understand countertransference and how it may play out in psychotherapy, some additional features and distinctions must be taken into account.

Chronic versus Acute Countertransference

This distinction has been around for a long time. Annie Reich (1951) appears to have been the first therapist to differentiate acute from chronic countertransference, and since she made this distinction, virtually everyone who has written about countertransference in any depth has made it part of their conception. When countertransference is acute, some quality or behavior of a particular patient connects to a soft spot or unresolved conflict in the therapist to bring about a countertransference response. For Reich, this kind of countertransference was seen as representing the therapist's identification with the patient in an effort to get some kind of gratification. For example, the therapist may support or reinforce the patient's dominance in his or her marriage because of the therapist's wish to be more dominant and/or the therapist's dissatisfaction with his or her self-perceived submissiveness. In fact, acute countertransference may be reflected in a wide range of needs: the therapist may have trouble listening to the patient because what the patient is expressing may be touching on a sore spot in the therapist; the therapist may withdraw from the patient who is aggressive because of the therapist's unresolved issues around a hyper-aggressive father; the therapist may become furious with a patient who might typically stir annoyance in most therapists by questioning if the therapy will be helpful because this particular therapist has intense achievement needs and feels doubtful of his or her adequacy; the therapist may reinforce submissiveness out of the therapist's need for dominance, which may be tied to many unresolved childhood issues; the therapist may begin talking too much because something the patient is doing stirs anxiety over the therapist's competence. These are only a few of the numerous possible examples of acute countertransference reactions.

Whereas acute countertransference is represented by the patient's behavior touching on a sore spot in the therapist, who then reacts in some way aimed at defending this vulnerability, the second kind of countertransference is not so particular. *Chronic countertransference* is a part of the therapist's personality, and represents a long-standing way of reacting in interpersonal situations. It represents unresolved conflicts and vulnerabilities that are part of the therapist and are enacted in all therapeutic situations. That is, chronic countertransference is a reaction to the frame of therapy, to the act of doing therapy, rather than to anything in particular that the patient does or is. For example, the therapist may be chronically oversupportive with all of his or her patients, tied to many unresolved conflicts stemming from early in life. Perhaps the therapist did not get enough support throughout childhood, or perhaps the therapist experiences guilt about not caring enough, as his parents did not care. Or the therapist may be highly active and intolerant of his patient's passivity out of fears and intolerance of his own passive side. The therapist may push for emotional expression in all her patients, regardless of whether emotional expression is called for, because of a childhood in which emotional expression was not tolerated. The point is that chronic countertransference represents a habitual way of responding to patients in general that is a reflection of unresolved problems or vulnerabilities in the therapist.

An example of chronic countertransference may be seen in the trainee who grew up in an intensely achievement-oriented family, where she had to get an A in every course, or feel insufficient as a person. She took this mindset into her work as a therapist-trainee, and every session represented an opportunity to fail. Needless to say, she was highly anxious about doing therapy and often miserable at not giving herself an A. She had this to say about her plight:

> Realizing that this anxiety about "getting a B" in doing therapy is what constrains me during sessions was of course the first step for me in overcoming this chronic countertransference problem of mine. However, at first it only served as a means to berate myself more after a session in which I was conscious of it being a problem. In fact, it just left me feeling like I'd had the ground pulled out from underneath me. I had no idea how to conceptualize my sessions without that "must-get-an-A" mindset. I hated that I did this to myself but had no idea what else to do.
> (see Gelso & Hayes, 2007, p. 35)

Both acute and chronic countertransferences need to be attended to. Acute countertransference may often be resolved by the therapist's self-examination, whereas chronic countertransference is more difficult. Because it is so much a part of the therapist, it is often impossible to see. The phrase, "the eye cannot see itself," seems apt here. Such countertransferences can be pernicious and it is important that the therapist, at a minimum, sense that there is something awry in how he or she is feeling and responding to patients. Fortunately, in the case example given above, the trainee clearly came to see the problem. However, she was helpless to resolve it. I believe that the most effective, perhaps the only, way to deal with chronic countertransference, especially when it is severe, is through the therapist's personal therapy. It is also important that psychotherapy supervisors be sensitive to this phenomenon, and help their supervisees see what is happening inside, as well as their enactments. When this happens, most supervisees are quite willing to seek psychotherapy for themselves.

Countertransference as Inner Experience versus Outer Behavior

Countertransference can be manifested at an inner level in terms of the therapist's feelings, thoughts, and sensations. It can also be enacted behaviorally. Regarding internal experience, I have found that therapists too often restrict what they allow themselves to feel about their patients. This is particularly true of therapist-trainees. As a rule, unless encouraged to become aware of whatever it is they feel in a nonjudgmental way, their feelings tend to be pretty bland. They want to be helpful and have always been good at it. They learn early on the importance of empathy, which is too often thought of in training as a kind of sympathetic understanding. Unsettling or unkind feelings or thoughts are quickly pushed to the side. In a word, these therapist-trainees are good Samaritans badly in need of some honest self-reflection. Early in my advanced psychotherapy practicum, I like to have my graduate students read Irvin Yalom's (2009) *The Gift of Therapy* in an effort to help them open up to themselves. One of the priceless quotes from Yalom's book is:

> When teaching students about empathy, Erich Fromm often cited Terence's statement from two thousand years ago – 'I am human and let nothing human be alien to me' – and urged us to be open to that part of ourselves that corresponds to any deed or fantasy offered by patients, no matter how heinous, violent, lustful, masochistic, or sadistic. If we didn't he suggested we investigate why we have chosen to close that part of ourselves.
>
> (p. 21)

Inner experience, whatever it is, and whether countertransference or non-countertransference, can be used as an aid to understanding the patient. It allows the therapist to get a glimpse of how the patient impacts others to whom s/he relates and also may serve as a telescope of what the patient experienced in significant childhood relationships. Regarding countertransference, the hardest part is for the therapist to separate his/her own conflicts from internal reactions that are what the patient is projecting into the therapist or the therapist's expectable reactions to the patient. Doing so requires considerable self-understanding, as well as a willingness to look honestly at one's feelings and experience. We usually only get it partly correct, and probably fail at this more times than any of us cares to admit. Still, with practice and a sense of openness to one's experience, we surely can improve in our detection and understanding of countertransference and other inner experience.

The other side of countertransference is behavioral, or that which is acted out in the hour. This acting out can be obvious or very subtle. The therapist can express any of a wide range of feelings directly or indirectly. Behaviors such as failing to listen to the patient, becoming hyperactive, feeling drowsy, giving advice, refusing to advise, expressing anger or contempt directly or indirectly, being excessively supportive or non-supportive may all be examples of countertransference enactments. The list of possibilities is large, indeed.

Generally, countertransference enactments are not helpful, and may be damaging to the therapeutic relationship, as has been empirically demonstrated (Hayes, Gelso, Kivlighan, & Goldberg, in press). Thus, it is important that the therapist keep a close look at him/herself in terms of such enactments. Still, it is clear that no matter how self-aware the therapist, such enactments do and will happen, and they do so in virtually all therapies, as Hayes and his collaborators found in their qualitative study (Hayes, et al., 1998). At times, such enactments can be helpful to the therapist in that they may be his or her first clue that something is amiss.

For example, I may not be aware of the issues that are being stirred up in me with given patients until I notice myself behaving in ways that are not customary for me. For me personally, talking too much, advising too much, falling silent, and withdrawing are what I often notice when I am in the midst of a countertransference experience that is being enacted. Unfortunately, we are too often unable to recognize countertransference behaviors as enactments, and our therapy will suffer for that. It is probably true that most therapies, imperfect as they are, will be able to tolerate a certain amount of countertransference enactment, depending of course on the specific nature and magnitude of those enactments.

I have noted that a wide range of therapist behaviors can reflect countertransference reactions. Below I list the behaviors included by Friedman and me (Friedman & Gelso, 2000) in our widely used measure of countertransference behavior. This measure was modified by Fuertes, Gelso, Owen, and Cheng (2015) so that potential users can see clarifications of the meaning of each item, as well as examples of in-session behaviors that might reflect that item. I am providing the clarifying statements for each item. Fuertes and his collaborators also provide examples in their article. Note that none of these countertransference behaviors occur to a very high degree in therapy sessions, but when they do occur, they tend to have an important and adverse effect on the treatment.

1. Colluded with the client in the session.

Clarifying Statement: Letting the client engage in unhelpful thoughts or patterns of behaviors without addressing.

2. Rejected the client in the session.

Clarifying Statement: Can be implicit or explicit – not validating the client when he/she should have been validated.

3. Over-supported the client in the session.

Clarifying Statement: Providing support in such a way that blocks the client from working through his problem.

4. Befriended the client in the session.

Clarifying Statement: Broke therapeutic boundaries, to act "friendly."

5. Was apathetic towards the client in the session.

Clarifying Statement: The therapist does not seem to care about the client or the outcome. Shows little investment in the client.

6. Behaved as if she or he were "somewhere else" during the session.

Clarifying Statement: Temporarily "zoned out."

7. Talked too much in the session.

Clarifying Statement: Your estimate is that the therapist spoke more than 50% of the time and it appeared excessive.

8. Frequently changed the topic during the session

Clarifying Statement: Changed topics inappropriately, no therapeutic reason evident.

9. Was critical of the client during the session.

Clarifying Statement: Harsh or hostile interventions, seeming to come from the therapist's own issues or frustration, not therapeutic.

10. Spent time complaining during the session.

Clarifying Statement: Burdening the client with "personal" complaints.

11. Treated the client in a punitive manner in the session.

Clarifying Statement: Punishment for a specific action, a demerit, could be subtle such as delaying the session, possibly belittling or infantilizing.

12. Inappropriately apologized to the client during the session.

Clarifying Statement: Clearly coming from therapist's own needs.

13. Acted in a submissive way with the client during the session.

Clarifying Statement: Relinquishing control and power of the session to the client in a way that seemed inappropriate and/or unprofessional.

14. Acted in a dependent manner during the session.

Clarifying Statement: Acted as though the therapist needed the client's approval.

15. Seemed to agree too often with the client during the session.

Clarifying Statement: Doesn't get the client out of a comfort zone. Therapist appears uncomfortable with confrontation, comes from therapist's own discomfort with tension.

16. Inappropriately took an advising tone with the client during the session.

Clarifying Statement: Too directive in the face of complexity, foreclosure of exploration of problems, appears defensive and not helpful or well timed.

17. Distanced him/herself from the client in the session.

Clarifying Statement: Active defense against the client or subject matter because of intensity, complexity, or an intimacy that was threatening.

18. Engaged in too much self-disclosure during the session.

Clarifying Statement: Therapist talked excessively about him/herself, related client's comments or experiences inappropriately back to him/herself.

19. Behaved as if she or he were absent during the session.

Clarifying Statement: Preoccupied, distracted, overall, was "not there" for the duration of the Session.

20. Inappropriately questioned the client's motives during the session.

Clarifying Statement: Conveys some suspicion or mistrust, suggests therapist can't accept client's views or motives.

21. Provided too much structure in the session.

Clarifying Statement: Imposed an excessive amount of structure on the session, let structure override clinical judgment.

Note that Positive countertransference items are: 1, 3, 4, 7, 8, 12, 13, 14, 15, 18. Negative countertransference items are: 2, 5, 6, 9, 10, 11, 16, 17, 19, 20, 21.

Countertransference as Too Much, Too Little, Too Positive, Too Negative

As implied, some key signs that the therapist is experiencing countertransference feelings and thoughts and/or is behaving countertransferentially is that his or her reactions deviate significantly from his or her personal norm. This, of course, assumes that the therapist's norm does not reflect a chronic countertransference reaction. Deviations from one's norm can be in the direction of too much or too little of some behavior. The therapist can say too much or too little, be emotionally hypervigilant or withdrawn, be too eager or too displeased to see the patient, feel too positively toward the patient or too negatively, enact too much anger or too little anger, be too supportive or too stingy with support. Deviations can also reflect feelings, thoughts, or behaviors that are too positive or too negative. The point is that it is important for the therapist to pay attention to both his or her inner experience and outward behavior and to be on the lookout for these excesses in either direction.

Of the many possible examples of deviations from one's norm representing countertransference, two fundamental dimensions emerge: over and underinvolvement, and positive and negative reactions. The reader is likely to readily see how overinvolvement, underinvolvement, and negative reactions can be countertransferential and injurious to the therapeutic work. However, a few additional words should be said about positive countertransference because it is perhaps the easiest of all to miss by the therapist. After all, positive feelings (apart from sexualized feelings) can only be a good sign and can only aid the therapeutic relationship, right? In fact, this is not so, and there is even some empirical evidence to this effect (e.g., Hayes et al., 1998). A rather obvious example of positivity being rooted in countertransference conflicts in the therapist is the therapist who is excessively warm and kind to his patient because of his (the therapist's) fear of not being sufficiently helpful as a human being and, in fact, of not being caring enough. This therapist, Dr. X, had unresolved issues around not feeling loved enough by his mother, and because of the pain this caused him, Dr. X was fearful of inflicting this on his patients. This dynamic was understood by Dr. X enough that he did not act it out with all of his patients, and thus it could not be considered a chronic countertransference reaction. However, he was vulnerable to patients who themselves did not feel cared for enough and who were good at stimulating guilt in their intimates whom they felt did not care. Dr. X usually had sufficient insight to grasp when this was happening, although it remained a soft spot in his psychotherapeutic work.

Hayes and his collaborators (1998) reported a perhaps more subtle example of the potentially deleterious effects of positive countertransference. In their qualitative study of expert therapists, these researchers noted a therapist who worried excessively about his own children's safety and who deeply empathized with a client when she expressed fears about not being able to protect her children from danger. According to this therapist,

> I understand the fear and worry and how terrible losing a kid would be for me, you know. And I certainly at times in my life have an ongoing fantasy about the atom bomb being dropped and what would I do and what route would I get out of the city, you know ... so I have some, I guess mostly just empathy of that situation.
>
> (p. 475)

Although in this case the therapist's vulnerabilities and perhaps their unconscious antecedents may have deepened empathy, one could readily see how, without the therapist's awareness, he could readily have become anxious and overprotective with particular patients.

Countertransference Management and the Two-Edged Sword

In my book with Jeff Hayes on countertransference and the therapist's inner experience (Gelso & Hayes, 2007), we used the subtitle "perils and possibilities." This was meant to capture the fact that countertransference can be for better or worse, and this two-edged nature of countertransference and other therapist inner experiences has been a theme of this chapter. Thus, left unmanaged, countertransference certainly can and often does damage and even destroy the therapeutic relationship. However, if managed properly, it can greatly benefit the work.

Countertransference "Management"

Why the quotation marks around the word, management? In presenting our work on countertransference management at meetings and workshops, it has become apparent to Hayes and me that the concept of management can easily create misunderstandings. Some therapists think of management as representing control, in which inner experiences are held back from the work, rather than being worked with. This is far from what we have meant by the term. Instead, *countertransference management is best seen as the therapist's effectiveness in attending to, understanding, and working with his or her inner experience.* As such, countertransference management is a key ingredient of effective psychotherapy of all persuasions, and its value in psychotherapy has been demonstrated across many studies (Hayes, et al., 2011; Hayes et al., in press).

The key question for the clinician revolves around just how one can effectively attend to, understand, and work with these reactions and experiences. A number of years ago, Jeffrey Hayes, Steven VanWagoner, who were at the time graduate students in a seminar I taught at the University of Maryland on the therapeutic relationship, worked together with me to develop the concept of countertransference management. We wanted to address this question of how the therapist can best attend to, understand, and work with countertransference, and we framed a theory of the therapist factors related to effective management of countertransference. Five such factors were postulated as importantly related to effective management. This theory was then put to the empirical test. In two studies, we found that the five factors taken together were more characteristic of therapists reputed to be excellent than they were of average therapists. We also found that these five factors were seen by therapists who were judged to be experts on countertransference as highly important for the therapist to possess (VanWagoner, Gelso, Hayes, & Diemer, 1991; Hayes, Gelso, VanWagoner, and Diemer, 1991).

What are the five factors that are related to good countertransference management? They are therapist (a) self-insight, (b) self-integration, (c) anxiety management, (d) empathy, and (e) conceptualizing ability. I shall discuss these factors shortly, but first it should be noted that, whereas the factors were originally theorized to be *related to* countertransference management ability, as our work unfolded, Hayes and I came to see the factors as *constituents of* countertransference management. In other words, these five factors may best be seen as being key parts of what management consists of, rather than merely being qualities that are related to effective management. An additional point about the factors is that they have trait-like qualities. That is, they have the status of skills that cut across any given therapist's work with patients. Naturally, the manifestation of these skills varies somewhat from patient to patient, but generally they represent ongoing qualities within the therapist.

In our most recent research on countertransference, my colleagues and I found that the five constituents of countertransference could be collapsed into two interrelated factors (Pérez-Rojas, Palma, Bhatia, Jackson, Norwood, Hayes, & Gelso, 2017). These may be labeled (1) *understanding self and client* and (2) *self-integration and regulation*. Below I discuss the five factors as embedded within these two overarching factors. (Note that each of the five factors is italicized.)

Understanding Self and Patient: The Bottom Line

The first factor, Understanding Self and Client, consists partly of the *therapist's insight into him/herself during psychotherapy sessions, including thoughts, feelings, and actions*. This insight may be both at a cognitive or intellectual level and a feeling level, which combines intellectual understanding with emotional awareness. It bespeaks an understanding of where the therapist's thoughts, feelings, and behavior come from, e.g., the extent to which they come from the therapist's inner world, the material the patient is sharing, and/or the interplay of the two. Also included within this factor is the *therapist's conceptualizing ability*. That is, the therapist has a conceptual grasp of the patient's dynamics (in whatever theoretical terms are suitable for the therapist and patient), the dynamics of the therapeutic relationship, and how the two go together. As this description implies, managing countertransference is at least partly a function of the therapist's having a theory, and the facility to use this theory to grasp the therapeutic relationship and what is happening in the treatment.

Finally, under the heading of understanding self and patient is the *therapist's empathic ability*. The ability to grasp the patient's world from the inside, which in this conception includes caring about the patient and partially identifying with the patient, is an important part of countertransference management. In other words, to the extent that the therapist is being empathic, s/he is ipso facto managing countertransference. The therapist is seeing the world as the patient sees it, without being clouded by the therapist's unresolved conflicts and vulnerabilities. This empathic ability, like self-insight, operates at both a cognitive and affective level. The therapist grasps the patient's inner world intellectually, and also is able to feel what the patient feels, although not to the extent that the therapist loses him/herself in the patient.

In sum, the three elements of therapist self-insight, conceptualizing ability, and empathy compose the first factor of Understanding Self and Client. The elements of this factor all work interrelatedly and in unison to facilitate the therapist's managing his/her countertransference, and in fostering the therapist's use of countertransference to benefit rather than hinder the work.

Self-Integration and Regulation: The Foundation

Although Understanding Self and Client may be the most important factor in countertransference management, the second factor may be the foundation for such understanding. As indicated, we have labeled this factor Therapist Self-Integration and Regulation. For starters, the therapist has a *high degree of self-integration,* possessing a solid sense of "where s/he stops and the patient starts." That is, the therapist has solid self-boundaries within the relationship, such that the therapist's identity is rarely if ever at risk. S/he carries a solid sense of who s/he is, and is differentiated from his/her patients. These boundaries are solid but permeable. What this means is that although the therapist knows who s/he is as a person, the patient's being and expressions can touch him or her, and this therapist can have strong feelings about the patient and with the patient. As perhaps the basis for these boundaries, the therapist carries with him or her into the relationship a solid sense of self-esteem and confidence.

In addition, the therapist is *effective in the anxiety management.* S/he certainly can experience anxiety in the therapeutic relationship, but the therapist is not overtaken by this anxiety. Thus, the therapist can be touched by the patient, at times feel the patient's anxiety, and feel anxious in response to certain material the patient is sharing. However, the therapist is also able to manage this anxiety, that is, to control and modulate the anxiety such that it does not bleed excessively into the relationship. In other words, the therapist's thoughts about and responses to the patient are not filled with and guided by anxiety. Here, too, the therapist's self-esteem and confidence are part of the work, for these qualities surely facilitate anxiety management. Similarly, the therapist who effectively manages anxiety does not possess high degrees of what has been termed trait anxiety. That is, such anxiety is not a part of his or her personality or being.

The great psychoanalyst, Erich Fromm, once commented that in good therapy, the patient's reactions to the therapist were like the ocean rushing through a sandy beach. The water permeates the sand, but then recedes. Anxiety management, and perhaps countertransference management in general, are like this. The therapist is able to be affected by the patient, to experience feelings that are often uncomfortable, but then allow these feelings to recede and not dominate the work.

Below I list the items from our most recently developed measure of countertransference management (Perez et al., 2017). This should provide for the therapist a clearer, more specific picture of the ingredients of countertransference management as I have discussed it. (Note the copies of the measure are available from Dr. Andres Perez-Rojas at Perez@gmail.com.)

Understanding Self and Client

-Understands the basis of his/her feelings, thoughts, and behaviors in sessions.
-Deeply understands clients from clients' point-of-view.
-Can identify the motives behind his/her behaviors in sessions.
-Uses his/her theoretical understanding of clients to inform the work during the therapeutic hour.
-Understands how his/her emotions, thoughts, and behaviors in sessions are connected.
-Is able to step into the clients' inner world.
-Effectively connects strands of clients' material in developing conceptualizations of clients.
-Effectively sorts out how his/her feelings relate to clients' feelings.
-Is able to conceptualize clients' dynamics clearly.
-Grasps theoretically clients' dynamics in terms of what goes on in the therapeutic relationship.
-Understands the basis for own atypical reactions to clients.
-Uses his/her understanding of the client–therapist relationship to inform the work during the therapeutic hour.

Self-Integration and Regulation

-Maintains a firm sense of who s/he is as a person in the sessions.
-Regulates his/her own nervousness well during sessions.
-Has a well-integrated self during sessions.
-Recognizes boundaries between him/herself and his/her clients during the psychotherapy hour.
-Does not let anxiety overwhelm him/her in the psychotherapy hour.
-Has appropriate confidence as a person during the psychotherapy hour.
-Presents a consistent sense of self in the psychotherapy hour.

–Demonstrates calm in the face of difficult client material.
–Deals effectively with his/her anxiety when working with difficult client problems.
–Allows him/herself to feel a range of affect without getting overly anxious.

Countertransference Management and Theoretical Orientation

As I have said, no theoretical orientation has a market on countertransference, and practitioners of every orientation need to be aware of their countertransference reactions and other inner experience. No one is immune to countertransference, and all therapists need to manage their countertransference reactions. In terms of managing, the general blueprint is essentially the same for all orientations: (1) seek to understand yourself and the patient, and (2) work on your own self-integration and emotional regulation.

Having pointed to the essential equivalence of the different theoretical orientations in terms of experiencing and managing countertransference, I conclude this chapter by discussing what appear to be the vulnerabilities of the three dominant theoretical orientations as regards countertransference management. It seems to me that each of the three orientations has a differing soft spot or key vulnerability around such management.

Psychoanalysis and the Disavowal of Responsibility

The psychodynamic/psychoanalytic orientation is of course where the concept of countertransference originated, and it has been a central construct in that orientation for the last three-quarters of a century. Because of this, it might seem that there is no particular soft spot among psychodynamic/psychoanalytic practitioners as regards countertransference. However, I believe that there is a key vulnerability, and that is the tendency to situate countertransference within the patient and view the therapist's countertransference reactions as an inevitable response to what the patient is projecting. For starters, it is worth repeating that the movement toward embracing the concept of countertransference in psychoanalysis began in the 1950s, and a big part of this embracing had to do with the widening scope of psychoanalysis. More severe disorders were being treated than in the early days of psychoanalysis. In particular, psychodynamic work with patients suffering from borderline personality disorders and other severe disorders became more prominent. Such patients seem to inevitably stir up strong emotional reactions in virtually all therapists. Thus, when working with these patients, intense emotional reactions in the therapist seemed normal and expectable, rather than being driven by the therapist's unresolved conflicts and vulnerabilities. It is a short half-step from here to the totalistic position that normalizes countertransference, and tends to look to the patient as the cause. These views are problematic because they represent a disavowal of the therapist's responsibility for countertransference, which in fact is fundamental, even when working with borderlines. Consider that with such patients, despite what the patient does indeed stir up, therapists vary widely in their reactions – in the intensity, excessiveness, and level of frustration involved in their inner reactions and how these bleed into the work. It is when the patient's behavior, including what is referred to as projective identification, touches the therapist's unresolved conflicts and vulnerabilities that what I refer to as countertransference occurs at an inner level, and must be managed. In most cases, this does happen when working with severely troubled patients because they excel at getting to our soft spots. And the psychodynamic therapist must continually look to his or her own unresolved issues and vulnerabilities when working with such patients, as well as the patient's projective identifications. Earlier I discussed how perhaps most therapist countertransference reactions blend with non-countertransference reactions. The two go together, and it is the psychodynamic therapist's job to grasp his or her own contribution to the problem tied to his/her own unresolved problems. To not do so allows the therapist to look away from his or her issues and reflects a subtle form of patient blaming.

Humanistic/Experiential Therapy and the Denial of the Negative

The humanistic/experiential therapist has a very different sort of vulnerability when it comes to managing countertransference. It is probably safe to say that most humanistic/experiential therapists have been influenced by the person-centered perspective of Carl Rogers and other current therapists. Similarly, the person-centered conditions, referred to as the necessary and sufficient conditions for therapeutic personality change (see the classic statement by Rogers, 1957) have been highly influential for these therapists. In his enormously heuristic statement, Rogers offered that three therapist conditions (along with three client conditions) were both necessary and sufficient for successful treatment: therapist empathic understanding, therapist unconditional positive regard for the patient, and therapist congruence or genuineness. When these conditions are combined with basic philosophical tenets of humanism, this can create a certain vulnerability in managing countertransference. The philosophical tenets to which I refer have to do with the belief that humans are basically good and trustworthy, and it is the therapist's job to create conditions (through empathy, unconditional positive regard, and genuineness) that will allow this basic trustworthiness and goodness to blossom into an actualization of the client's potentials (see the early statement by Grummon, 1965, on the basic assumptions of humanism in psychotherapy).

Tied to Rogers' (1957) necessary and sufficient conditions, as well as the humanistic philosophical foundation, the humanistic/experiential therapist who is worth his or her salt must respond to clients in a caring and empathic manner, and have regard for the client without conditions. To not have these qualities, or to have them compromised by more negative feelings, is to provide ineffective treatment. This, I believe, creates a difficulty for the humanistic therapist to become aware of and accept the inevitable negative effects that will occur in psychotherapy, especially with particular patients suffering from particular disorders. The fact that person-centered therapy also places a premium on genuineness does counter to an extent the inhibition of negative affect I have just noted. This, however, puts the humanistic therapist in a quandary of sorts. S/he must feel unconditional positive regard, be warm, empathic, and caring, on the one hand, and be genuine about what s/he feels on the other. In order to resolve this conundrum, it is important for the humanistic/experiential therapist to both understand that s/he will at times have negative, even intensely negative feelings, for the patient, while also having positive regard for the patient's inner being. This is a lot to ask of the therapist, and yet it seems essential to effective humanistic/experiential psychotherapy in terms of countertransference management.

There certainly is an awareness in the humanistic/experiential therapies of both countertransference and non-countertransference feelings on the part of the therapist. Elliott (2013), for example, has discussed in detail, how the person-centered/experiential therapist should address negative reactions to clients. However, he also points to how the experience of negative reactions runs counter to key elements of person-centered/experiential theory of how therapists are supposed to feel toward their clients. Although not referring explicitly to countertransference, Elliott's chapter should be read by all humanistic/experiential therapists who seek to manage their countertransference reactions effectively.

Cognitive-Behavioral Therapy (CBT) and the Repudiation of Affect

If the countertransference management soft spot of the psychodynamic therapist is the tendency to attribute the responsibility for countertransference to the patient, and the soft spot of the humanistic therapist is the tendency to repress or deny negative feelings for the patient, the soft spot for the CBT therapist is the tendency to focus on technique at the expense of staying attuned to his or her own feelings toward the patient. This is particularly relevant to countertransference reactions that stem from the therapist's unresolved conflicts and vulnerabilities. For example, CBT therapists, Levendusky and Rosmarin (2013) suggest that

> a cursory review of the literature on empirically supported CBT treatments suggests that therapists' emotional reactions are to be controlled, or perhaps altogether discouraged, through the utilization of precisely scripted treatment protocols. The effort to rigorously standardize treatment gives the impression that there is little or no place for the contemplation or evaluation of emotional experiences in therapy. Furthermore, given its historical roots within animal models, the foundation of CBT is broadly perceived as placing an emphasis on technique and being primarily nonrelational.
>
> (p. 46)

Although Levendusky and Rosmarin (2013) discuss in some depth how this viewpoint is changing in CBT, and there is some beginning research on countertransference in dialectical behavior therapy, a version of CBT (Aafjes-van Doorn, Kamsteeg, Portier, & Geetali, 2019 under review), the therapist's focus on technique, and tendency to not focus on his or her inner experience, especially when it is countertransferential, is still part of the orientation. Even very enlightened CBT therapists, such as Persons (2008) or McMain and Wiebe (2013), do not focus on countertransference. They do pay close attention to the therapist's feelings in response to the patient, but there is an almost total neglect of the countertransference basis for some of those feelings and for the necessity of the therapist paying close attention to his or her unresolved issues and vulnerabilities. One can easily get the impression from even the current wave of CBT authors who pay attention to therapist's feelings that countertransference is a rare occurrence and can be done away with through proper training and technique. I think this is far from the reality of the psychotherapy situation for CBT therapists, as well as therapists of all persuasions.

References

Aafjes-van Doorn, K., Kamsteeg, C. D., Portier, C. H., & Geetali, C. A. (2019, under review). Dialectical behavior therapy skills group in a psychoanalytic community service: A pilot study of assimilative integration.

Elliott, R. (2013). Therapist negative reactions: A person-centered and experiential psychotherapy perspective. In A. W. Wolf, M. R. Goldfried, & J. C. Muran (Eds.) *Transforming negative reactions to clients: From frustration to compassion* (pp. 69–90). Washington, DC: American Psychological Association.

Epstein, L., & Feiner, A. H. (1988). Countertransference: The therapist's contribution to treatment. In B. Wolstein (Ed.), *Essential papers on Countertransference* (pp. 282–303). New York: New York University Press.

Freud, S. (1959). The future prospects of psychoanalytic therapy. In E. Jones, (Ed.), & J. Riviere (Trans.), *Collected papers of Sigmund Freud* (Vol. 2, pp. 139–151). Oxford, England: Basic Books. (Original work published in 1910.)

Freud, S. (1959). Recommendations for physicians on the psychoanalytic method of treatment. In J. Riviere (Ed. and trans.), *Collected papers of Sigmund Freud* (Vol. 2, pp. 323–341). Oxford, England: Basic Books. (Original work published in 1912.)

Friedman, S. M., & Gelso, C. J. (2000). The development of the inventory of countertransference behavior. *Journal of Clinical Psychology, 56*(9), 1221–1235.

Fuertes, J., Gelso, C. J., Owen, J. & Cheng, D. (2015). Using the Inventory of Countertransference Behavior as an observer-rated measure. *Psychoanalytic Psychotherapy, 29*(1), 38–56. doi:10.1080/02668734.2014.1002417

Gelso, C. J., & Hayes, J. A. (2007). *Countertransference and the therapist's inner experience: Perils and possibilities.* Mahwah, NJ: Erlbaum.

Grummon, D. L. (1965). Client-centered theory. *Theories of counseling.* New York: McGraw Hill.

Hayes, J. A., Gelso, C. J., & Hummel, A. M. (2011). Managing countertransference. *Psychotherapy, 48*(1), 88.

Hayes, J., Gelso, C., Kivlighan, M., & Goldberg, S. (in press). Countertransference management. In J. Norcross & M. Lambert (Eds.), *Psychotherapy relationships that work* (3rd ed). New York, NY: Oxford.

Hayes, J. A., Gelso, C. J., VanWagoner, S. L., & Diemer, R. A. (1991). Managing countertransference: What the experts think. *Psychological Reports*, 69(1), 139–148.

Hayes, J. A., McCracken, J. E., McClanahan, M. K., Hill, C. E., Harp, J. S., & Carozzoni, P. (1998). Therapist perspectives on countertransference: Qualitative date in search of a theory. *Journal of Counseling Psychology*, 45(4), 468–482.

Kohut, H. (1984). *How does analysis cure?* New York: International Universities Press.

Levendusky, P. G., & Rosmarin, D. H. (2013). Cognitive behavior therapy: A rich but implicit relational framework within which to deal with therapist frustrations. In A. W. Wolf, M. R. Goldfried, & J. C. Muran (Eds.) *Transforming negative reactions to clients: From frustration to compassion*. Washington, D.C.: American Psychological Association.

McMain, S., & Wiebe, C. (2013). *Psychotherapy essentials to go: Dialectical behavior therapy for emotion dysregulation*. New York, NY: WW Norton & Company.

Mitchell, S. A. (1988). *Relational concepts in psychoanalysis*. Cambridge, MA: Harvard University Press.

Mitchell, S. A. (1997). Psychoanalysis and the degradation of romance. *Psychoanalytic Dialogues*, 7(1), 23–41.

Mohr, J. J., Gelso, C. J., & Hill, C. E. (2005). Client and counselor trainee attachment as predictors of session evaluation and countertransference behavior in first-counseling sessions. *Journal of Counseling Psychology*, 52(3), 298.

Pérez-Rojas, A., Palma, B., Bhatia, A., Jackson, J., Norwood, E., Hayes, J., & Gelso, C. (2017). The development and initial validation of the Countertransference Management Scale. *Psychotherapy*, 54, 307–319. doi:10.1037/pst0000126

Persons, J. B. (2008). *The case formulation approach to cognitive-behavior therapy: Guides to individualized evidence-based treatment*. New York: Guilford Press.

Racker, H. (1957). The meanings and uses of countertransference. *The Psychoanalytic Quarterly*, 26(3), 303–357.

Racker, H. (1968). *Transference and countertransference*. London: Karnac Books.

Reich, A. (1951). On countertransference. *International Journal of Psychoanalysis*, 32, 25–31.

Rogers, C. (1957). The necessary and sufficient conditions of therapeutic personality change. *Journal of Consulting Psychology*, 21(2), 95–103.

Stefana, A. (2017). *History of countertransference: From Freud to the British object relations school*. NY: Routledge.

VanWagoner, S. L., Gelso, C. J., Hayes, J. A., & Diemer, R. (1991). Countertransference and the reputedly excellent psychotherapist. *Psychotherapy: Theory, Research, and Practice*, 28, 411–421.

Winnicott, D. (1949). Hate in the counter-transference. *The International Journal of Psychoanalysis*, 30, 69–74.

Yalom, I. (2009). *The gift of therapy: Reflections on being a therapist*. London: Piatkus. (Original work published in 2002.)

6 Love, Hate, and Other "Inadmissible" Feelings in the Psychotherapist

When intense feelings in psychotherapy are written about, the focus is almost always on the patient. Yet the therapist, too, experiences intense feelings. Indeed, some therapists very often experience intense affects, and some patients clearly stir such reactions in most therapists. Naturally, it is important that these feelings in the therapist be understood and managed. The present chapter is an extension of Chapter 5. I explore intense inner experiences that are particularly difficult for the therapist to admit, even to oneself. The focus will be on the therapist's experience of love (including sexuality) and hate.

Over the years, a large literature has accumulated about intense feelings that patients have for their therapists. If we think of what may be the two most common states, or at least the most commonly addressed ones – love and hate – we see much clinical writing from the beginnings of the "talking cure." For example, Freud, more than 100 years ago, wrote about transference love that some patients experienced toward their therapists. Patients' hateful feelings, too, have been addressed in depth, particularly as analysts and therapists have worked increasingly with the more severe of the psychopathologies, for example, patients suffering from borderline personality disorders.

Whereas the feelings of love and hate in the patient have been the topic of much attention in the clinical and theoretical literature in psychotherapy, those of the therapist have been sadly neglected. Yet, as Annie Rogers (1996) put it in *A Shining Affliction*, "The psychotherapy relationship is two-sided, whether we acknowledge it or not ... [It] is an interchange of love, longing, frustration, and anger in the vicissitudes of a real relationship" (p. 19). The therapist's feelings, including the more intense ones such as love and hate, are surely a key part of the process.

Rather than simply being neglected, I believe that these intense and/or difficult affects on the part of the therapist have actually been avoided, perhaps because they are experienced as shameful, and in the case of sexual feelings, dangerous to therapeutic relationships. In this chapter, I counter this avoidance and focus on the therapist side of the equation. Although love and hate will take center stage, it should be added that there certainly are other difficult and/ or intense therapist states or inner experiences that creep into and at times may pervade the work of therapy. These difficult and intense states may occur especially when the therapy is longer-term and the patients are more difficult, but they also appear even in briefer work with those closer to the normal range. Some examples of such states are dislike for the person of the patient, disinterest in the patient, and envy of the patient. Why do I call the states that are addressed in this chapter inadmissible? I use this label because love and hate, as well as the other experiences I have mentioned, are felt by us therapists to be shameful and bad, and thus I believe they are very often not admissible to our awareness as therapists, as well as to public examination in the form of case presentations and writing. In the present chapter, I shall explore from where feelings of love and hate originate, their meaning for the treatment, and how they may be "worked with" so that they benefit rather than damage or destroy the treatment.

Love and Sexuality in Psychotherapy

Some years ago, I participated in a psychotherapy roundtable in which leading psychotherapy scholars discussed what they perceived as the key elements of the treatment process. A significant part of the discussion focused on the therapist's contributions to the treatment, including the usual attention to the person-centered triad of therapist empathy, unconditional positive regard, and congruence. I was struck, however, by the fact that more intense and/or difficult feelings were not even mentioned. For example, not a word was uttered about the therapist's loving feelings toward the patient. This troubled me, but something in me said, "keep this to yourself, don't bring it up," and I followed this inner voice. At the end of the first day of meetings, I brought up my observation to a senior colleague who cautioned me not to bring the topic up. It seems that talking about love in psychotherapy connects to sexuality and to fears of ethical violations around acting out of sexuality. Perhaps at a deeper level, we therapists are fearful of knowing our loving feelings because caring too deeply may create a sense of vulnerability, of not being in control, and perhaps, too, of loss in the sense that the relationship inevitably ends. In any event, it seemed to me then, and even more so now, that it is important not to avoid the topic of love, and the often attendant topic of sexuality, in therapy. This is so because therapists' feelings around these topics have the potential to greatly benefit, damage, or even destroy the therapeutic relationship, depending on how they are handled by the therapist.

What Kind of Love?

As therapists and human beings, we all know that love is complex. There is not a single kind of love, and in seeking to understand love in psychotherapy, we must ask, what kind of love. It is also important to explore just how love relates to sexuality in therapy. I think the great existential psychoanalyst, Rollo May, hit on something important for the therapeutic relationship when he underscored four kinds of love, as follows:

> There are four kinds of love in Western tradition. One is *sex*, or what we call lust, libido. The second is *eros*, the drive of love to procreate or create the urge, as the Greeks put it, toward higher forms of being and relationship. A third is *philia*, or friendship, brotherly love. The fourth is *agape* or *caritas* as the Latins called it, the love that is devoted to the welfare of the other, the prototype of which is the love of God for man. Every human experience of authentic love is a blending, in varying proportions, of these four.
>
> (May, 1969, p. 38)

This mixture may occur in the therapeutic relationship as well, particularly in longer-term work where the therapist gets to know the patient deeply. The kind of love that I believe most often and most clearly emerges in therapeutic relationships is what May refers to as philia and/or agape, the deep caring, often with a brotherly or sisterly element, of one human being for another, in which the well-being of the other is the center of the relationship. Because this form of love exists in a relationship in which the therapist knows the patient intimately and has a realistic and genuine feeling for the inner being of the patient, I see it as mostly residing within the realm of the real relationship (as described in Chapters 1 and 3). This kind of love is likely, in and of itself, to be mutative. That is, although it is not the only thing that helps the patient change, it is an important ingredient of what fosters growth. Being cared for deeply by another human being who knows one well, has one's best interests at heart, and is respected or admired, is bound to strengthen the patient's self-regard. It also facilitates the patient's healthy risk-taking and further opening up in a way that is insight-rendering and behavior changing. Moreover, when working with patients in longer-term work, one should not be as concerned when loving feelings are part of the relationship as when they are not.

When Sexuality Enters the Picture

The discussion so far is likely not very controversial. However, in keeping with Rollo May's description, the loving feelings on the part of the therapist may contain a sexual element, and this is where things can get more complicated and contentious. Several decades ago, Blum (1973) wrote about the concept of erotic transference, and Blum's observations pertain directly to the therapist's feelings, as well. For Blum, such feelings were a normal and healthy part of a therapeutic relationship in which each participant is of a gender to which the other is attracted. Because these feelings are experienced toward a person the therapist cares for and is coming to know deeply, they are likely to be mostly reality-based and genuine, and thus be part of the real relationship. The caring and attraction can be psychologically healthy.

Whether caring combined with sexual attraction is indeed a healthy expression of the real relationship depends, among other things, on the frequency, intensity, and duration of these feelings. The more intense, frequent, and pervasive feelings of sexual attraction in the therapist are indicative of the kind of loving feeling that May refers to as lust. The greater the frequency, intensity, and duration of such lustful feelings, the more likely they are to represent unresolved countertransference-based feelings and to disrupt the therapeutic relationship. Why is this so? As one of my psychotherapy trainees asked recently, "why cannot the therapist simply fall in love with the patient, and be intensely attracted to him or her without that representing the therapist's unresolved issues?" My response has been that because the therapeutic relationship most fundamentally revolves around the therapist's understanding the patient deeply, and providing a nurturant and emotionally safe relationship in which the patient is encouraged to "tell all" (while the therapist is not so encouraged), the emergence in the therapist of intense sexual attraction and feelings that pervade the therapeutic relationship bespeaks a violation of the implicit or explicit therapeutic contact. For this contract to be so violated by the therapist, whom we must assume is well-intentioned, something must be amiss in his or her inner world. Emotional wounds exist that have not healed sufficiently and are seeping into the therapeutic relationship.

At the same time, it is also true that therapists' sexual feelings and responses may be stirred by the patient's behavior. Such behavior may seek consciously or unconsciously to stimulate the therapist's sexuality. An example of this is the case of Teresa, with whom I worked a number of years ago (see Gelso, Perez-Rojas & Marmarosh, 2014, p. 127):

> Teresa had made her way through several therapists by the time I began working with her. No one seemed good enough for her, for one reason or another. Although there was an unspoken sexuality that Teresa seemed to exude, her fundamental problems seemed deeply rooted in very early attachment experiences with a mother who sounded to me to be critical and ungiving, clearly not a secure base or safe haven in attachment terms. An image of Teresa's early trauma was revealed in a dream she described when we were exploring her painful childhood interactions with her mother. In the dream, Teresa was in a swimming pool enjoying being enveloped by the rather warm water when all of a sudden the water turned into dead babies. Based on our exploration, the dream seemed to represent both Teresa's deep yearning for mothering and the profound deadness of a very young part of her self.
>
> After the sessions in which we worked with this dream, Teresa seemed more sexual, more seductive, and more difficult to reach. Then during one session, she got up from her chair and turned the lights off in the room. I felt a slightly dizzying rush of sexual feeling, along with sadness. I asked her to turn the lights back on, and we proceeded to explore feelings around her yearning for mothering she never received. To my mind, Teresa was being unconsciously sexual as a way of defending against terrifying and overwhelming dependency needs, which had developed early in her life and were beginning to be touched upon in our work, as well as dread

around the death of a part of her self that was immensely undernourished. In a psychoanalytic sense, Teresa's unacknowledged but intense sexuality was a defense against more deep-seated and frightening needs that were fundamentally oral (pertaining to dependency).

In this case, my sexual reactions were stirred by the patient's sexuality. These reactions were fleeting and tied to the patient's unconscious material and defenses. The reactions did not represent a caring or sexual attraction toward the other person (although I did find her attractive and did care about her), but were stimulated by the patient's behaviors, which in turn had a defensive basis. Perhaps most often, however, the therapist's sexual reactions stem from a combination of the patient's unmet needs and behavior and the therapist's unmet needs. As I have said, if the frequency, intensity, and duration of the therapist's sexual attraction are low and are in the context of May's philia or agape, they are likely part of a sound real relationship and often do not need particular attention. However, even when these reactions are not intense, they may relate importantly to the treatment, and can often serve a defensive function for both therapist and patient. An example comes from the work of Dr. Andres Perez-Rojas, who was at the time of this treatment doing an internship at a university counseling center:

> Emma and I worked together in time-limited individual psychotherapy. She came to treatment to address anxiety around starting graduate school and adjusting to living by herself in a new town and being in a long-distance relationship. She was an attractive, petite, talkative young woman with a great sense of humor. Humor, in fact, was the first clue of a budding attraction between us. I could tell that she enjoyed making me laugh, which was all too easy to do. Soon I discovered that I, too, could make her laugh, and really liked doing so. At first this wasn't a big barrier to treatment. But as the work progressed, and we uncovered more of her pain around loss and unmet needs in relationships, our use of humor—and the attraction that stirred underneath—inhibited deeper exploration and processing of her feelings and attachment anxieties.
>
> At the time that Emma and I started working together, I too had just moved to a new area to start my position at the center. I too had to adjust to a new situation away from loved ones. I also related to the theme of loss and unmet needs that Emma had begun to recognize in her history. Although I never directly shared my past or my feelings, I conveyed them indirectly (mostly non-verbally), which furthered a sense of camaraderie between us. I didn't want to admit it at first, but I felt less lonely with her. That we both enjoyed making each other laugh was very gratifying, too. I thought, at some point, that it was unfair that we had met under such circumstances. What could have been if we'd met out in the "real world"?
>
> To overcome the barrier that our mutual attraction posed to the treatment, and to step back from the fantasy rabbit hole I was staring into,

I had to first become aware of my attraction toward Emma and how it affected my behavior. Then I had to come to terms with the vulnerabilities it was connected to. For that, supervision was vital: it helped me unpack and understand what was real and genuine in the therapy relationship, and what was transference and countertransference.

Eventually, I found better ways to respond to Emma. In one session, she again made me laugh, quite genuinely, with an anecdote about struggling with a school subject with which I, too, often struggled. I paused for a moment; I could feel myself wanting to reciprocate. While still feeling, and probably showing, the aftereffects of laughing, I said that in times like these, I could be quite taken with her. (A half-smile touched the corner of her mouth.) I said that I had been wondering, though, whether my being taken with her like that wasn't actually distracting us from talking about the difficult feelings that had brought her to therapy in the first place. And wasn't that a disservice to her—more of the same, yet another way in which she wasn't getting her needs met?

Emma's smile waned, and she looked down at the floor. Neither of us said anything; the silence must have lasted just a few seconds, but to me, it felt eternal. I thought maybe I had revealed too much of my feelings, or that maybe she felt ashamed. Finally she spoke, and answered my question simply with, "It's possible." There was a hint of disappointment in her voice—the gig was up—but afterward, the session felt much different. She went on to talk about a recent fight with her boyfriend, and the feelings of anger, sadness, and loneliness that accompanied the fight—which we then connected to dynamics in her early attachments within her family.

I believe that my intervention—in which I first acknowledged, albeit indirectly, the flirting, and then wondered whether it kept us from going deeper in the work—allowed Emma to switch her attention to the feelings she was defending against, in a way that wasn't shaming. It helped to frame that switch in attention not as a rejection of her and her feelings, but as something that needed to happen to attend to her needs. It all started, however, with an awareness of my contribution to our dynamic: that she was not just flirting with me but that I, too, was flirting with her; and that the flirting came from my desire to fill a void currently in my life. Acknowledging my feelings and their likely source freed me from having to worry about them, which left more room to be congruent and to actually listen and help Emma understand.

After that session, the frequency, duration, and intensity of my attraction to Emma lessened. There still was some laughing and flirting: not enough to be disruptive, but enough that we could learn from it. Indeed, with time, it became clearer that flirting was an expression of the idea that Emma felt the need to be charming and pleasing to others to ensure their availability in her life. We continued working together productively until we reached her session limit. Despite the relatively short duration of our work together, termination was difficult for us both; it was hard to say goodbye. It helped, however, to know that she was walking away with a deeper, better understanding of the dynamics that contributed to her adjustment difficulties.

(Personal communication, Andres Perez-Rojas, December 2017)

The two examples I have provided involved heterosexual pairings of male therapists and female patients. For a wonderfully detailed example of how therapist and patient sexuality may surface in a female therapist–male patient dyad, see the case presented by Dr. Cheri Marmarosh in Gelso, Perez-Rojas & Marmarosh (2014). The issues I am describing in heterosexual dyads ought to be essentially the same for dyads in which one or more members is not heterosexual, but this is a topic that certainly deserves our attention and study.

What to Do About It

As I have implied throughout, how the therapist should deal with his or her loving and sexual feelings depends greatly on (a) what kind of loving feelings predominate (see May's four kinds of love); (b) the frequency, intensity, and duration of these feelings; (c) from where the feelings originate; and (d) the nature of the therapy that is being conducted. The first step for the therapist is to acknowledge such feelings to him or herself. Left unacknowledged, loving and sexual feelings are likely to spill over into the work in a way that hinders progress and, indeed, damages or even destroys the therapeutic efforts. The next step goes beyond mere acknowledgment. If one ingredient of "what to do about it" stands out, it is the need for the therapist to study both him/herself and the patient. Thus, if there is a prescription, it may be best captured by the phrase "understand, understand, and understand." Again, this applies both to the therapist's self- understanding and his/her understanding of the patient. I believe that there is a natural unconscious resistance to self-understanding in the case of the therapist's sexual attraction. The conflicts that intense attractions almost invariably reflect are repressed for a reason. Thus, the therapist's task is virtually to try to understand something s/he does not want to understand. This is of course a tall order, and yet it is a fundamental part of the therapist's management of countertransference, which itself has been found to be substantially related to treatment success (see the research summary by Hayes, Gelso, Kivlighan, & Goldberg, in press).

Beyond self-acknowledgment and self-understanding on the therapist's part, there remains the question of whether the therapist's loving feelings and sexual attraction should be shared with the patient. Should the therapist explicitly express his or her loving and/or sexual feelings toward the patient? Although therapist self-disclosure can be a powerful tool that fosters positive movement in therapies of all orientations (see Farber, 2006; Pinto-Coelho, Hill, & Kivlighan Jr, 2015), it is important that it fits the needs of the patient, and not be used for the therapist's gratification.

The possible answers to the question of the therapist's disclosure of his or her loving and sexual feelings may well vary for those feelings involving primarily May's agape or philia versus sexual attraction. In the case of sexual attraction, my reactions are similar to those of Maroda (2004) and Lijtmaer (2004). That is, it is hard to see how sharing such feelings will foster growth in the patient or strengthen the therapeutic relationship in useful ways. More often than not, such revelations are likely to place an unneeded burden on the patient or be confusing to him or her. I suspect that sharing such feelings more likely gratifies the therapist rather than the patient. Thus, it is best that the therapist's sexual attractions be subjected to self-analysis and, as in the case examples presented above, used to foster the patient's self-understanding. An exception to this position is when the therapist points to attraction in a modulated way with the aim of helping the patient see the ways in which this attraction may hinder exploration and serve defensive functions. For example, in the case just presented, when Perez-Rojas points to how he told his patient that "at times like these I could be quite taken with her" and then sought to explore how that kept him and the patient from deeper exploration, the treatment became more effective.

The question of the therapist's sharing of sexual attraction becomes more complicated, however, when the patient has expressed sexual feelings for the therapist (Gelso, Perez-Rojas, & Marmarosh, 2014). Should the therapist tell the patient that s/he too feels an attraction? That s/he does not, when that is the case? As I have discussed recently (Gelso et al. 2014; Gelso & Perez-Rojas, 2017), it is preferable for the therapist to treat such feelings in the patient like all other feelings: accept them and seek to understand them, rather than sharing whether or not the therapist too experiences such feelings. At the same time, the patient should not be shamed for his or her feelings. I have found it helpful to communicate something like "I appreciate what you feel, and in fact I'm flattered by it; but it is important that we deal with these feelings like the other feelings you have shared – let's try to understand them" (Gelso et al., 2014, p. 128). Also in a way that is not shaming, it is at times helpful for the therapist to communicate that such feelings can never be acted out during or even after treatment. This serves as a needed protection for the patient (and the therapist), creating a safe haven to explore whatever s/he feels in the hour.

As for loving feelings, those most embodied in May's philia or agape, I believe the answer to the question of sharing is somewhat different. Most often it is useful to help the patient explore why he or she would doubt the therapist's caring, rather than state that "I care deeply for you" or "I have loving feelings for you." A concern about explicitly communicating loving feelings is that, as Freud worried, this will foster the patient's substituting the need to be treated for the need to be cured. In other words, the treatment experience will be so rewarding that it becomes the end in itself. To my mind, this is worth worrying about, to the point that I believe it best to show the patient one cares through the caring and loving way the therapist does his or her job, e.g., asks questions, attends empathically and nonjudgmentally to the patient's feelings, shows up on time, demonstrates pleasure in seeing the patient, exhibits abiding interest in the patient and his or her welfare, demonstrates in myriad ways that the patient is a worthwhile human being, etc. It is also worth noting that direct expressions of loving feelings by the therapist may be experienced as oppressive by the patient, and may actually inhibit the patient's expression of negative feelings toward the therapist.

Still, there are certain times in therapy in which the therapist's expression of caring is likely to benefit the patient, for example, during times of crisis, when the patient may feel particularly unworthy of caring, during moments of deep connection, or when therapy is coming to an end. Just what does or should the therapist say to communicate love or loving feelings? I must admit that I have never been able to tell a patient directly that I love him or her, feeling that this is too likely to be experienced as a boundary crossing and felt by the patient to be beyond what is appropriate for a therapy relationship. It may feel good to the therapist but be either a burden or provocative to the patient. However, when such feelings are part of the real relationship, and especially after complicated transference (and countertransference) feelings have been worked through, expressions such as "I think you can see that I care very much about you" or "I certainly experience you as a good and lovable person" can be deeply meaningful to some patients. It is often helpful to follow up such expressions with a question about how these therapist reactions made the patient feel.

Hate in the Countertransference

Love and sexuality are difficult for the therapist to admit to him/herself and to deal with. Hateful feelings, however, are even more difficult, as these seem fundamentally inimical to any good relationship, to say nothing of a therapeutic relationship. Yet feelings such as these are often part of the therapeutic process. This was highlighted several decades ago by the great psychoanalyst Winnicott (1949) in his seminal paper, "Hate in the Counter-Transference." Winnicott noted that when working with severely troubled patients, such feelings were essentially inevitable. They could also be helpful to the therapeutic process in that they provide a window into the patient's inner world and give the therapist a telescope of sorts into the patient's childhood and what s/he experienced in early life. Winnicott likened the inevitable hateful feelings the analyst has toward his/her troubled (and thus emotionally very young) patient with those a mother has toward her infant. He lists 18 reasons why a mother hates her infant (while also pointing to the reality and marvel of her loving feelings). For example, the baby was a danger to her body in pregnancy and birth; the baby is ruthless and treats her as scum ... an unpaid servant and slave; she is forced to love the baby, excretions and all; and the baby has no appreciation of all she sacrifices for him/her. Similarly, the more troubled patients say, feel, and demand many things in treatment that engender negative reactions, often intense ones. Like the good mother, however, the therapist must not act out the hateful feelings in treatment, but instead must understand them and perhaps share a toned-down version of them later in treatment as the patient is getting better.

To return to the point of the difficulty therapists have facing hateful feelings in themselves and letting others know about these feelings, the reasons for this are captured with great clarity by Dr. Jean A. Carter (2006), a highly gifted therapist who does exceptional long-term work with very troubled patients:

> As I have thought about my own experiences of hateful countertransference, I feel a depth of shame. Those hateful feelings are unacceptable to one's self .... They are unacceptable because they threaten our own self-concept and self-esteem. They bring up our own sense of failure .... We want to avoid those feelings because they are the feelings of shame, and shame leads to a wish to conceal, to hide, to remain blind to our own shameful experiences.

As I have implied, when working with patients suffering from severe psychopathology, such as borderline personality disorder (BPD), intense feelings such as hate and rage on the part of the therapist seem almost inevitable, and have been noted by therapists from virtually all theoretical orientations (see Wolf, Goldfried, & Muran, 2013, 2017). Such feelings in the therapist are stimulated by the defenses of the patient, which aim to disown the patient's hateful feelings and instead stir them in the therapist. This allows the patient not to face his or her own intensely negative affect and also protects the patient from dreaded dangers of a close relationship with the therapist. The patient may then tend to reject their therapist because of the therapist's negative reactions. In the psychodynamic literature, this defense is often referred to as projective identification. In work with BPD, the therapist must be able to successfully navigate the minefield of projective identification if the treatment is to be effective, and a key part of it is learning to manage, in Winnicott's terms, hate in the countertransference.

Although there is no doubt that patients suffering from BPD do regularly create negative reactions in their therapists, the great focus in the psychoanalytic literature has tended to be on the patient as the sole perpetrator of the therapist's rage and hate. Some psychoanalytic descriptions make it appear that all of what the therapist feels is due to the patient and his or her defenses. At times, it almost seems like the patient's hateful feelings are magically transported into the therapist through a mystical process known as projective identification. At the core, such characterizations represent little more than muddy thinking. What is missing from conceptualizations is often just what behaviors, however subtle, the patient manifests that create hateful feelings in the therapist and how the therapist's dynamics play into the therapist's feelings toward the patient. Indeed, although the patient's behavior is the precipitant of hateful feelings in the therapist, the frequency, intensity, duration, and specific form of those feelings are also partly due to the therapist and his/her unresolved conflicts and vulnerabilities. In this sense, as I discussed in Chapter 5, the countertransference interaction hypothesis is centrally implicated in the therapist's reactions. This lapse in the discourse on BPD, projective identification, and countertransference is an important one because the therapist's denial of his/her role in hateful feelings is bound to limit the efficacy of treatment.

A Case in Point

The countertransference interaction hypothesis was evidenced in my work with a patient early in my career. The patient, a 27-year-old White woman whom I shall call Jane, had seen several therapists prior to our work, and none were good enough for her. We worked together for two years, mostly in twice-a-week psychodynamic therapy. During most of this time, I was being supervised by a well-known and gifted psychoanalyst in the Washington DC area who specialized in the treatment of narcissistic and borderline disorders. At the time, I was in my mid-30s and had worked with few deeply troubled patients. Jane was married, had no close friends, and was unemployed, despite having a BA degree in anthropology. Her presenting problems revolved around severe generalized anxiety, severe enough that she was essentially homebound. Jane was tightly wound, critical, and compulsive. In our work together, whenever we took a step forward, I could count on the next several sessions being filled with criticism of me and our work. The criticism was usually presented in a sneering way, and with a kind of laughter that reminded me of the devil child in the movie, *The Exorcist*. During most sessions, in fact, she expressed doubt that therapy could help her, and doubt that I was effective enough as a therapist to be of help. I recall being left in an emotional hovel when Jane told me that our problem was that I was from a lower class background than she, that I must not have had sisters because I didn't understand women, and that the treatment I provided was ineffective because I probably didn't know what I was doing. I tried several approaches to our work, each working well for a short time, followed by Jane's sneering depreciation that the approach was useless for one reason or another (a behavioral approach was stupidly superficial, a more humanistic approach was smarmy and useless). I had many hateful fantasies revolving around harming this patient, and these were, of course, upsetting and unnerving.

In my supervision, I often shared my frustration in working with Jane, and my more hateful feelings, as well. I periodically expressed the feeling that Jane was untreatable and that her particular form of narcissistic injury made it impossible to move forward. My supervisor, instead, commented that the problem was not Jane's narcissism, but rather my narcissism. After two years of stalemated therapy, and after a "trial period" of a few months, I brought the treatment to an end, stating that the patient's ambivalence was just too much to allow us to continue with any chance of success. I referred her to a more seasoned therapist who was effective at working with the kind of assaultiveness that Jane exhibited.

By any yardstick, Jane was a difficult patient, the kind of patient that is often written about in the psychoanalytic literature on BPD, projective identification, and the therapist's rage.

Clearly, her own rage was defended against through stirring my emotional pot, so that I rather than she was the angry one. However, what is missing from such an analysis is my role in the frequency, intensity, duration, and specific form of my rage. At that point in my career, my own sense of competence was too shaky to tolerate effectively the kinds of criticisms repeatedly leveled by Jane, while at the same time, I had too many unresolved conflicts around achievement and a need to excel. Indeed, my sense of self as a therapist and as a person was not yet solid enough, and that is what my supervisor was referring to when he commented that the problem was not Jane's narcissism but instead my narcissism. That is why I often changed approaches with Jane, rather than understanding that her pushing me to do so was a manifestation of her defenses, and also why I would have been unable to tolerate effectively the hit that would inevitably come if I remained more steadfast in my approach. In retrospect, had I understood myself more and attained a higher level of maturation, I would have had less intense countertransference problems with Jane and managed better the countertransference I did have.

The point here is that, even when the therapist's hateful countertransference is strongly stirred by the patient's defenses, it is important that the therapist also look inward to his/her own conflicts and complexes as the partial cause and to try to work with those conflicts and complexes in him/herself. Doing so will help at least mitigate the otherwise intense hate in the countertransference, diminish acting out the countertransference, and allow the therapist to better work with the patient.

A Less Troubled Case

Hateful feelings in the therapist can also surely occur with less troubled patients, where projective identification and other similar defenses (e.g., splitting, primitive projection) are not primary. An example, also from early in my career, was my work with a patient whom I shall call David (see Gelso and Perez-Rojas, 2017). David was a 19-year-old university student when we began our work, and the treatment was on a once-a-week basis over a period of 20 months. David was emotionally young, and he yearned to be loved and appreciated. Although functioning well in school, David seemed quite needy, and this was manifested in his pulling for love, caring, and sympathy from others, even when they did not really feel sympathetic and loving. Friends either had to come through with the loving and sympathetic feelings that David wanted from them or these friends ended up feeling guilty that they did not care as they should. Needless to say, David's friendships did not last very long. I was able to conceptualize these dynamics in David and his relationships pretty quickly in our work. However, I did not see just how much the dynamics were invading our relationship, even when a telling event occurred between us. During one session in which David was sharing his pain stemming from a particular relationship, he asked that I hug him. Although I am not at all a hugger in therapy, I did hug David, while also feeling uncomfortable doing so and not feeling the kind of positivity that one ordinarily feels when hugging another person. The source of the discomfort was unclear to me until I had a dream the night before our next session. In the dream, I was on top of David on the floor and was choking him. And I was getting pleasure from this. Naturally I was unsettled when I awoke. The obvious became clear to me at that point. I had been manipulated into caring for him over a period of several weeks, just as others had felt in his extra-therapy life, and I was furious at him for that. As this seeped in, I also became aware that on the mornings of our session, I was grouchy, often sniping at my wife and kids.

My emerging understanding of the countertransference hate helped our therapy considerably. As I have stated in reviewing this case:

> I was able to be more in touch with my feelings in the moment with David, and to be in touch with the deeper fears that caused him to pull for love and affection. This awareness in me served to modulate my feelings toward David, and use them to frame helpful interpretations to him about what he was doing with me and with others, as well as the needs underlying his interpersonal patterns and others' reactions to him. It was also more possible to refrain from falsely sympathizing with David and acting like I felt more positively than I did. My ability to modulate my feelings was aided by an understanding of my own personal conflicts around giving and receiving, and a tendency toward guilt about not giving enough. The intensity of my reactions was fueled by my revulsion of my own neediness, a conflict of which I was only dimly aware at the time. These conflicts made me both an easy target for David's affective yearnings and pull for affection, and they also fueled the intensity of my unconscious hateful reaction.
>
> (Gelso & Perez-Rojas, 2017, p. 108)

I never told David of my dream, but the feelings I came to understand in myself became key to the success of this treatment. I was able to share with David some of the feelings he stirred in me as he became emotionally stronger and was able to hear and benefit from this disclosure. This is in keeping with suggestions by Winnicott (1949) and, in particular, Mehlman and Glickauf-Hughes (1994), who suggest that the therapist communicate a metabolized or toned-down version of his or her feelings when the patient is strong enough to integrate these.

Owning the Negative

The two cases I have described represent different levels and kinds of psycho-pathology. In the case of Jane, her depreciation of me was palpable, and my hateful countertransference reactions were expectable, what Winnicott (1949) referred to as objective countertransference. The case of David was somewhat different. My hateful reactions were more clearly tied to my unresolved conflicts that were, in turn, a response to his pulls for love and affection, making me vulnerable to those pulls. However, in both cases, the therapist's unresolved conflicts came into play and were part of the hateful reactions. Perhaps influenced by our own self idealizations as therapists, it is difficult to face these tendencies in ourselves, and that is likely part of the reason we have tended to make the patient the culprit in our hateful countertransferences. Finally, in both cases, and indeed in perhaps all cases, the therapist's self-understanding, as well as his or her emotional integration and strength, are fundamentally important in facilitating effective management of hate in the countertransference.

Postscript

Psychotherapy is a relationship of passions. Although it is the patient who does most of the self-exploration in psychotherapy, and thus feels the most and the most deeply, if the therapist is fully present in the therapeutic relationship, s/he, too, feels a lot, and at times those feelings are of such intensity that we may capture them with words such as love and hate. Although such intense feelings are often experienced as shameful to therapists, they need not and should not be such. Instead, they should be brought to our awareness and be the subject of our scrutiny. This is so because understanding these feelings, and the patient's needs that are likely at least partly driving this intensity, is bound to aid therapeutic progress, and at times be the key to understanding and working with the patient. At other times, intense feelings, such as certain kinds of love, should be prized by the therapist, for when genuinely felt and part of the real relationship, they may be the most important curative factor in helping our patients learn to love themselves and love others. Finally, there will be times when therapists cannot figure it out on their own. The feelings may be too frequent, intense, and of too long a duration; and they may be stemming from internal conflicts that the therapist is simply unable to understand. That is time to seek help in the form of case discussion with colleagues or further supervision. Naturally, the therapist's personal therapy may also be crucial when deeper conflicts preclude understanding.

References

Blum, H. P. (1973). The concept of erotized transference. *Journal of the American Psychoanalytic Association*, 21(1), 61–76.

Carter, J. A. (2006, August). The eye can't see itself because the eye hides in shame. Paper presented at the Annual Convention of the American Psychological Association, Washington, D.C.

Farber, B. A. (2006). *Self-disclosure in psychotherapy*. New York, NY: Guilford.

Gelso, C. (2014). A tripartite model of the therapeutic relationship: Theory, research, and practice. *Psychotherapy Research*, 24(2), 117–131.

Gelso, C. J., & Perez-Rojas, A. (2017). Inner experience and the good psychotherapist. In L. Castonuay, & C. Hill (Eds.), *How and why some therapists are better than others? Understanding therapist effects.* (pp. 101–116). Washington, DC: American Psychological Association.

Gelso, C. J., Perez-Rojas, A. E., & Marmarosh, C. (2014). Love and sexuality in the therapeutic relationship. *Journal of Clinical Psychology*, 70(2), 123–134.

Glickauf-Hughes, C. (1994). Characterological resistances in psychotherapy supervision. *Psychotherapy: Theory, Research, Practice, Training*, 31(1), 58.

Hayes, J., Gelso, C., Kivlighan, M., & Goldberg, S. (in press). Countertransference management. In J. Norcross & M. Lambert (Eds.), *Psychotherapy relationships that work* (3rd ed.). New York, NY: Oxford.

Lijtmaer, R. M. (2004). The place of erotic transference and countertransference in clinical practice. *Journal of the American Academy of Psychoanalysis & Dynamic Psychiatry*, 32(3), 483–498. doi:10.1521/jaap.32.3.483.44775

Maroda, K. (2004). *The power of countertransference: Innovations in analytic technique.* Hillsdale, NJ: The Analytic Press.

May, R. (1969). *Love and will.* New York, NY: WW Norton & Company.

Mehlman, E., & Glickauf-Hughes, C. (1994). The underside of psychotherapy:Confronting hateful feelings toward clients. *Psychotherapy: Theory, Research, Practice, Training*, *31*, 434–439. https://protect-us.mimecast.com/s/XApWClYvpnu26KyJqfG3x1-?domain=dx.doi.org doi:http://dx.doi.org/10.1037/0033-3204.31.3.434

Pinto-Coelho, K. G., Hill, C. E. & KivlighanJr., D. M. (2015). Therapist self-disclosure in psychodynamic psychotherapy: A mixed methods investigation. *Counselling Psychology Quarterly*, 29(1), 29–52. doi:doi:10.1080/09515070.2015.1072496

Rogers, A. G. (1996). *A shining affliction: A story of harm and healing in psychotherapy.* New York, NY: Penguin.

Winnicott, D. W. (1949). Hate in the countertransference. *The International Journal of Psycho Analysis*, 30, 69.

Wolf, A. W., Goldfried, M. R., & Muran, J. (2013). *Transforming negative reactions to clients: From frustration to compassion.* Washington, DC: American Psychological Association.

Wolf, A. W., Goldfried, M. R., & Muran, J. C. (2017). Therapist negative reactions: How to transform toxic experiences. In L. Castonguay & C. Hill (Eds.), *How and why are some therapists better than others? Therapist effects* (pp. 175–192). Washington, DC: American Psychological Association.

7 Good Therapist, Good Relationship

A Summing Up

In this final summing up, I shall review key points in the book and offer conclusions regarding the therapeutic relationship. The conclusions are presented as statements and followed by discussion, and they are made with clinical practice centrally in mind. Much of this material summarizes key points in the book, but some of it extends those points and adds new material. The statements are based on clinical theory, research, and my own practice of psychotherapy and supervision over more than five decades. Because my career as a psychotherapist has been joined by my career as a therapy researcher, I naturally bring research to bear in these suggestions, but the main focus shall be on clinical theory and practice.

1. The therapeutic relationship is complex and multidimensional, and it includes the contributions of both the therapist and the patient.

Throughout the history of theory and research on psychotherapy of all persuasions, there has been a tendency to view the therapy relationship as unidimensional and/or something created by the therapist alone. The primary examples of these views are the tendency to equate the relationship with the working alliance between therapist and patient, as well as the therapist-offered conditions of empathy, unconditional positive regard, and congruence. Both of these conceptualizations are deeply deficient, capturing only a fraction of the therapeutic relationship. They have been maintained out of convenience at best and theoretical laziness at worst. It is as if we have found useful constructs (working alliance and therapist-offered conditions) that certainly account for some of the effects of treatment, but have not then gone on to attempt to grasp what else might be needed to capture the wonderful complexity of the therapeutic relationship.

It is important to consider why the two conceptualizations I have mentioned are insufficient. First, the working alliance is but a single element of the relationship, and the work connection that therapist and patient have could not possibly be the totality of the relationship. When one considers all of the wide range of feelings and attitudes that go into any relationship, it is a bit shocking that therapists could possibly reduce the relationship to this one element. Perhaps the reality is that therapists have not actually done so. It may be that therapy researchers have created the problem in their wish to simplify for the purpose of getting on with their research. This may not be problematic, except to the extent that academics and academic researchers use this monochromatic conception, then students who are naturally taught by these academics learn to adopt it and carry it into practice. The point for the practitioner is to appreciate and ponder the complexity of the therapeutic relationship and thus to abandon what they may have learned in graduate school!

As for the therapist-offered conditions, despite what may be considered an elegant and powerful theory from which these conditions emanate (Carl Rogers', 1957, theory of the necessary and sufficient conditions for therapeutic personality change), they only pertain to the therapist, whereas, as we all know, the therapeutic relationship is bipersonal. So the therapist side of it can only be part of the relationship, and it is important that we therapists think of the therapeutic relationship as a function of both therapists' and their patients' contributions.

Nearly a decade ago, both Adam Horvath and I agreed that the time had come to shed single-construct conceptions of the therapeutic relationship (Gelso, 2009; Horvath, 2009). The fact that Horvath shared this viewpoint was especially significant because he has been arguably the greatest contributor to the study of the working alliance in psychotherapy. However, one-sided and singular conceptions of the relationship continue to rule the theoretical roost. Practicing therapists need to guide researchers here in appreciating, working with, and studying the complex, multidimensional, and bipersonal nature of the therapeutic relationship.

2. All therapeutic relationships may be seen as consisting of three interlocking components: a real relationship, a working alliance, and a transference–countertransference configuration.

There are many ways to capture the multidimensional nature of the therapeutic relationship. The tripartite model I have developed is one such attempt, and it has been explored considerably over the years. The three elements of this model are interrelated, and in the case of the working alliance and real relationship, considerably interrelated. All three are present from the first moment of contact between therapist and patient, and in the case of patient transference, from even prior to the first session in the form of preformed transferences. That is, the patient develops a kind of transference based on fantasies about his or her expected therapist, and these fantasies are further stirred by initial correspondences or phone contacts.

In Chapter 1, I described the interrelations among the elements of the tripartite model, and here I shall briefly summarize them. First, as described in Chapter 2, the real relationship and working alliance very clearly and strongly relate to one another. Indeed, both seem cut from the same cloth. As the term implies, though, the working alliance may be seen as forming from the work that needs to be done if treatment is to be successful, whereas the real relationship is the personal or person-to-person part of the overall relationship, and it is part of each and every relationship formed between two persons. While highly interrelated, the two elements also contribute independently to treatment process and outcome.

The real relationship and the working alliance obviously relate to client transference in the sense that the stronger the real relationship and the working alliance, at least in part, the less the patient's perceptions of and projections onto the therapist are guided by transference. However, in the case of the real relationship, because transference is not the inverse of the real relationship, and also because the two may be seen as existing on separate dimensions of experience, the real relationship and transference are not nearly perfectly inversely related to one another. Patients, for example, can have a strong real relationship with their therapists and simultaneously experience a significant amount of negative transference. In such cases, the real relationship can be a major aid in working with and through these negative transferences. The working alliance, too, can repair the potentially damaging effects of negative transference and facilitate the patient's exploration of transference.

On the negative side, transference, especially negative transference, can damage or poison both the real relationship and the working alliance if efforts are not made to work through the patient's negative perceptions of and projections onto the therapist (assuming the therapist has not "earned" these reactions). Especially when negative transference emerges before the establishment of strong working alliance and real relationship, it is important that therapists of any and all theoretical persuasions help their patients come to see these negative reactions for what they are. Thus, CBT and humanistic/experiential therapists must help their patients see that these therapists are not the negative figures occupying their patients' psyches when the patients are manifesting negative transference. Usually this involves asking the patient, in one way or another, questions such as "who am I being to you now?" and "where are you coming from?" The delicate task is to help the patient see that s/he is coming from somewhere other than a realistic and accurate perception of the therapist, while also not making the patient feel negated or dismissed.

The therapist's countertransference is also related to transference, the real relationship, and the working alliance. If we think of countertransference as the therapist's reactions to the patient based on the therapist's unresolved conflicts and vulnerabilities, it makes sense that it will be injurious to the therapeutic relationship and process, thus weakening the real relationship and the working alliance, and also both stemming from and fostering transference. Similarly, countertransference is affected by the other components. A sound working alliance and a good real relationship, as well as diminished transference, will all tend to reduce the countertransference and its potentially pernicious effects on treatment.

Given these interrelations, it behooves the therapist to pay attention not only to the three interlocking elements of the relationship (working alliance, real relationship, and transference–countertransference), but to how each is affecting the other during the hour. The bottom line, however, is that the therapist needs to focus on building and preserving a sound working alliance and real relationship, understanding and helping the patient understand transference (especially when it is negative and/or may injure the therapeutic relationship), and understanding and managing countertransference.

3. Techniques and the relationship go hand in hand, each affecting the other and at times being part of the other.

There has been an overriding tendency in the psychotherapy field to divide the therapeutic work into two parts, the relationship and the techniques used by the therapist. The two are often treated as separate entities. This division makes little sense, as the therapeutic relationship and therapist techniques are not only deeply intertwined, but are, in a certain sense, one and the same.

The relationship does not simply happen out of thin air, or out of therapist and patient meeting each other. From the therapist's side, something must be done; and beyond greetings and perhaps small talk, what is done – the therapist's therapeutic behavior – is generally in the form of techniques. In this way, techniques become the relationship. That is, what it is said and how it is said are manifestations of techniques and the relationship. This convergence may best be explained through examining reasonable definitions of the relationship and of technique. Earlier I defined the relationship as *the feelings and attitudes the psychotherapy participants have toward one another and the manner in which they are expressed*. Technique, on the other hand, may be viewed as *a defined method or tool that is used by the therapist to facilitate therapy and bring about change in the patient*. I am proposing that the manifestation of technique reflects the relationship and influences the relationship to the extent that at times and in a certain sense the two are interchangeable. For example, consider the "technique" called interpretation. This term typically indicates a response made by the therapist in which causal connections are pointed out between the patient's past and present behavior or between the patient's outward behavior and underlying inner experience. In making an interpretation, the therapist is both expressing the relationship and influencing the relationship. Stated another way, the depth, emotional tone, valence, duration, and content of any given interpretation are displays or manifestations of the feelings and attitudes the therapist has toward the patient, and further affect the relationship, as well.

From the patient's side, we do not talk about patient techniques. Instead, we refer simply to the patient's behavior. Here again, the patient's behavior (the parallel to the therapist's techniques) reflects and affects the therapeutic relationship to the extent that in practice they are impossible to separate.

Is there any reason to separate therapist technique or patient behavior from the therapeutic relationship? It is probably wise to do so when we wish to empirically study these phenomena, for science, at least quantitative psychotherapy science, does benefit from partitioning phenomena into parts. But in doing so, it is important to keep mindful of the reality that the therapist's technique and the therapeutic relationship are deeply interconnected and in a certain sense inseparable theoretically and in practice.

4. The preservation and strengthening of the working alliance should take center stage from the very beginning of treatment.

The most fundamentally important element of the therapeutic relationship is likely the working alliance. That is, if the work of therapy is to be successful, there must be at least a sound working alliance between patient and therapist. If there is not this sound connection around the work itself, it is hard to imagine treatment being successful, or perhaps even being done. In this sense, I would suggest that research on the working alliance actually underestimates the importance of the alliance. When the numerous studies on the working alliance are combined, it has been found consistently that the working alliance accounts for about 5–8% of the variance in therapy outcomes (see meta-analysis by Horvath, Del Re, Fluckiger, & Symonds, 2018). The percentage may not seem like much, but when one considers all of the variables at play, the fact that just one of them may account for up to 8% of outcomes is impressive. And yet, it also makes sense that this amount is an underestimate when one considers that the working bond between the participants, their agreement on the goals of treatment, as well as their agreement on the tasks needed to attain those goals is even more fundamentally important than implied by the 5–8% figure. Consider all of the extraneous material, or error variance, involved in any given study, and it is unlikely that a given variable could be found to account for much more variance, even when it is crucial to success.

To get a sense of the importance of the working alliance, consider what the chances of success in treatment are if the patient does not believe in or trust the therapist's abilities, the therapist does not believe the patient has the personal qualities needed to form a connection with him or her, and the two do not agree much on the goals of treatment and the tasks needed to attain useful goals. The prognosis for such a case would be exceptionally poor. This, I believe, means that at least a minimally sound working alliance is necessary if the work is even to proceed. I do not think that research studies have addressed this phenomenon, in that rarely have dyads with very poor initial alliances been examined, perhaps because patients in such dyads do not stay in treatment long enough to even be studied.

The therapist's first task is to form a sound working alliance, and the therapist's second task may well be to maintain and preserve the alliance. I have discussed in Chapter 3 how that may be done. From the therapist's side, the bottom line in alliance development is for the therapist to show the patient that the therapist understands the patient, sees some of the basic issues facing the patient, and can communicate in a way that the patient trusts that the therapist and patient can work successfully together to help the patient get better. Part of this alliance formation involves the therapist using techniques with sufficient expertise that the patient will have a sense of the therapist's competence.

On the negative side, alliance formation is not fostered by the therapist siding with the patient in the patient's struggles in relationships or by joining the patient in his or her efforts to avoid facing the central issues. Perhaps what these antitherapeutic behaviors lead to may be best termed pseudo-alliances. In seeking to use techniques expertly, a sense of timing is vital to alliance formation. Without colluding with the patient, the therapist's main task in working alliance formation and preservation is knowing when and how to say what to the patient. The therapist's empathy or ability to enter the patient's inner world deeply is perhaps the most basic element of good timing. If we know the patient from the inside out, we are usually able to have effective timing in what to say and how.

It is important to underscore that there often will be one or more ruptures in the working alliance, and therapists must be highly sensitive to such ruptures. These occur especially as the therapist seeks to move forward in helping the patient confront his or her conflicts and problems. No matter how sensitive and empathic the therapist, s/he does need to help the patient face material that is avoided, and doing so is likely to create some ruptures. The therapist needs to be on the look-out for ruptures, help the patient explore them, and when appropriate, own mistakes that are made. I have noticed, though, that novice therapists often too readily apologize for mistakes, fearing the patient's negative reactions. Such avoidance results more often in a pseudo-alliance and does not lead to successful treatment. The suggestion is to seek to understand and help the patient understand the rupture, and only apologize when a mistake has indeed been made.

Ruptures are also caused by empathic failures on the therapist's part. Such failures, often very slight, are an inevitable part of therapeutic work. And with certain disorders, empathic failures on the therapist's part are a key element of the success of treatment. (See Heinz Kohut's, 1971, 1977 discussion of the importance and growth-rendering aspects of empathic failures in patients suffering from narcissistic personality disorders.) Again, the rupture may be partly resolved by the therapist's apology. But my suggestion, particularly to inexperienced therapists, is don't overdo it. Make the apology, own it, and then help the patient look at what was upsetting and how that relates to the patient's dynamics and issues.

5. What may be termed a real or personal relationship exists from the first moment of contact between therapists and patients and must be attended to by therapists if treatment is to have its maximal impact.

Whereas the working alliance is the necessary catalyst for treatment success, the real or person-to-person relationship is the most fundamental element of the therapeutic relationship, and a strong real relationship is an important element in successful outcomes (see meta-analyses by Gelso, Kivlighan, & Markin, 2018).

It will be recalled that the real relationship is the part of the overall therapeutic relationship that is marked by the extent to which the participants are genuine with each other and experience/perceive each other realistically (without transference). It is also the non-work aspect of the relationship in the sense that it reflects how the patient and therapist are connecting as persons, how much they "take to" each other as persons, rather than as professional therapists and patients. In the strong real relationship, the therapist and patient experience mutual appreciation and enjoyment. Because of its importance to the success of treatment, therapists need to pay attention to it from the beginning. In part, the real relationship merely exists, and nothing can be done to strengthen it. This part reflects the extent to which the two participants in the relationship connect as persons, share certain values, and moreover are "in the same tribe" in ways that matter for the success of treatment. Still, in other ways, the therapist can work to maintain and strengthen the real relationship. The key is to be genuine and to strive to experience and perceive the patient without being clouded by one's own unresolved conflicts (countertransference).

One of the great paradoxes about the concept of genuineness is that the therapist can be truly him/herself without much deliberate self-disclosure, although therapist self-disclosure does increase the likelihood modestly that the therapist will be seen as genuine by the patient. In the absence of deliberate self-disclosure, the therapist will reveal much about him/herself simply by being there. Not only does the therapist's office décor and personal attire communicate information about the person of the therapist, but so do the therapist's sense of humor, non-verbal behavior, and both what material s/he attends to and how s/he goes about attending to that patient material.

Another way in which the therapist communicates genuineness is by not deceiving the patient. "Thou shall not lie to thy patient" ought to be the first commandment of the therapeutic relationship. As therapists, we need to tell our patients what we believe, with timing and tact, but not with sugar-coating. If honest feedback is not called for, or if self-disclosure is not part of the therapist's theoretical approach, then it behooves the therapist to communicate this to the patient. The genuine therapist can say that s/he would rather not share certain material with the patient, and give the reason for not sharing.

Perhaps a bottom line about self-disclosure is that if it is not relevant to the patient's needs, it will not be helpful. This has been documented in several studies, and of course makes obvious clinical sense. So as therapists, we need to be careful about our motivations for self-disclosing, as well as careful about how much and when we disclose.

6. Empathy, caring, and affirmation are key elements of successful treatments of all theoretical persuasions.

Carl Rogers' conceptualization of the importance of therapist empathy, unconditional positive regard, and congruence is one of the most profound and valuable theories in the history of psychotherapy. My conception of the role of empathy, caring, and affirmation dovetails with Rogers' statement, but it is not the same. One aspect that does fully overlap, though, is the emphasis placed on the therapist's empathy. It is hard to imagine successful therapy if the therapist does not experience and demonstrate empathy. Research evidence over several decades provides powerful support for the importance of empathy. At the same time, empathy continues to be a frequently misunderstood concept. It often gets conflated with states and behaviors such as agreement, warmth, caring, and genuineness. I believe it is important to be clear about what empathy is and to separate it from these other states. Empathy is best seen as understanding the patient's inner experience, partially and temporarily identifying with that inner state, while not losing one's self and maintaining one's separateness. So conceived, empathy aids patient improvement in two ways: it is curative in and of itself and it fosters and deepens the patient's self-exploration. The curative element of empathy pertains to the fact that human beings seem to grow and benefit from being known. Also, being known fosters a sense of being knowable, in contrast to the pathology-fostering feeling of being so crazy that one could not possibly be known.

Although empathy in itself helps a great deal, its benefits are multiplied by the therapist's actual caring for the patient. The experience of being cared about and for is bound to foster growth, especially when one considers the fact that so many of our patients do not feel worthy of being cared for, feel unlovable, and were indeed not loved and cared for in a healthy way by those who mattered most to them in childhood.

Caring for the patient does not mean always having positive feelings. At times, for most patients with whom I have worked, I have experienced negative feelings, e.g., annoyance, anger, dislike, and at some points, even hate. However, it is important that the most fundamental feeling be caring, and this is most effective when it incorporates actual liking for the basic person of the patient. I know I do my best work when I like the patient, am eager to see him or her, and enjoy spending the time with them. When we do not have such caring, it is important to wonder why, and to see what is blocking it. I invite the reader to consider his or her history of working with clients or patients, and think about how many you believe you have helped substantially under conditions of not caring much for them as persons. My personal percentage would be quite low.

The concepts and importance of therapist empathy and caring are rather easily digested. The importance of affirmation, however, is much trickier. What does it mean to affirm the other? We would probably all agree with the value of the patient having the right to feel what s/he feels. If this does not involve taking sides on the appropriateness, defensiveness, and realism of the feelings, it is easy – and important – to affirm. However, there is a part of affirmation that goes beyond the patient having a right to feel his or her feelings. There is a part that communicates that the patient is justified in his or her feelings. This part pertains to cases in which the patient was indeed wronged or harmed in a way that was not deserved. The harm may have come from broad institutions, cultural groups, and the patient's intimates, including those most responsible for his growth and well-being during childhood and beyond. I have offered in Chapter 2 that in such cases, it is useful for the therapist to affirm that, indeed, the patient was wronged. In my own work, I have offered such affirmation most often in long-term therapy, often lasting several years (at times a decade or more), where it was clear that the patient was treated poorly, sometimes devastatingly so, and that this indeed was not fair. However, there are times when such acknowledgment does not require years of therapy. For example, cases in which the patient was unjustly treated (e.g., racism, sexual assault, abuse in the workplace) often warrant affirmation. Naturally, the therapist needs to be careful that s/he is not just feeding the patient's externalizing defenses, as this will foster the patient's blaming of others or the world, but not help the patient work through more fundamental internal conflicts or build a stronger sense of self. The material of the case will reveal to the therapist who is watchful whether his or her comments are truly affirming or simply feeding the patient's externalizing defenses.

7. Within the context of empathy, caring, and affirmation, therapy is most successful when the therapist maintains a stance of benevolent neutrality.

At a time in the history of psychotherapy in which therapists are more open and supportive with their patients than ever before, proposing that we return to a re-constructed concept of therapist neutrality borders on heresy. Still, I have proposed that if the aim of treatment is patient self-understanding, insight, and awareness, then it is important that the therapist maintain a kind of neutrality. In training settings in particular, I have observed a powerful tendency for the therapist to side with the patient in the patient's difficulties with others in his or her life, and to believe that this siding-with was a demonstration of therapist empathy. Empathy, of course, does not mean siding with your patient.

If the kind of neutrality I am advancing is to be effective, it must be carried out in a context of empathy, caring, and affirmation on the part of the therapist. This is why I use the term "benevolent neutrality." Still, neutrality is a key element of successful treatment in that therapy aimed at understanding, insight, and awareness is most effective when the therapist does not take sides with the patient when the patient is expressing negative reactions in relationships in his or her life; does not side with one or the other side when the patient is experiencing internal conflicts; does not push or manipulate the patient into experiencing emotions before the patient is ready to do so; and does follow some rules of thumb about when to satisfy the patient's wishes for support, reassurance, advice, and explicit statements that the therapist cares. I believe Freud had it right when he worried that if the therapist takes care of the patient too much (gratification in Freud's terms), the patient is likely to give up the need to grow and change, and get hooked on the treatment itself.

It is important to be thoughtful about when to support a given patient, and in what way. Some patients do indeed need the therapist's support (e.g., advice, structuring, explicit statements of caring), and might move backwards without it. On the other hand, most do best when the therapist adopts a more neutral stance (with some deviations along the way), so long as the neutrality is in a context of empathy, caring, and affirmation.

8. Transference exists in all relationships and may be for better or worse, depending on its nature and intensity, as well as how the therapist responds to it.

The time to view transference as a part of only the psychoanalytic and psychodynamic treatments is long past. There is empirical, theoretical, and clinical evidence to support the assertion that transference happens in psychotherapies of all persuasions, and I would add that it is likely an element in virtually every therapy relationship. The question is no longer whether it exists but how to address it.

In Chapter 4, I have provided examples of how it can be exhibited and addressed in treatments beyond the psychodynamic. For this summary chapter, the key assertion is that it is most important that transference be addressed when it interferes with the progress of therapy. This interference most often happens when the transference is negative – when the patient projects onto the therapist negative reactions (e.g., dislike, anger, hate, disinterest, criticalness, etc.) that either are not what the therapist is feeling or are the therapist's almost inevitable responses to what the patient is projecting onto or into the therapist. The interference due to negative transference may take many forms, ranging from blocking exploration of the most threatening affects in the patient to actually destroying the treatment. There are cases in which the therapist is sure that the patient's negative reactions to the therapist and the work are transferential, but the patient will simply not go there. In such cases, the therapist should first look inward to see if the problem is more countertransference than transference. Sometimes it is, and sometimes it is a mixture of transference and countertransference. Still, despite our best efforts to understand ourselves and our patients, I believe many of our failure cases are a result of such impenetrable negative transferences, in which the patient takes what is transferential to be realistic reactions. In other words, the patient believes that transferential reactions to the therapist are, in fact, the therapist's problem and is unable to look inward for at least part of the reason for the negative transference.

Fortunately, most negative transferences are capable of being understood, especially if the patient and therapist have sound working alliances and real relationships. Just how the therapist chooses to deal with transference will depend heavily on his or her theoretical orientation, as explored in Chapter 4.

At times, the positive transferences will also create impediments to treatment. For example, the patient's projection of positive qualities onto the therapist that go beyond the reality of the therapist (the therapist is experienced as warmer, kinder, more expert than is the case) may serve as a barrier to the patient's understanding of hidden negative feelings ... feelings pervade the patient's intimate relationships. Here, too, it is important that the positive transferences be explored in a way and at a time that works for the patient, and that fit the therapist's belief system and theoretical approach.

Finally, transference may be for better as well as worse. Freud pointed to unobjectionable positive transferences, which may help build rapport and sound working alliances. Other than in psychoanalysis per se, I do not believe that such transferences need to be addressed as transference. However, when transferences are idealizing (see Chapter 4), they do eventually have to be worked with and through.

9. Countertransference can be for better or worse, depending upon how the therapist manages it.

Countertransference can be for better or worse. If understood and worked with (i.e., managed) by the therapist, countertransference can help the therapist deepen his or her understanding of the patient and what is needed in the work. (See meta-analysis of relation to countertransference management to treatment outcome by Hayes, Gelso, Kivlighan, & Goldberg, 2018.) If ignored or poorly managed, countertransference will likely damage or even destroy the therapeutic relationship. Again, the key is managing the countertransference, and it appears that there are two overriding factors that determine how well it is managed: (1) understanding oneself and one's patient and (2) being personally integrated, including being able to regulate one's emotions in the treatment hour. The therapist's understanding is deepest and most effective when it represents both intellect and affect. That is, therapists must have an intellectual or cognitive grasp of their inner experience and what goes in patients' minds during the hour; and therapists need to be aware of and, to an extent, actually experience the patient's and his/her own feelings. As well, the therapist's empathy for the patient is a key element of this countertransference management process.

In addition to understanding the patient and him/herself, as I have said, if the therapist is to effectively manage countertransference feelings, s/he must be personally integrated in the hour and be able to regulate and control his or her feelings. What this means is that the therapist is able to manage countertransference to the extent that s/he is not suffering from too many unresolved conflicts, is able to maintain separateness from the patient while not building a wall around him/herself, and also is able to experience anxiety without being overwhelmed or controlled by it.

Although the patient's behavior is likely a precipitant or trigger for countertransference reactions, the therapist's unresolved conflicts are the origin. Thus, countertransference is best conceptualized in terms of the *countertransference– interaction hypothesis*, wherein the patient's behavior (including highly subtle nonverbal behavior) interacts with the therapist's emotional vulnerabilities to produce countertransference. It is important to note that countertransference as an internal event (feelings, thoughts, visceral sensations) are not problematic in and of themselves. They are, however, problematic when they spill into the therapy hour and affect the therapist's reactions to the patient.

Because the enactment of countertransference in the session can be so damaging to treatment, it is important that therapists try to prevent or manage this through their attempts to understand themselves. This becomes difficult, if not impossible, when the countertransference reaction is chronic, that is, something carried within the therapist and set in motion simply by doing therapy (the therapeutic frame). Here the therapist is trapped in his or her own way of being, so to speak, and often cannot even see that there is a problem. For example, the therapist who is chronically oversupportive with patients typically cannot see this. Instead, it must be brought to his or her attention by patients' reactions, colleagues, or supervisors. If there is a solution to such chronic countertransference, it is the therapist's own personal psychotherapy.

Fortunately, because most therapists have sought personal therapy and are reasonably integrated, chronic countertransference is not pervasive. We are indeed able to manage countertransference with some conscious and direct effort. For example, Knapp, Gottlieb, and Handelsman (2017) recommend that therapists periodically take their own emotional temperatures before and after sessions. They also suggest that we try to identify the predominant feelings expressed by the patient in the session, and identify their own reaction to those feelings. This strikes me as sound advice to therapists, so long as we understand that when countertransference is at work, we often do not want to see. Thus, we therapists need to get in touch with this avoidance and seek to overcome it.

10. Intense therapist affects are present in some therapeutic relationships and must be acknowledged and understood if they are to help rather than hinder treatment.

Intense feelings, such as love and hate, are easy to suppress, or look away from. What I have written about countertransference management in Statement 9 is even more applicable to countertransference reflecting these intense states. They need to be looked at, owned, and understood – beyond attributing them to patients. They also need to be worked with so that they may benefit rather than damage the treatment. Managing intense countertransference reactions, however, is much harder when it comes to these intense states. They are so often worrisome and shameful to the therapist, and we have an even greater investment in avoiding them. It may be impossible to manage intense countertransference without outside help. Here psychotherapy supervision, even for the seasoned therapist, may be necessary. For the less seasoned therapist, therapy supervision is even more often needed, as in the case example provided below. The therapist in this case was in the fourth year of her doctoral program. She had three prior therapy practica, and was doing an externship at our psychodynamic clinic at the University of Maryland. I was her therapy supervisor, and in this role met with her weekly for supervision. The therapist was an enormously gifted trainee who worked effectively with difficult patients. Below is her description of intense reactions to a patient with whom she was working and the blind spots she experienced around her own intense affects that she encountered and worked through.

> Steve and I had worked together for a year and a half in individual psychotherapy. He was a 52-year-old early retiree who sought therapy to manage his depression and explore his pervasive and intense feelings of isolation. He had few friends or family who spoke with him. Although he desired a romantic partner, he limited himself in his search and stated that seeing his hairdresser and me would suffice for him. As I got to know Steve, it became clear that he was deeply narcissistically wounded. Thus, he developed an idealized and erotic transference toward me, which was particularly unsettling given that I was 26 years his junior. He needed to see me as an omnipotent figure to which he was a part of in order to lift himself from his core shame.
> Oftentimes when Steve and I were on the verge of insight into one of his core issues, he would stop and stare saying, "It's just so lovely gazing into your eyes. Can I just do that?" I was angry when Steve derailed us from our work in this way. It felt like a power play with gender and age undertones toward which I had strong countertransference reactions. With the help of my supervisor, I began to understand that this erotic transference was a form of unconscious resistance. Through much reflection and guidance, I began to start making small successful interpretations of what was happening between Steve and me, and how this was holding him back from finding an intimate relationship outside of therapy.
> Although our work surrounding the erotic transference gradually improved by Steve exploring his pattern of desiring unattainable relationships, it took a major downturn during one session. I had gotten engaged the weekend prior, and I knew going into session that Steve could have very difficult reactions to seeing the new piece of jewelry on my left ring finger. At first he congratulated me, and noted his self-defeating pattern of desiring the unattainable. Consciously he had always been aware that we could never be together romantically, but this was the final nail in that fantasy's coffin. As the session progressed, Steve began to talk about how impressed the women he took to bed were by his opening up, and how I will never know that side of him. An internal fit of fury grew toward his bragging about the women he brought to bed and insinuating that I could have been one of them, which I perceived only as another power play to make me uncomfortable. However, my rage made me miss the deeper issue this flaunting symbolized for him. I subsequently became defensive and made intellectualized interpretations he was not ready to hear. He left feeling very misunderstood and ashamed.

In my next supervision session, I was still feeling rage toward Steve. My supervisor expressed a different perspective. He explained that because Steve was feeling vulnerable about the engagement news, which likely intensified his feelings of being alone and fundamentally flawed, he needed to escape that vulnerability by flaunting about times when he took pleasure in being able to open up and be himself. As I understood that this flaunting represented a covering up of his self-contempt, feelings of shame in the form of tears began to surface in me. How could I have been so depleted in empathy toward Steve, and how awful that I felt so viciously angry toward this deeply wounded and isolated man?

When I reflected on my rage, I came to understand that part of it was revulsion toward my own need to flaunt and receive external validation when I am feeling insecure. In addition, I could not tolerate feeling placed in a submissive position, which is related to my discomfort with my passive side. However, a deeper issue surrounding fear and anger toward myself about not being good enough explained the intensity of my reactions. I had little efficacy working with erotic transference and felt rage when I had to do so because it exposed my incompetence. When I did, in fact, fail Steve regarding his transference, I felt intense shame about my inadequacy. Interestingly, shame over his defectiveness is one of Steve's core issues. Thus, I was faced with the question of how I could help Steve with this when I had such trouble facing it in myself—highlighting my incompetence yet again. When I reflect on the entirety of this case, I know it was partly human that I responded to Steve the way I did. It did not feel good to be put in a submissive, uncomfortable position as a younger female therapist trainee. However, I came to realize the importance of understanding why he did this and what he was escaping, as well as why I reacted so strongly, in order to continue meaningful work with Steve.

11. There is more

In this book, I have presented a conception of the structure of the patient–therapist relationship as it is manifested in all therapeutic relationships, regardless of the therapist's theoretical orientation, the duration of treatment, the frequency of sessions, and the particular characteristics of the participants. I have proposed that all therapeutic relationships consist of a real relationship, a working alliance, and a transference–countertransference configuration. Within this context, I have sought to elaborate key ingredients of effective therapeutic relationships: a strong real relationship; sound working alliance; transference that is not highly negative and/or is capable of being worked with; countertransference that is effectively managed, including when the therapist experiences intense affects such as love and hate; a therapist who is empathic, caring, and affirming; and a therapeutic stance of benevolent neutrality.

Taken together, the structure and factors that have been addressed may serve as a rough blueprint for a sound therapeutic relationship and effective psychotherapy. However, it is important to also clarify that in this book, I have not been comprehensive. That is, there are certainly relational factors that have not been examined or have been addressed in only a cursory manner. I have not explored therapist and patient personality or stylistic factors that are a key part of the therapeutic relationship and the success or failure of treatment. For example, therapist and patient attachment patterns and behavior have not been delved into, although there is evidence that these play an important role (see review by Levy, Ellison, Scott, & Bernecker, 2011; Strauss & Petrowski, 2017). Therapist qualities such as emotional presence (Hayes & Vinca, 2017), what has been termed appropriate responsiveness (Stiles & Horvath, 2017), and therapist credibility (Gibbons, 2018) have not been examined explicitly, although the qualities and behaviors involved in these constructs have been incorporated into our discussion.

One factor that has not been sufficiently explored is that of culture, both the patient and the therapist's cultural background. Culture may be considered in the narrow sense, having to do with the therapist's and the patient's race/ethnicity, or it can be used in a much broader way, pertaining to both client and therapist gender, sexual orientation, religious background and, moreover, any qualities reflecting cultural belief systems. There is some empirical support for the importance of therapists' attentiveness and comfort in working with cultural elements of their clients' lives (Hayes, Owen, & Nissen-Lie, 2017). Although rare, there are some excellent case examples of therapists' dismissively minimizing cultural experiences of patients (Hayes, Owen, & Nissen-Lie, 2017; Tummala-Narra, 2016) and, on the other hand, incorporating cultural understandings into the treatment process in helpful and creative ways. (See Martinez-Taboas, 2005, for an example of incorporating religious/spiritual beliefs into the therapy with a very spiritual patient suffering from psychogenic seizures.) Cultural elements are important for therapists to attend to and address if the therapeutic relationship is to be strong and to have the positive impact that we all seek. In working with patients who are members of culturally oppressed groups, an affirming attitude in which the role of oppression in the patient's life is understood and explored can have a major impact on the therapeutic relationship and the progress of therapy.

As this book draws to an end, it seems fitting to note another neglected topic (in this book and in the field) that has great relevance to the therapeutic relationship. The termination phase of therapy has much to do with everything that has gone on before this phase, and it also has a bearing on what the patient carries from the therapy relationship into life after treatment has ended. Practicing therapists make clear that there is indeed a termination phase in most therapies, that at least about 15% of the treatment time is taken up with issues around termination (Bhatia & Gelso, 2017), and that certain therapist behaviors are highly characteristic of this phase (Gelso & Woodhouse, 2002; Norcross, Zimmerman, Greenberg, & Swift, 2017). These behaviors may serve as a guide to the therapist on the features of an effective termination phase. The termination behaviors revolve around the therapist helping the patient look at what has been accomplished and what still remains (looking back and looking forward) and in sharing the final good-bye. The real relationship is usually at the forefront during this ending phase; and, especially in longer-term work, patients often talk about how they want and need to carry with them the internalization of "the good therapist" that has developed over the course of the treatment.

The quality of the therapeutic relationship is reflected in how the termination phase unfolds, and I would offer that the final saying goodbye usually captures what has been the nature and quality of the therapeutic relationship. How this final goodbye is shared by the patient and therapist, and indeed how the termination phase has been addressed, will both likely have an impact on the internalized therapeutic relationship that the patient carries into the future.

References

Bhatia, A., & Gelso, C. J. (2017). The termination phase: Therapists' perspective on the therapeutic relationship and outcome. *Psychotherapy*, 54, 76–87. doi:10.1037/pst0000100

Gelso, C. J. (2009). The time has come: The real relationship in psychotherapy. *Psychotherapy Research*, 19, 278–282. doi:1080/10503300902777155

Gelso, C. J., Kivlighan, D. M., & Markin, R. D. (2018). The real relationship. In J. Norcross, & M. Lambert (Eds.), *Psychotherapy relationships that work* (3rd ed.). New York, NY: Oxford.

Gelso, C. J., & Woodhouse, S. S. (2002). The termination of psychotherapy: What research tells up about the process of ending treatment. In Tryon, G. S. (Ed.), *Counseling based on process research: Applying what we know.* (pp. 344–369) Boston, MA: Allyn & Bacon.

Gibbons, M. B. C. (2018). Credibility. In J. C. Norcross, & M. J. Lambert (Eds.), *Psychotherapy relationships that work* (3rd ed.). New York, NY: Oxford.

Hayes, J. A., Gelso, C. J., Kivlighan, M., & Goldberg, S. (2018). Managing countertransference. In J. Norcross, & M. Lambert (Eds.), *Psychotherapy relationships that work* (3rd ed). New York, NY: Oxford.

Hayes, J. A., Owen, J., & Nissen-Lie, H. A. (2017). The contributions of client culture to differential therapist effectiveness. In L. G. Castonguay, & C. E. Hill (Eds.), *How and why are some therapists better than others? Understanding therapist effects.* (pp. 159–174) Washington, DC: American Psychological Association.

Hayes, J. A., & Vinca, M. (2017). Therapist presence, absence, and extraordinary presence. In L. G. Castonguay, & C. E. Hill (Eds.), *How and why are some therapists better than others? Understanding therapist effects.* (pp. 85–100) Washington, DC: American Psychological Association.

Horvath, A. O. (2009). How real is the "real relationship"? *Psychotherapy Research*, 19, 273–277. doi:1080/10503300802592506

Horvath, A. O., Del Re, A., Fluckiger, C., & Symonds, D. (2018). Alliance in individual psychotherapy. In J. Norcross, & M. Lambert (Eds.), *Psychotherapy relationships that work* (3rd ed.). New York, NY: Oxford University Press.

Knapp, S., Gottlieb, M. S., & Handelsman, M. M. (2017). Self-awareness questions for effective psychotherapists: Helping good psychotherapists become even better. *Practice Innovations*, 2, 163–172. doi:10.1037/pr0000051

Kohut, H. (1971). *The analysis of the self*. New York, NY: International Universities Press.

Kohut, H. (1977). *The restoration of the self*. New York, NY: International Universities Press.

Levy, K. N., Ellison, W. D., Scott, L. N., & Bernecker, S. L. (2011). Attachment style. In J. N. Norcross (Ed.), *Psychotherapy relationships that work* (2nd ed.) (pp. 377–401). New York, NY: Oxford University Press.

Martinez-Taboas, A. (2005). Psychogenic seizures in an espiritismo context: The role of culturally sensitive psychotherapy. *Psychotherapy*, 42, 6–13. doi:10.1037/0033-3204.42.1.6

Norcross, J. C., Zimmerman, B. E., Greenberg, R. P., & Swift, J. K. (2017). Do all therapists do that when saying goodbye? A study of commonalities in termination behaviors. *Psychotherapy*, 54, 66–75. http://dx.doi.org/10.1037/pst0000097

Rogers, C. (1957). The necessary and sufficient conditions of therapeutic personality change. *Journal of Consulting Psychology*, 21(2), 95–103.

Stiles, W. B., & Horvath, A. O. (2017). Appropriate responsiveness as a contribution to therapist effects. In L. G. Castonguay, & C. E. Hill (Eds.), *How and why are some therapists better than others? Understanding therapist effects*. (pp. 71–84) Washington, DC: American Psychological Association.

Strauss, B. M., & Petrowski, K. (2017). The role of therapist attachment in the process and outcome of psychotherapy. In L. G. Castonguay, & C. E. Hill (Eds.), *How and why are some therapists better than others? Understanding therapist effects*. (pp. 117–138) Washington, DC: American Psychological Association.

Tummala-Narra, P. (2016). *Psychoanalytic theory and cultural competence in psychotherapy*. Washington, D.C.: American Psychological Association.

Index

abstinence, vs. gratification 40, 45–9, 148
accommodation, vs. assimilation 11–12, 77
affirmation (of patient) 35, 38–9, 67, 146–8, 154
ambivalence *see* hidden ambivalence
analytic attitude 90
Andersen, Susan M. 12, 80
anxiety management, and countertransference 19, 117, 118–19, 150
appropriate responsiveness 154
assimilation, vs. accommodation 11–12, 77
attachment patterns 154

Bachelor, A. 9, 66–7
Barber, J. 89
behavioral therapy *see* cognitive/behavioral therapies (CBT); dialectical behavior therapy (DBT)
benevolent neutrality: chapter overview vii, 29–30; issues 39–40; not taking sides in patients' outer struggles 42–3; refraining from manipulating patients into emotional expression 43–5; refraining from taking sides in patients' inner struggles 41–2; rules of abstinence and gratification 40, 45–9; summing up 148–9; taking an observer position 40–1; *see also* empathic way
Bergman, Ingmar, *Face to Face* 39
Bhatia, A. 12, 57, 79–80
Blum. H. P. 37, 127
Bohart, A. C. 34, 55, 94
borderline personality disorders: and capriciousness 87; and caring 36; and countertransference 103, 120–1; and dialectical behavior therapy 8; and gratification 48, 49; and hate 125, 134–5, 136; and hidden ambivalence 86; and reflection of feeling technique 33; and transference 95
Bordin, E. S. 3, 9, 67
Bowlby, J. 11–12, 77, 106
Bozarth, J. D. 34
brief therapies: vs. long-term therapies vi–vii, 1; and negative transference 14–15; vs. patience 68–9; and transference 90–1; and working alliance 9–10

capriciousness, as marker of transference 87
caring: vs. empathy 33; and empathy 35–8, 146–7; and working alliance 67
Carter, Jean A. 3, 8, 10, 63, 134
CBT *see* cognitive/behavioral therapies (CBT)
Cheng, D. 112
client-centered therapy 13, 32, 41; *see also* person-centered therapy; Rogers, Carl R.
client-therapist collaboration 67
co-construction (in transference) 11, 13, 75, 77, 83, 97
cognitive/behavioral therapies (CBT) vii, 2; behavioral techniques 4; and benevolent neutrality 40; and countertransference management 122–3; and curiosity 69; and empathy 30, 35, 39; and lived/living therapeutic relationship 24; and negative transference 142; and real (or personal) relationship 8; and real relationship/working alliance interrelation 53; and transference 14, 91–3; and working alliance 9, 10–11; *see also* dialectical behavior therapy (DBT)
competence (expertise) 67–8

conceptualizing ability, and countertransference management 19, 41, 117–18
congruence (or genuineness) 2, 13, 94, 121, 122, 146–7; *see also* genuineness
consistency/constancy, and strengthening of real relationship 56–7
countertransference: chronic vs. acute 109–11, 151; concept and definitions 102–5; countertransference interaction hypothesis 106, 135–6, 150–1; countertransference vs. non-countertransference reactions 102, 107–9; and empathy 18, 19, 32, 117, 118; inner experience vs. enactments 111–16; integrative perspective 15–17, 23, 57, 105–6; management of 17–19, 41, 116–20, 150–1; management of and cognitive-behavioral therapies 122–3; management of and humanistic/experential therapies 121–2; management of and psychoanalytic therapies 120–1; management of and strength of real relationship 57–8; negative countertransference 22, 105, 115; objective countertransference (Winnicott) 107, 138; positive countertransference 22, 105, 115–16; and real (or personal) relationship 22–3, 142; and transference 23–4, 25, 142; and tripartite model 4, 11; and working alliance 21, 22, 142; *see also* hate; love
credibility (of therapist) 154
cultural factors 154
curiosity 69, 90

Davison, G. C. 14, 91, 93
dialectical behavior therapy (DBT) 8, 123
Diemer, R. A. 17
distortions (in transference) 6, 76–7
drive theory 89

Eagle, M. 31
ego analysis 89
Electra complex 74
Elliott, R. 33–4, 55, 122
emotional intensity/flatness, as marker of transference 84–6
emotional presence 154
emotion-focused therapies 7, 94–5
empathic mirroring 35
empathic understanding (Rogers) 2, 13, 30–1, 32, 34, 94, 121, 146–7

empathic way: chapter overview vii, 29–30; empathy and affirmation of patient 35, 38–9, 146–8; empathy and caring for patient 35–8, 146–7; empathy and countertransference 18, 19, 32, 117, 118; empathy vs. sympathy 33, 68, 111; expressing empathy 34; and fostering of real relationship 55–6; and fostering of working alliance 67, 68, 145; what empathy is 30–2, 147; what empathy is not 32–4, 147; why empathy helps 34–5, 147; *see also* benevolent neutrality
empty-chair technique 4, 95
Eubanks-Carter, C. 64
experiential therapies *see* humanistic/experiential therapies; process-experiential therapy
expertise (competence) 67–8

Freud, Anna 41–2
Freud, Sigmund: abstinence vs. gratification 40, 45–9, 148; countertransference 102–3; sadism and good analytic work 63; self-insight 17–18; therapist's communication of loving feelings 132; transference 11, 12, 73, 79, 81–2, 150; transference and distortions 76; transference love 125
Friedman, S. M. 112
Fromm, Erich 111, 119
Fromm-Reichmann, Frieda 14, 75
Fuertes, J. 112

genuineness: congruence or genuineness (Rogers) 2, 13, 94, 121, 122, 146–7; and real (or personal) relationship 5, 6–7, 53, 146
gestalt therapy: and real (or personal) relationship 7; and transference 13, 14, 95, 97
Glickauf-Hughes, C. 137
Glover, E. 87
Goldfried, M. R. 14, 91, 93
Goldman, Rhonda 94–5
Gottlieb, M. S. 151
gratification: vs. abstinence 40, 45–9, 148; therapist's gratification 109, 131
Greenberg, L. S. 7, 33–4, 55
Greenson, Ralph R.: affective atherosclerosis 40; horrific losses and neutrality/abstinence 48; transference 21; transference markers 83, 87;

working alliance 9; working alliance and real relationship 20, 52
Grummon, D. L. 121

Handelsman, M. M. 151
hate: and borderline personality disorders 125, 134–5, 136; and countertransference 36, 40, 133–8, 151–3; as "inadmissible" feeling in psychotherapist 125–6, 138
Hayes, Jeffrey A. 15–17, 57, 74, 105–6, 108, 112, 115–17
hidden ambivalence, as marker of transference 86–7
Hill, C. E. 7, 58
Horvath, Adam O. 141
humanistic/experiential therapies vii, 2; and benevolent neutrality 40; and countertransference management 121–2; and empathy 30–1, 34, 35; and lived/living therapeutic relationship 24; and negative transference 142; and present, past and therapeutic change 96; and real (or personal) relationship 6–7; and real relationship/working alliance interrelation 52–3; and transference 13–14, 93–5; two-chair technique 9; and working alliance 9, 10–11, 66; *see also* emotion-focused therapies; gestalt therapy; person-centered therapy
Hummel, A. M. 57

idealizing transferences 87, 98–9, 150
inappropriateness, as marker of transference 83–4
insight *see* integrative insight; intellectual insight; self-insight (self-understanding); triangle of insight
integrative insight 17, 96
intellectual insight 96–7
interpersonal therapies 7, 14, 74–5, 105
interpretation technique 4, 143
intersubjective-relational psychoanalysis: and countertransference 105; and transference 75, 76, 95

Jackson, J. 57

Kanninen, Katri M. 29–30, 33, 40, 43, 44
Killingmo, B. 38, 39
Knapp, S. 151
Knox, S. 7, 58
Kohut, Heinz 31, 32, 55, 75, 87, 98, 145

Levendusky, P. G. 122
Levy, K. N. 48
long-term therapies: vs. brief therapies vi–vii, 1; and working alliance 9–10
love: as "inadmissible" feeling in psychotherapist 125–6, 138; love and sexuality in psychotherapy 127–31, 151; Rollo May's four kinds of love 36–7, 126–7, 128, 129, 131–2; therapist's self-acknowledgment/understanding 131; therapist's self-disclosure or not 131–3
Luborsky, L. 11

McMain, S. 123
magnitude (of real/personal relationship) 5, 53–4
Marmarosh, C. 37, 131
masochism 99
May, Rollo 36–7, 126–7, 128, 129, 131–2
Mehlman, E. 137
Menaker, Esther 99
Mitchell, S. 75
moving (the session) forward 69–70
Muran, J. C. 64, 68
Murdock, N. L. 14

narcissistic personality disorders: and countertransference management 19, 135–6; and idealizing transferences 87, 98–9; and rupture-repair process 145; and strengthening of real relationship 59–62; and tenaciousness of transferences 87–8
negative transference: and brief therapies 14–15; definition 11; and person-centered/emotion-focused therapies 95; vs. positive transference 77–8, 97–9; and progress of therapy 15, 21, 85, 149; and real (or personal) relationship 6, 25, 142; and working alliance 21, 25, 142
neutrality: psychoanalytic conception of 41–2; *see also* benevolent neutrality
Norcross, J. 3
Norwood, E. 57
nurturant working relationship 66

object relations theory 89
observer, therapist as 40–1
Oedipus complex 74, 75
Owen, J. 112

pain, and analytical work 63–4
Palma, B. 57
participant-observer, therapist as 40–1
patience 68–9, 95
Pérez-Rojas, A. E. 37, 57, 119, 129–31, 132
Perls, Fritz 7, 13, 95, 97
personal relationship *see* real (or personal) relationship
person-centered therapy: and countertransference management 121–2; person-to-person relationship 41; and real (or personal) relationship 7; and real relationship/working alliance interrelation 52–3; reflection of feeling technique 3–4, 32–3; and transference 13, 94, 95; *see also* client-centered therapy; Rogers, Carl R.
Persons, J. B. 8, 91–3, 123
Piaget, Jean 11–12, 77
Plato 17
"playing with your cards face up" 54, 58–9; *see also* self-disclosure
process-experiential therapy, empty-chair/two chair techniques 4
projective identification 98, 121, 134–5, 136
Przybylinski, E. 80
psychoanalysis: and affirmation (of patient) 38; countertransference 102–3, 120–1; Electra complex 74; and empathy 31; neutrality concept 41–2; Oedipus complex 74, 75; projective identification 98, 121, 134–5, 136; and real relationship/working alliance interrelation 53; relational tilt 12, 14; transference 11, 12–13, 15, 73–4, 75, 89; and working alliance 9; *see also* drive theory; ego analysis; Freud, Sigmund; intersubjective-relational psychoanalysis; object relations theory; psychoanalytic self psychology; psychoanalytic/psychodynamic therapies; relational psychoanalysis
psychoanalytic self psychology 31, 35, 55, 75, 89, 98, 105
psychoanalytic/psychodynamic therapies vii, 1–2; and benevolent neutrality 40; and countertransference management 120–1; and empathy 30, 31, 34, 35; essence of psychodynamic therapy 89; integrative insight 17, 96; interpretation technique 4, 143; and lived/living therapeutic relationship 24; and real (or personal) relationship 7–8; and real relationship/working alliance interrelation 52–3; and transference 8, 11, 12–13, 15, 89–91; and working alliance 9, 10–11, 67; *see also* interpersonal therapies; psychoanalysis

Racker, Heinrich 105
rage *see* hate
real (or personal) relationship: in cognitive/behavioral therapies 8; definition and qualities 5–6, 53–4, 145–6; in humanistic/experiential therapies 6–7; and love 127; in psychoanalytic/psychodynamic therapies 7–8; and sexuality 127; strength vs. salience 54, 58; strengthening of (case example) 59–62; strengthening of (negative case) 54–5, 146; strengthening of (positive case) 55–9, 146; and termination phase (of therapy) 155; and transference/countertransference 6, 22–3, 25, 142; and tripartite model 4; and working alliance 20–1, 52–3, 62–3, 141–2
realism (of real relationship) 5, 6, 53
reflection of feeling technique 4, 32–3, 34, 68
Reich, Annie 109
relational psychoanalysis 75–6, 105
relational-intersubjective psychoanalysis *see* intersubjective-relational psychoanalysis
Renik, O. 7, 54; *see also* "playing with your cards face up"
Rogers, Annie 37, 125
Rogers, Carl R.: congruence (genuineness) 2, 13, 94, 121, 122, 146–7; empathic understanding 2, 13, 30–1, 32, 34, 94, 121, 146–7; immersion in client's experience 41; nondirectiveness and competence 68; person-to-person relationship 7; therapist-offered relationship 66, 141; therapy with Gloria and neutrality 42; transference 13, 94; unconditional positive regard 2, 13, 35–6, 94, 121, 122, 146–7
Rosmarin, D. H. 122
rupture-repair process 10, 64–6, 68, 145

Safran, J. D. 64, 68
salience (of real relationship), vs. strength of 54, 58

Sampson, H. 83
Scala, J. W. 48
Schaeffer, J. A. 80–1, 93
Schafer, R. 90
"self differentiation" 19
self-disclosure 58–9, 60, 131–3, 146
self-insight (self-understanding): and countertransference management 17–18, 19, 117, 118, 138, 150; and therapist's sexual attraction 131; and working alliance 66–7
self-integration: and countertransference management 18, 19, 117, 138; "therapist self-integration and regulation" 117, 118–20, 150
sexuality: erotic transference 127; *see also* love
Silberberg, Ayelet 54, 55, 60–2
storytelling (as defensive function) 69–70
strength (of real relationship), vs. salience of 54, 58
Sullivan, Harry Stack 14, 40, 75
Summers, R. 89
sympathy, vs. empathy 33, 68, 111

tear-and-repair process 10; *see also* rupture-repair process
tenacity, as marker of transference 87–8
Terence 111
termination phase (of therapy) 154–5
Teyber, E. 7
therapeutic movement 69–70
therapeutic relationship: defining 2–3, 143; multidimensional nature of 140; and termination phase (of therapy) 154–5; and therapist techniques 3–4, 143–4; unexamined factors 153–5; *see also* brief therapies; long-term therapies; tripartite model
therapist techniques 3–4, 143–4; *see also specific techniques*
The Tired Therapist case 76–7, 84
transference: in brief therapies 90–1; co-construction 11, 13, 75, 77, 83, 97; in cognitive/behavioral therapies 14, 91–3; conceptions and definitions 11–12, 73–7; core relational transference theme 88–9; and countertransference 23–4, 25, 142; distortions 6, 76–7; erotic transference 127; feelingful vs. intellectual exploration 96–7; fundamentals (rules-of-thumb) 77–9; in humanistic/experiential therapies 13–14, 93–5;

Index 161

idealizing transferences 87, 98–9, 150; integrative conception of transference 11–12, 76–7; markers of transference 83–9; patient insight and success of therapy 15; and patient's life outside therapy 99; present, past and therapeutic change 96; in psychoanalytic/psychodynamic therapies 8, 11, 12–13, 15, 89–91; and real (or personal) relationship 6, 22–3, 25, 142; reasons for transference 81–3; resistance to transference 85–6; summing up 149–50; transference love 125; and tripartite model 4, 11; as universal phenomenon 79–81; and working alliance 21–2; *see also* countertransference; negative transference
triangle of insight 90, 91
tripartite model: chapter overview vii, 1–2; defining the therapeutic relationship 2–3, 143; interactions between relationship and therapist techniques 3–4, 143–4; lived and living relationship 24–5; overview of tripartite model 4–5, 141–3; real (or personal) relationship 4, 5–8; real (or personal) relationship and transference/countertransference 22–3, 24–5; transference-countertransference configuration 4, 11–19; transference-countertransference inter-relations 23–4; working alliance 4, 8–11; working alliance and real relationship 20–1; working alliance and transference/countertransference 21–2, 25
two-chair techniques 4, 9

unconditional positive regard (Rogers) 2, 13, 35–6, 94, 121, 122, 146–7
"understanding self and others/clients" 19, 57–8, 117–18, 119, 150

valence (of real/personal relationship) 5–6, 54
Van Wagoner, S. L. 17, 116–17

Watson, J. C. 55
Weiss, J. 84
Wiebe, C. 123
Winnicott, D. W. 36, 40, 107, 133–4, 137, 138
Wolitzky, D. L. 31

working alliance: definition 8–9, 63; and different therapies 9, 10–11; fostering/preservation of 66–70, 144–5; high-low-high patterns in 10; and long-term vs. brief therapies 9–10; and multidimensional nature of therapeutic relationship 140–1; paradox in alliance formation 63–4; and real (or personal) relationship 20–1, 52–3, 62–3, 141–2; rupture-repair process 10, 64–6, 68, 145; and transference/ countertransference 21–2, 25, 142; and tripartite model 4

Yalom, I. D. 7, 111